THE METAPHOR EXPLAINED, NOW WHAT?

OMAR AHMAD

Copyright © 2023 Omar Ahmad.

All rights reserved. No part of this book may be reproduced, stored, or transmitted by any means—whether auditory, graphic, mechanical, or electronic—without written permission of both publisher and author, except in the case of brief excerpts used in critical articles and reviews. Unauthorized reproduction of any part of this work is illegal and is punishable by law.

ISBN: 979-8-89031-276-1 (sc)
ISBN: 979-8-89031-277-8 (hc)
ISBN: 979-8-89031-278-5 (e)

Because of the dynamic nature of the Internet, any web addresses or links contained in this book may have changed since publication and may no longer be valid. The views expressed in this work are solely those of the author and do not necessarily reflect the views of the publisher, and the publisher hereby disclaims any responsibility for them.

One Galleria Blvd., Suite 1900, Metairie, LA 70001
(504) 702-6708

CONTENTS

Commemorations iv

Introduction v

Preface vii

Chapter 1   Some Teachings of Mine Over the Years
I Have Been Writing Here 1

Chapter 2   Some Words of Wisdom About Biblical
Lore We Have and Related Topics 55

Chapter 3   Some Veracity Of Quranic Verses I Have 105

Chapter 4   Some General Teachings Here From
My Page On Facebook 156

Chapter 5   Some Additional Articles From My Facebook Page ... 203

Chapter 6   Ahmadi Issues in Islam We Have 226

Chapter 7   Prophet Muhammad in Scriptures
and Writings We Have 251

Epilogue Here 263

COMMEMORATIONS

This book is dedicated to me, the American people, who are me in identity and like to listen to my lecture for them and their distaste is over for the most part as they have found me to be true to their ideals and their values have evolved with time that I have been teaching them and they are reluctant to sin like they used to and further, they are kind to me and find avenues for me to stay with them and live in their land in freedom and with the ability to write on and teach in lecture form as well.

In addition, they have allowed the publication of material and books I write and have made them available to the public to learn from, not just n this land but worldwide my literature prevails with them and they are responsible for allowing me the identity of saint Dabbat Al-Ard which many agree with in your land of the free, at least in literature we can publish with you, as I profess to be this saint that appeared in the West from the Eastern lands as a doctor and then turned to teaching when his license was relinquished for teaching them edicts of Islam we have for you of Ahmadiyyat which you find distasteful not and find pleasurable to know and live with.

Omar.

INTRODUCTION

Please see the introduction here where I teach stuff to you from Allah some and also from other dignitaries in Islam where talkeen or to be subversive in a good sense occurs as I am gradual in it and you accept me because I am late in issues for you but some alacricity does result on major issues and my book star has yet to be published in a way that I get proceeds from it but it is so my books have got published now and I may get some money from them but I don't know how much will be forwarded to me.

Please know it is clear my book got published there in 2015 and I did not receive any money for it so I sue the federal employee with your ability for me in the American public as you know it changed world history in that you all became me in things and so forth results you are my rahber or helper there where I file my lawsuit with them (as a metaphor of course as you hold the reins of court on me) for their theft of my proceeds so that you pocket my money and so forth results I am paid handsomely as it is Allah's guarantee that it be so that I get some of the proceeds for myself and so forth I really don't need it, that much anyway, so I give to those who need it, why should the federal employee disburse it while we can and Africa is fed where there is need and so forth results.

Please see alacrity is required in issues that concern death of community members and abortion and fornication issues must be handled adeptly and quickly as a child lost is a tragedy that must be prevented if at all possible you say, nay, it is not a minor matter with God and He punishes immediately these acts on carnage on an innocent one He has for us but it is so you must have alacrity in this issue and ban abortion in the land and export this sentiment worldwide it is murder actually you do and liberal views are to be fought with that allow lax sexual contact to occur and sex is for marriage and God does not accept leeway in this regard so it is imperative you act immediately to save life He creates in you.

Please see the country is aware I teach well yet they insane me in court and force medication on me through conservators and other avenues they have but they are coming around to peace as well with your anvil on them and Mehdi people emerge in this land and elsewhere where freedom of speech and religion is pursued as that is what the statutes allow and it has come about that we are allowed freedom now with harassment kept to a minimum as people have taken over my case and allow children and adults to seek life as they wish, more here is sane, yes, the American ideals are coming forth but evil must be fought, yes, evil that is in the sight of our Creator and we must not compromise on values of goodness that He sees fit for you and your country at large, and the West as well, and the struggle or jihad must go on until piety occurs with you in the world forum, yes, struggle with me to make it occur through peaceful means of teach and cajole on them, the people at large, where we are one body under Him, the Creator there.

Omar.

PREFACE

Please see the title of my book is 'now what' actually as I am complete in issues of the metaphor from before but will explain things more here but it is so we are 1 entity and I need uniformity in you and I need to teach you issues you like you like to know about the universe and science as well and other topics of Shiaism and Judaic law that is now outcast as they were too evil to survive with flourish and you know my car is to appreciate people from whatever background they are but they must leave evil edicts of their clan and conform to civilization values we have in Islam for you.

Please know there is a precedent here that I am sued eventually by some people in the sense they take away my rights but you won't allow it overtly in this country, at least after what you've done to me previously where I've been jailed for minor irregularities and so forth you're kind now as I gave you One God structure with you and you are pleased you are going to make it Heaven Abode eventually as the law has become apparent to you as sane to follow from Him, your Creat, and so forth you are kind in issues and want my peace as I am kind to you as well.

It is clear you have come a long way and many of your former values you had are not dear to you and you like to live piously under Him, your Creator, Who talkeens not but tells you in straightforward way in the Quran to you how you are going to make to Heaven and if you wish otherwise so be it He will take care of it eventually as Hell awaits the disobedient one to Him and your life will be merry not and hardship is your door here if you do not conform to His ways on you, more here is necessary, there is an element that wants fornication crimes to continue that used to be the norm in your land but it is so the majority do want to conform to His law that is in the Old Testament, the Quran and Jesus' teach there and it is here we give pause for thought, was there any good in that life where you left the norms of society Islam has and started killing your children that you beget in you and adultery was your norm as well, these are not values Jesus taught you and Allah in the Quran dissuades you from it as well so there are many of you that fight fornication rites you had and you want to make it a more stable society for you in future so your children have a better life and happier one as well.

As usual, I am indebted to websites I use resources of for my literature and the Lahore Ahmadiyya group for making Muhammad Ali's Quran available for us to read and use in my literature, which I do, and I am indebted to the publishing house I use that have made my books available for you to peruse and read at your leisure, and pleasure if you will, and I am indebted to family who allow me leeway in publishing my books as before they used to be averse in things that I do with my literature there.

Finally, I would like to say I am thankful for Allah's intervention for me in guiding me how to get our literature to people and now you have it He is the deciding factor in my life throughout my sojourn with you as saint Dabbat Al-Ard when I made that claim many years ago and He and my Prophet are responsible for my acclaim with you.

Omar.
April, 2023.

CHAPTER ONE

SOME TEACHINGS OF MINE OVER THE YEARS I HAVE BEEN WRITING HERE

Intro.
Please see the anwan or topic today is how we get there to heaven in one piece without going through hellfire extensively like my predecessor Jesus there did when he taught you the metaphor and so forth you became compliant but did he reach it, Paradise there, he did, and now he resides in Heaven with others but it is so he deterred things and let it occur that the metaphor took hold and you became trinity in views, something he did not envision but still it occurs to his detriment but it so occurs you were closer to Islam than pagan gods you have then and he was innocent in it by Allah and he had left the country when it took hold, the concept of him being son materially and then Paul did the rest, as I have shown you previously.

Please know it is clear I am published by you now so I say this that you have been kind to me to allow this format on Facebook to continue over the years where my views get air and now you succumb to One God the Quran has for you and most of you come forth willingly to Him, but keep me afloat as there are many adversaries here who don't like my literature coming forth where you convert materially to me and what I teach here on Facebook book format here and my books to you as you will deter it some but i know kind is your name here so you deter not actually and give me statutes I need for my speech to be free and so forth I'm One God with you concept there, inshallah it will be so, so that Islam is 1 belief with you in this forum you have of world literature to follow. Omar.

please see the meaning of life here and my beauty is what you covet all of you and it is enough that your heart is at peace that eternal ways you will be with me and i will manifest myself to you so that your peace results with me in your personal journey with me and then you shall see it the utter joy of your creation there say i allah to you

please see the reason i create you is for heart to know your worth and your heart rests in peace at your hierarchy in things of the nature i teach you in that your following of me must be like the one coveted by you yes it is muhammad who is the best in submission to me and then others occur in their worth they know they are not he and so your peace results yes thats why i create you here so that your peace occur and rancor occurs no more in your heart

please see this verse and hadith on the subject of time that we have and i have to tell you time always existed and i was alone from always then i wanted to be known so i created mankind that they would recognize me and serve me in my needs you think nay i am self-sufficient but in my wish to be known and loved by others so thats why i created you in this world as a separate conscious being and gave you living and things you like and reserve my blessings for heaven for you where you will have all you wish yes i made you all my creation for you to worship not as i dont need that but in my creation of things i have hierarchy in ways and you must know the best of you is he who serves me the best to bring all of you to me and that person is muhammad and he has the quran to serve you and there is no other book like it but it is so i gave you a destiny or qadr in things that you may know my hierarchy exists but when you come to heaven you will all be equal to me but my grace is most on him who you call my beloved one and you will not be jealous there but all will know your place is not to be him but yet you will love us all humanity with peace from us but you have to get there before then everything falls into place and you know i am kind to tell you this there is no rancor there you will all be fulfilled in your need for love and joy will be there for you but remember my first creation was he who you call me not but muhammad there around 20 billion years ago when i decided to create but first i create your destiny with the pen i write there so you understand that how this thing came about but it is so you dont

THE METAPHOR EXPLAINED, NOW WHAT?

know it your destiny there so vie with one another with good deeds and show your worth to us and mary was the next i create 7 billion years before this time and from these two spring mankind in their gene there which was spirit from them and this spirit is you on earth as well and you evolve here while there you are static in your spirit you are then so there you have it time did not begin but was ongoing as long as i was there but you date it from my first creation dont i was always there and time is a dimension not but i am time from immemorial times and there you have it there is no beginning to it and it goes on unending like the way we are once i created you but it is so you are safe to understand it has no beginning it just exists like i do and i wished to be known to the lover of me and satisfy my urge to take care of you once you have shown your worth and know your hierarchy with me and so there you have it my history is here in my words say i allah there and there you have it i was a beauty and i was satisfied by what i am there but eventually i knew i would create you to know me but it was so i would create my perfect one to let humanity know about me and he would teach me as i would remain hidden from view but the heart i did create to comprehend me and it desires my company so it submits to me but it is so i create evil for people to do if they wished and so i would see which person succumbs to my teach through muhammads pen and my voice coming here and you have a choice always i give that to my creations to come willingly until i force you through hell in you so that it occurs when hell transpires you have shown your worth to humanity and me and you wont vie with me about the fact why did i give my favorite one the best position for you there you have it your hell is written by your own hands and i give you a term there depending upon how bad youve been and so you know my wisdom is consummate and there is a purpose for your create and eventually you will be in heaven with me but you must face your term in hell before you come to me and some i will forgive on the day i judge you and some i will send for reform to hell where the fire consumes you and you see your worth which you did not see before and now you have it i am your company forever after you know your evil in things you do there in your life before you enter my abode with me so be aware of me in what i ask you as it is my wish you obey me in my laws here and if you wish to do it evil in your life at the beck of yourself or the devil so be it i will punish you all together in it and i know you know it is over you have understood the meaning of life but know your creation is to keep me company in loving embrace i give you when you are like my muhammad to me who wouldnt dare me in things and so you know your hierarchy depends on that yes your submission to me in my law structure there through the ages ever since i created you

allah here to you personally on this page here

Al-Dhariyat

51:56 And I have not created the jinn and the men except that they should serve Me.

51:57 I desire no sustenance from them, nor do I desire that they should feed Me.

51:58 Surely Allah is the Bestower of sustenance, the Lord of Power, the Strong.

Hadith here

"We have come to ask you about this matter" He said, "First of all, there was nothing but Allah, and his throne was over the water, and He wrote everything in the Book (in the Heaven) and created the heavens and the earth..."

– Sahih Al Bukhari, Volume 4, Book 54, Hadith 414.

Hadith also

Ubadah b. al Samit said to his son:

I heard the Messenger of Allah say: "The first thing Allah created was the pen. He said to it: 'Write.' It asked: 'What should I write, my Lord?' He said: 'Write what was decreed about everything till the Last Hour comes.'" Son! I heard the Messenger of Allah say: "He who dies on something other than this does not belong to me (on qadr)."

– Sunan Abu Dawud Book 41, Hadith 4683,

Hadith Qudsi

I was a hidden beauty and I wanted to be known so I created My creation so that they would know Me.

THE METAPHOR EXPLAINED, NOW WHAT?

please see there is one god who taught this to me that the word can be understand with ease actually

why do i write like this so you can develop your acumen and decipher words without all these rules being applied by law they make and in a few generations you will like to write like this in languages you use and apostrophes need not be used as one can decipher the word without it and capitals are needed not either commas are useful but not required and so there you have it you apply your head to it and if people have difficulty they can use punctuations and other assets they want but it is true it is like the arabic language of prophet muhammads time and he wrote like this in language he use but enough they think you are making too many changes and our children are getting affected but it is good fun for them to learn this dictum style we have then and in a few generations it wont be a problem to decipher languages like this and allah and the prophet know love occurs this way as rules make you stilted in things you do and ideas float freely this way with you and you develop your intellect as well

omar

see the universe is a fragment here and allah is there giving you his impression that you are small actually even though you want to be my size but no one is me so rest assured you will never be gods like i am to you and mine body is a delight to you more than the seven heavens combined

see the universe is flat not but sphere-like and there is no end to space as it is the dimension we live in and other heavens exist which we can warp into as spirits and not in our body format and it is true the universe is expanding in this dimension we live in as it was created in it by force of nature allah has there around 20 billion light years not but years of your reckoning when he decided to make me human being not but muhammad who would know him and teach me here omar here as i teach others and i learn as you learn from my pen from him allah there and now you know it is a dimension we live in as space is empty and the suns are created in it from allahs body not but his spirit which is a form *of matter which is pure energy units and his body is his spirit and soul thats all for now you already know his spirit created us and all matter*

please see the universe is a fragment here in this dimension of the lower dimension of the material essence i create says i to you the creator here and the next dimension is oblique and covers this one and so forth with all seven of them each one a grain of sand compared to the one above it and i reside above my creation in unend i am and infinite in length and breadth we are not but i allah am and my energy is unend as well i have no limits and my book is the quran of muhammad which entails all the laws to get you there to the 7th heaven not only but to reach my grace to you in that it is grace i give you with me so obey me in it and we will be happy to meet there where i will greet my beloved with grace of myself and gift heaven to her and him who loves to meet me in person

please see know your worth is to sin to get this to your comprehension but if you are sinful i will punish you and know yourself as a child who serves me your creator as a child who is my servant who i will bless in this world with things mundane to you but valuable too as peace in this world has no price attached and in heaven there is unend i give of things you wish but your fruits are your good deeds here and there you will see love from people and marriage to them and sex with children born to you and travel with knowledge from me and so forth houses of gold and silver if you wish them and embroidered cloth for you of silken brocade and it goes on from my reservoir of unend i have for you but you must be good and obey my word in my book to you yes muhammad to me as it has the ingredient for the potion of joy you have now in your life and bear my trial here with patience yes this material world is a trial for you but gain strength and wisdom and your fruits will come to light in paradise i create for you as you were good here and becoming space is for you there for all eternity a gift never to be cut off

omar and muhammad here and allah as well yes we wrote this
Hud.
11:108 And as for those who are made happy, they will be in the Garden abiding therein so long as the heavens and the earth endure, except as thy Lord please — a gift never to be cut off.

THE METAPHOR EXPLAINED, NOW WHAT?

an atheists asks what is the purpose of religion when we can live with the laws of society with us but i ask you what is the purpose of life if you want to live that way without him your creator there

please know religion gives us peace there is creator of us who will take care of us and when we die will give us another life where the meaning of life comes to our comprehension and that we will eventually go to paradise which he has prepared for us when we are clean with you and him as well

please see you have understood he exists as the one cell dna code is perfect for us to exist and you see the immense structure of the universe we study at enormous distance from us of billions of light years and you know there has to be a creator there and you see the perfection of this world in order for us to live in it with its oxygen in due proportion so that our body lives with no toxicity in it and the inert nitrogen that sustains us and so forth our chemical milieu that the earth has and the plants that produce oxygen and scrub out the toxins of other gases and the alternation of the day and night and the perfect distance of the sun to us and you know this universe is perfect to us earthlings and so you know he exists to create this perfect world for us and so you succumb to his existence and you know the law he has sent to us is perfect through the times and most of you believe the quran is his book as well with the law in it for us to submit to and with this submission to his will we find peace here in us and without as well so you know religion is meant to be obeyed and there is a purpose for this submission and to see who is the best in it and when we face hardships in life who submits better than others and so forth who is patient and does not lose faith in him no matter the consequences of hardship on us yes the world is a test for us as to see who submits better and therefore has a higher heaven than you who berate him for hardships and sufferings you face yes each moment he is test on us and now you know the atheists question is answer to it why is there suffering and death and so forth misery here yes it is to test you but he gives you respite too where you have fun and gaity but he expects you to follow his law to you now you know he exists there the creator of this perfect place a speck in the universe we know and thus you know our creation too is perfect to understand him in the frontal lobe he gave us to understand concepts about him and thus if you deny him after this it is your evil you wish that you dont want to be answerable to him your creator and your denial of truth is a punishable offense by him and there let the matter rest that you see squalor in this life when you dont obey him and death of yourself in spirit in the world to come as well

omar

Al-Imran

3:190 In the creation of the heavens and the earth and the alternation of the night and the day, there are surely signs for people of understanding.

3:191 Those who remember Allah standing and sitting and (lying) on their sides, and reflect on the creation of the heavens and the earth: Our Lord, Thou hast not created this in vain! Glory be to Thee! Save us from the chastisement of the Fire.

please see the difference between me and omar here say i muhammad there as i am the emissary of allah and he represents us in his views to you

please see this verse that signifies prophethood has come to an end and that we are saints who have communication from him who creates us to be servants of his grace and i know it is complicated but a prophet is an emissary of him allah who has sovereignty over us and a saint is not a prophet in that sense of having authority over you from him who is the creator there

please see the communication of a saint is also different in that it is his message that comes to his or her mind while the prophet is given a message through the agency of an angel though thought form of message do occur as well to them but it is concrete their role over you and they must be obeyed if you want him your creator to do you good and let you enter paradise with him your savior on earth

please know communication from the prophets do exist to saints and in that context they can be said to be their representative and it is so it a metaphor association we have with him the prophet but it appears we are the prophet as the message is from him but we dont have authority *and his teachings coming to us through our pen and tongue have to be adapt to our culture if it makes sense to people and even if we say this is from him the prophet it does not carry weight like a prophets word does and there you have it that role as an emissary from him the creator is no longer seen in the world and things have to be taken in the context of the book of the prophet and we believe muhammad is the last one and no one will appear now so take my words in reference to the quran and if i adjust religious edicts it is from him the prophet on his behalf the creator there and it is temporary as the words of the quran cannot be altered when they were revealed in their original words so you see i am a lieu only and the quran is permanent there so there you have it jesus was similar in that he was a prophet like me say i muhammad here and his words had to be obeyed for his people otherwise they were not going to make it and thats what occurred to the bani-israel tribe of his land yes they did not make it with their creator and have to go for rehab in hell in the hereafter for them and there it is in your book that he was the way and his follower did have life from his teach and was carried to life in the hereafter if he or she stayed true to his teach there and later christianity with polytheism in it did not have life and they went for rehab in the hereafter as they followed another other than jesus christ your savior there*

omar and muhammad here
Al-Ahzab

33:40 Muhammad is not the father of any of your men, but he is the Messenger of Allah and the Seal of the prophets. And Allah is ever Knower of all things.

John 14

6 Jesus answered, "I am the way and the truth and the life. No one comes to the Father except through me."

please see your defiance is your death on you and if you don't submit here it will be a long while before i let you enter heaven in submission to me say i allah there

please see there is observable area of the universe and there is area that we cannot perceive as it is too far away and its light cannot be seen here but it is so you can travel there after you die so rest assured your sight will see it but do use your telescopes and search the cosmos as it will give you awe of me your creator as i am big more than it the observable sight not but the cosmos and you are a speck to me yet you rise in defiance to me why because you are incomplete and dont appreciate my nature to let you grow through trial and error for some until you come to me after your death then you will succumb more but i know its late for some that they succumb there as well why because you hate to give into my grandeur and people will be there in barzakh who will not succumb even though they know its true that my universe is vast and i am even more so why this attitude to me yes i wish it if they didnt succumb on earth then i will delay them there by taking their soul from them as that is how you evolve enough of you i say there now pray and see if you can recover your peace yes it will occur after you are judged say i as then the soul recurs and you can fast and pray like some of you did not on earth life you live

allah here and over to you man and wife and child to do your bid and see consequences for you

please see your soul is the seat of your learning and if you diminish it or bury it it causes your death of intellect in you and intelligence is remote as well

please see allah is the soul to you and he communicates with you if your soul grows and comes in sync with your conscious state and then if you follow his bid on you you become one with him like isa and myself were and muhammad was perfect in it but did adjust allahs beckoning on him for the will of the people as can be seen in hadith law that he circumvent his opinion for their sake when they couldnt do something he asked them to but he was wise more and as the lead for men he knew their limits so he would adjust law in some issues but not the quran if at all possible for him but it is so he is our lead and he may adjust the law later again to please him who is the creator there who likes it that his word is followed through with

please see the soul is our ruh that is breathed into us at inception and conception and stays with us always not but when we sleep it goes to

THE METAPHOR EXPLAINED, NOW WHAT?

him the creat for repair in things as many turmoils occur some with man and women during their day but it is true the soul communicates with us from allah to our mind as then we see and understand his knowledge and it adds knowledge to us in our mind and heart as well

please see allah is one but he is in us as well as the quran says

please know it is complex not as his spirit is everywhere

please see our spirit is from him as well but he communicates through his soul and if we diminish it we dont see or understand things we read or see or hear as it doesnt reach our soul which is the seat of our understanding of things and if we dont understand issues our mind and heart do not learn and some wander on blindly not seeing reality of truth to us

please see the minds eye is your seat of seeing which is your soul and if you cause it to grow your mind sees clearly

please see when you break your spirit your soul diminishes and you dont see clear ways which is what sex does

please see other sins like abort kills your spirit and your soul doesnt communicate with your mind and your heart doesnt learn things and you become animal-like not knowing stuff your creator creates you for so there you have it your soul leaves you in essence and you dont learn what life is about

please cause it to grow with repentance so that he can forgive you and your soul becomes the seat of learning again like when you were a child yes you become living when he forgives you and your soul fills your spirit again

please know regular prayer causes your soul to replenish you and your understanding of things occur and you can read literature such as mine and the quran as well which makes sense to you then

please know great minds know they repent their evil constantly as minor or major qualms are allayed and they develop peace in them

please see to inhibit evil in you as this breaks the spirit and your mind becomes confused in issues it faces

please see a confused mind is the devils car in that it drives the wrong path to him your god and its destination is hellfire

omar

Al-Hijr

15:28 And when thy Lord said to the angels: I am going to create a mortal of sounding clay, of black mud fashioned into shape.

15:29 So when I have made him complete and breathed into him of My spirit, fall down making obeisance to him.

Al-Sajdah

32:7 Who made beautiful everything that He created, and He began the creation of man from dust.

32:8 Then He made his progeny of an extract, of worthless water.

32:9 Then He made him complete and breathed into him of His spirit, and gave you ears and eyes and hearts; little it is that you give thanks!

Qaf

50:16 And certainly We created man, and We know what his mind suggests to him — and We are nearer to him than his jugular vein.

Al-Anum

6:71 Say: Shall we call, besides Allah, on that which profits us not nor harms us, and shall we be turned back on our heels after Allah has guided us? Like one whom the devils cause to follow his low desires, in bewilderment in the earth — ...

Al-Shams

91:7 And the soul and its perfection!

91:8 So He reveals to it its way of evil and its way of good;

91:9 He is indeed successful who causes it to grow,

91:10 And he indeed fails who buries it.

please see the soul beckons you to do good and forbids evil on you as it is from your god as a guide to you so let it flourish with regular prayer and charity in you and if you cause it to diminish by ignoring its edicts on you you will have nature worse than animals who dont sin by nature they have

please see this verse that we have a nature and that is upright in piety we are and i know you think you are upright when you dont lie or cheat others but upright is law-abiding in us as the verse says here that you have a duty to keep so you know the law he allah to you enacts is sane for you in that your soul rejects it if you break your spirit-law you have and diminishes in light it has thereby limiting your sight in issues you have there you have it when you break your spirit-law you lose your soul and thats why we say all religions taught the same law as taught by the prophets there and homosexual law was never condoned in any law structure i had says i allah there there you have it i would never allow it and when you follow secularism that allows this freedom to men and womenkind they break them in it and they suffer in their life so ban it for their repose that it is abnormal act and it should never be accepted by man or child he has

please know other laws entailed in the quran are there for your review if you break any of them your fiber will break and your spirit will be lost in that its fiber will break and its mettle will be weak and you wont be able to accomplish much and you will lose faith in yourself and allah as well and that will remain until you are judged as guilt with you unless you relent to forgive you by repent you do

please know fornication and adultery and homosexual acts are major sins by which you will lose faith as your spirit will break and you will lose sight as your soul diminishes and your soul is my tool that i give you in order for you to discern between right and wrong you have it in this world after you die i take it from you and your trial is end and you await judge on you on how you lived your life say i omar not but allah there so there occurs omar is sane to learn the reason the soul is given to man and mankind on earth so they know through pangs of conscience when they err and that is my soul beckon you to correct itself your heart to you in sin you live except some who follow my law perfectly which are few as yet

allah here

Al-Rum

30:30 So set thy face for religion, being upright, the nature made by Allah in which He has created men. There is no altering Allah's creation. That is the right religion — but most people know not—

30:31 Turning to Him; and keep your duty to Him, and keep up prayer and be not of the polytheists, please see the unitarians are one body with us of islam and that the country is founded on unitarian principles by their founding fathers

please see sanity emerge here that the unitarians were an offshoot of islam emerging in christianity in the 16th century and adopted jesus as a man incarnate not of him who creates and many great minds have emerged with them but now the time has come for the quran to dominate you and illihoon quran is what you adopt but it is true when the west saw the truth of islam they adopt it in the form of this church and it was good move on their part

please see the views of the unitarians in that they align to those of islam for the most part and now you know america was based on unitarian principles you will succumb more to me in islam of illihoon to you with the prayer we have and us being one body under him our creat and many great minds did it beget like isaac newton george washington thomas jefferson quincy adams amongst many other american and european nationals who were against monotheism not they produced in its edicts in the christian church and many united states presidents were also from this church and they knew the truth of islam but couldnt muster more until it is now apparent the quran is the book preserved mainly intact by him your creat and thats why your race considers its motto to be one nation under god

Extract from Wikipedia page on Unitarian church

Although there is no specific authority on convictions of Unitarian belief aside from rejection of the Trinity, the following beliefs are generally accepted:

One God and the oneness or unity of God.

The life and teachings of Jesus Christ constitute the exemplar model for living one's own life.

Reason, rational thought, science, and philosophy coexist with faith in God.

Humans have the ability to exercise free will in a responsible, constructive and ethical manner with the assistance of religion.

Human nature in its present condition is neither inherently corrupt nor depraved (see original Sin) but capable of both good and evil, as God intended.

THE METAPHOR EXPLAINED, NOW WHAT?

No religion can claim an absolute monopoly on the Holy Spirit or theological truth.

Though the authors of the Bible were inspired by God, they were humans and therefore subject to human error.

The traditional doctrines of predestination, eternal damnation, and the vicarious sacrifice and satisfaction theories of the Atonement are invalid because they malign God's character and veil the true nature and mission of Jesus Christ.

End of section

please see this verse this applies to the followers of christ in the unitarian church as they are true to his word and we consider them muslims like the apostles were considered so in the vernacular of god in the quran and there you have it early christians were muslims by us and the ebionites were a muslim sect that followed christs disciples in things so we are one body with them

omar

Al-Imran

3:50 And (I am) a verifier of that which is before me of the Torah, and I allow you part of that which was forbidden to you; and I have come to you with a sign from your Lord, so keep your duty to Allah and obey me.

3:51 Surely Allah is my Lord and your Lord, so serve Him. This is the right path.

3:52 But when Jesus perceived disbelief on their part, he said: Who will be my helpers in Allah's way? The disciples said: We are Allah's helpers: we believe in Allah, and bear thou witness that we are submitting ones (Muslims).

please see this note from your president who didnt make it but had some piety with him in that he liked one god concepts the quran had and adopted it for his country

i had many flaws and killed many men of indian descent but i know muhammad was right in issues and we joined the unitarian movement thomas and myself and taught one god principle to people we talked to and the quran was available to us and we read it but more importantly it was translations of the quran by muslim hands that we saw correct as these people who gave us the quran were vicious in it about our man muhammad there but we knew he was a saint at least as he had a book and so it occur many of us in the movement of independence were unitarians and we knew one god principles apply but i was bad in many ways and suffered hell in my hereafter but it is so we brought unitarianism to you here and we are forgiven for our sins quincy made it but thomas and myself were immured in debt to others but it is so there was a black slave who was saint who told us we would be unitarianism as a nation one day thats why we stuck to the principle of one god for us as a nation to us

omar not but his pen as george washington here

please see the american indians were sad at your arrival though they welcomed you initially but it is so you broke pacts with them and fought them rather than assimilating them in your culture

please see the american indian race was massacred by you and they lost heart when you did abysmal things by me to subjugate them to rule you had yes you raped their child in front of her and him and took their body parts for booty ornaments you had and people like geronimo lost heart yes he was a believer in me his creator and he died a broken man thats what you did to the spirit of them

geronimo was a stalwart believer in me but it is so they made captives of most indians who survived the deluge they did when they massacred them in these states but it is so they were sad living in camps in their forts after their captivity occurred and it is sad to see a race gone away by you but you are better now and protect their gene from expiry in this land of illihoon people you are but do compensate them with riches and lifestyle adequate for their needs and i will come forth with you in forgiveness for your race as there was some good in you you did adopt me your creator in your prayers you do and teach them as well what they lost when you taught trinity there instead of their god allah there

omar not but allah to you here

isaac newtons note here for your perusal

please see this comment from this esteemed colleague of ours where he says we were exposed to excerpts of the quran in our literature and i was a young man when that occur and we saw the truth of what the unitarians or monotheists were saying so i adopt it and researched our book the bible and saw what omar writes about and i saw ikhlas in the quran excerpts i had and so became a believer in it the teachings of this man who they call muhammad there and i taught arianism was sane but i was a true muslim and said so they were a good race in my literature there but it is so thats all i could muster say i isaac here

isaac newton here from omars pen

please see atheism is the bane for your society as you attempt to bring god back into your life

please see atheism has reigned here

please know your founding fathers founded this land in the worship of god and not atheistic principles it adopt in its course

please see they looked down on the worship of a man and did not want the church to interfere with government of the country even if it was a christian land but the minds that formulated the country were not as they were muslim bent and called themselves unitarians and they worshipped him who create them

please see they did not want the worship of jesus in government offices so they relinquished it the church there but they did keep the worship of god intact and so you have become atheists where you dont allow islam of worship of him who you call god in your vernacular publicly in government offices and schools at large and this is evil car you have

please see islam is served here by my telling you you do have islam if you take out the worship of man out of the building of religion you adopt

please know the church has to succumb to you as it is your country and you dont want this base instinct that you would call him who you call jesus as your god to you while he did not create you in your dna car you have and so the quranic verse rings true that your founding father and others thought that god was omniscient and all-powerful and prayed there for this day that you would institutionalize prayer there for him in your public arena and you would allow prayer for your kids in school they have and there you have it supreme court is outcast for adopting atheism in your culture where god used to be centerpiece of your life

please see constitutional amendments are required to allow you god in your life where you work where he can be discussed freely and that you allow prayer for him there as well

omar

Al-Baqarah

2:163 And your God is one God; there is no God but He! He is the Beneficent, the Merciful.

Al-Imran

3:29 Say: Whether you hide what is in your hearts or manifest it, Allah knows it. And He knows whatever is in the heavens and whatever is in the earth. And Allah is Possessor of power over all things.

please see these words are solace here as you lost ground in the last century when you became atheists in things and left god in your prayers you had not with you

please see thomas was a unitarian no he was me a muslim of ahmadiyya bent and thats why your country adopts me as we believe like thomas jefferson in normal births in all humans and also god is omniscient and worthy of taking care of us in all respects of life yes he was a muslim like me says george washington and there were many like us who hated church structure and beliefs and so there you have it we separated church from us in the government of man and wife but that doesnt mean we were areligious we prayed too but like i said before our sins were many with the christians not as we let them be but with the american indian man and woman and their child so we didnt make it to heaven but we were all influenced by church not but by muslim literature and adopt universalism and unity concepts for our government not allowing jesus worship in it and so there you have it we were monotheists and submitting to the one god in his teachings to us and quincy adams and john adams made it with universalist ideology but thomas was wrong and universalism did not catch on the mainstream as he wished and now it has in the mainstream of american fabric and i support here this move of ahmadiyya religion as it is sane

THE METAPHOR EXPLAINED, NOW WHAT?

for us and stay away from the miracles islam has i say but you have accepted him omar here thats why i say it now otherwise he would be mischief to write from us for his betterment to occur but yes we are deists in the american government there so let it rest with you we are one body with islam worldwide now and it is over our war there which subsequent governments did in their ignorance of our religion yes the founding fathers were us in islam of monotheism and thats the best we could muster yes the unitarian principles islam has of our country

omar not but george here

please see repentance in your heart is key to your survival after you say the shahada

please see the shahada means repentance in it and it means you are going to forge for yourself a new life and it entails forgiveness from your creator but the intent is that you will turn over a new leaf to you and you will not commit misdeeds otherwise you are not forgiven in that sense and only when it is associated with repentance in your heart is it accepted as peace for you as to become a muslim means that you have the car to be upright now

please see we all commit sins in our lives and sometimes mistakes occur even after we say the shahada but as hud here says turn back not in wrongs you do before after accepting me your creator as your god and as al-zumar says i forgive you all sins if i feel you are sincere to me in repentance act you have and i ask you continue to live your life in forbearing to others and things i do to you say i the august one to you allah there and there you have it you will be forgiven if i see you are pure in yourself and the intent is there not to do it again the sin you did

omar not only

Al-Zumar

39:53 Say: O My servants who have been prodigal regarding their souls, despair not of the mercy of Allah; surely Allah forgives sins altogether. He is indeed the Forgiving, the Merciful.

Al-Imran

3:132 And obey Allah and the Messenger, that you may be shown mercy.

3:133 And hasten to forgiveness from your Lord and a Garden, as wide as the heavens and the earth; it is prepared for those who keep their duty:

Hud

11:51 O my people, I ask of you no reward for it. My reward is only with Him Who created me. Do you not then understand?

11:52 And, O my people, ask forgiveness of your Lord, then turn to Him, He will send on you clouds pouring down abundance of rain and add strength to your strength, and turn not back, guilty.

please see this chapter ya sin which has the concept that you will be raised one day even if you are an open disputant here

please see the concepts in the quran about me your creator are safe to be with and also the law structure i give you is safe for your culture wherever in the world you are and i know its late for some lands that you adopt me formally in my book to you but it is so there is much good in it and when comprehension occurs it is sane in its entirety for you to adopt then you will be safe from my wrath say i allah there as i will exact punishment on those communities who lag behind in my edicts to you thinking your culture is superior while it is not only illihoon is safe for you and there are many inconstancies in you which are not sane by you and if you adopt the illihoon quran you will be sane in issues like the west has become and 1 god is their watchword as to how they became pliant to my pen here and i know your culture worldwide recognizes me as your god but rest assured i am not willing to relent on piety principles i enact for you in illihoon you are and my word in the quran is extant see here how i give life to the earth in the form of a green tree that you use for yourself and i am complete in knowledge as your creator and i know whats best for you and you dont so submit to me in the quran i teach and with clarity of intellect you realize which is in muhammad alis translation and not in other qurans where they carry the baggage of some imbecile concepts they have so use only muhammad alis version and his notes are sane for you but amend them with my teach from omars pen and tongue as he teaches daily the quran there and there you have it my word is from muhammad the prophet there in this quran i teach to you so adopt it and no else and it is my humble request to man to do so why humble because i enact it though i am explicit and can order but i want you to come through in illihoon yourself

omar not at all here but his pen as me allah there

Al-Hadid

57:1 Whatever is in the heavens and the earth declares the glory of Allah, and He is the Mighty, the Wise.

57:2 His is the kingdom of the heavens and the earth. He gives life and causes death; and He is Possessor of power over all things.

57:3 He is the First and the Last and the Manifest and the Hidden, and He is Knower of all things.

57:4 He it is Who created the heavens and the earth in six periods, and He is established on the Throne of Power. He knows that which goes down into the earth and that which comes forth out of it, and that which comes down from heaven and that which goes up to it. And He is with you wherever you are. And Allah is Seer of what you do.

57:5 His is the kingdom of the heavens and the earth; and to Allah are (all) affairs returned.

Ya Sin

36:77 Does not man see that We have created him from the small life-germ? Then lo! he is an open disputant.

36:78 And he strikes out a likeness for Us and forgets his own creation. Says he: Who will give life to the bones, when they are rotten?

36:79 Say: He will give life to them, Who brought them into existence at first, and He is Knower of all creation,

36:80 Who produced fire for you out of the green tree, so that with it you kindle.

36:81 Is not He Who created the heavens and the earth able to create the like of them? Yea! And He is the Creator (of all), the Knower.

Please see the abort of a child is heinous crime but to single out girls is detrimental to society there.

Please see this verse from Nahl where it says that the man would bury his daughter alive for shame that it caused him.

Please know it is true in present day India it is the same in that they abort the female and carry the male pregnancy till term.

Please know this is abominable to do.

Please know Islam does not allow this and when it came to Arabia this practice of burial of their daughters passed away in the dust of time and was never practiced again in that land.

Please know we cherish our womenfolk and give them respect and honor in Islam.

Please know my daughter knows the respect she has in the religion and is grateful for it, Islam I mean here.

Please know it is clear India is a problem state.

Please know it is actually illegal to do this abortion there yet it is widely practiced.

Please know it is culture they have that a daughter is a burden.

Please know it is rampant there.

Please know it is practiced somewhat in other countries as well but Muslim lands are immune from this evil practice due to this verse here. Omar.

The Bee.

16:57 And they ascribe daughters to Allah. Glory be to Him! And for themselves is what they desire!

16:58 And when the birth of a daughter is announced to one of them, his face becomes black and he is full of wrath.

16:59 He hides himself from the people because of the evil of what is announced to him. Shall he keep it with disgrace or bury it (alive) in the dust? Now surely evil is what they judge!

please see there is one god and he has one law on us from forever and there are certain deviances in it that creep into it when man interferes with it his law-bearing on us

please see anum here where it says there is no changing allahs words in that the law entailed there is unchanged from the beginning of mankinds creation and we cannot disregard the law in its entirety as it is our nature these laws are please see from the beginning even when we were spirits these laws were in place but we werent coming through and disregarded him except a few like muhammad and some with him why it was because there was no punishment enact then

please see eventually we were created here where he gave instructs for our punishment if we broke the law of significance which fornication is then and he said we would be punished in the hereafter if we did it here so there was no escape from his law there

please see it was here that i showed you the prophets always told them his people not to disregard the law and punishment was enact by the people on the errant one who disobeyed the law of significance and there you have it there is no altering his word on us till we are judged

please see it is our nature though yes this law on us and we know we break our fiber in that our spirit goes from us when we sin

please see from time immemorable people have tried to circumvent gods law on them and buddhist took god away from their scriptures and so did the chinese who followed law not by confucius and kept it as wisdom as they did not want law from him the creator where they will be obliged to follow through in obedience and they would have to have law of fornication not there with them so it occurred to make excuses in culture to make it occur that sex was permitted to them

please know paul abrogated law similarly when he said what he did that jesus took away your sins and you would enter paradise while jesus never indicated that in his teachings to them and asked them to ask forgiveness from him his creator as was jewish custom then so he abrogated law this way and he also said there was no law there

please see you know what hardship follows when you have sex outside the marriage realm and that is gods punishment there that you abhor now but it is so his word will not change and all religions have similar laws as given by prophet there at the outset and jesus was no exception he upheld it the law on fornication not and sex not outside marriage clan you have now so there you have it god is not going to change nature and his law as long as mankind is on earth and there are no exceptions in any culture and the quran is the final word in that it enacts punishment for it please see the reward is immense if you follow through with islamic custom of punish the act by law-making of it in a public setting as god requests you there and if your culture does so it will raise itself to heights where intellect reigns and in heaven you will have pleasures where he will permit relationships in marriage you will be for all eternity when you get there so ive done my bid and shown you rewards and punishments he has and now it is up to your culture to adapt to it and make law enact by you in humble poise to his greatness there the creator i mean who is above us in peace one day in heaven abode when we make it there for ourselves

omar

Al-Anum

6:114 Shall I then seek a judge other than Allah, when He it is Who has sent down to you the Book fully explained. And those whom We have given the Book know that it is revealed by thy Lord with truth, so be not thou of the disputers.

6:115 And the word of thy Lord has been accomplished truly and justly. There is none who can change His words; and He is the Hearer, the Knower.

6:116 And if thou obey most of those in the earth, they will lead thee astray from Allah's way. They follow naught but conjecture, and they only lie.

6:117 Surely thy Lord — He knows best who goes astray from His way, and He knows best the guided ones.

please see it is the worship of me that i create you and you are pleased in it as it is your peace that you worship the one who created you from himself and gave you a conscious mind to think for yourself from him to me you say

please see this verse that you flee to me your creator and that i created you but to serve me in worship i do you say but it is so you succumb to me now and you fear consequences if you dont serve me in worship

please see i admonish but am loving if you come through in your escape to me in my command to you do i ask you to be but it is so there are some who escape not this culture and break my edict and i am severe in it

please know i ask you to worship me why it is because when you do you become me in repose and i am your thoughts in worship mode you have and your need is addressed by me eventually i do take care of you if you worship me your creat to you if you do so with no pride and i know you do otherwise but it is so you come through with one god in you now you know your fiber is me and that you are meant to be holy personages not ones doing your bid in things which is unholy for the most part and rebellious of you say i omar not but allah to you

allah here

Al-Dhariyat

51:47 And the heaven, We raised it high with power, and We are Makers of the vast extent.

51:48 And the earth, We have spread it out. How well We prepared it!

51:49 And of everything We have created pairs that you may be mindful.

51:50 So flee to Allah. Surely I am a plain warner to you from Him.

51:51 And do not set up with Allah another god. Surely I am a plain warner to you from Him.

51:52 Thus there came not a messenger to those before them but they said: An enchanter or a madman!

51:53 Have they charged each other with this? Nay, they are an inordinate people.

51:54 So turn away from them, for thou art not to blame;

51:55 And remind, for reminding profits the believers.

51:56 And I have not created the jinn and the men except that they should serve Me.

51:57 I desire no sustenance from them, nor do I desire that they should feed Me.

51:58 Surely Allah is the Bestower of sustenance, the Lord of Power, the Strong.

please see to be holy in your dealings with me your creator and others in islam who beckon you to persevere in good behavior to them and others

please see rum here where he talks about the nature of man and child

please see upright is holy to us in our vernacular and you know its clear such people are not polytheists and thats a part of being a hanif or upright person like abraham and muhammad and others in islam like myself and jesus as well

please see upright is holy when you speak the truth about him your creator and in other matters being upright as well

please see those who disbelieve are called unholy or the worst of creatures

please see this includes the animals as creatures are mentioned here in this verse from bayyinah so raise yourself up in holiness to be upright and testify your god is one god like the quran says here

please know being holy or upright is a muslim creed and by nature man is supposed to be holy

please see according to hadith a child is a muslim or upright and it is with the passage of time his or her parents change their views and some become polytheists and lose their upright state

please see those who follow their low desires are not holy and it is the nature of man to be upright so succumb to it in the laws he has the creator there

please see it is over and you cant be holy if you profess polytheism or call jesus your god or bow down to idols

please observe the law which is your nature in you

please see there is no changing allahs law or his nature in us

please see your soul is allahs essence in you and is holy and if you are holy in your deeds and words then you are in sync with him your creat and your essence emerges in you and you are happy with peace and joy in your life as well

please see when you sync yourself with him your creator with your actions and words of truth you say you become him as well becoming 'we' people as allah uses the word 'we' in the quran for himself and others with him and the metaphor applies if we are allah in essence in our nature we become him and our attributes are his then

please know it is over and you have understood you cannot sin if you want nature of upright with you so observe the law as a community being upright in testimony about him your creator and so forth testimony in court settings where you are asked things and commit not sins of the nature we talk about on this page of mine which are low desires in you or in other words do not take your low desires to be your god to you beckoning to them rather than him your creator to you and there you have it in a nutshell what it means to be holy in your life

omar

Al-Rum

30:29 Nay, those who are unjust follow their low desires without any knowledge; so who can guide him whom Allah leaves in error? And they shall have no helpers.

30:30 So set thy face for religion, being upright, the nature made by Allah in which He has created men. There is no altering Allah's creation. That is the right religion — but most people know not—

30:31 Turning to Him; and keep your duty to Him, and keep up prayer and be not of the polytheists,

Al-Imran

3:67 Abraham was not a Jew nor a Christian, but he was (an) upright (man), a Muslim; and he was not one of the polytheists.

Al-Imran

3:95 Say: Allah speaks the truth; so follow the religion of Abraham, the upright one. And he was not one of the polytheists.

Al-Bayyinnah

98:4 Nor did those to whom the Book was given become divided till clear evidence came to them.

98:5 And they are enjoined naught but to serve Allah, being sincere to Him in obedience, upright, and to keep up prayer and pay the poor-rate, and that is the right religion.

98:6 Those who disbelieve from among the People of the Book and the idolaters will be in the Fire of hell, abiding therein. They are the worst of creatures.

98:7 Those who believe and do good, they are the best of creatures.

98:8 Their reward is with their Lord: Gardens of perpetuity wherein flow rivers, abiding therein forever. Allah is well pleased with them and they are well pleased with Him. That is for him who fears his Lord.

Al-Furqan

25:43 Hast thou seen him who takes his low desires for his god? Wilt thou be a guardian over him?

25:44 Or thinkest thou that most of them hear or understand? They are but as the cattle; nay, they are farther astray from the path.

please see the first command of his to obey him in worship alone for all major revealed religions though the matter has been made obscure in some of their books by changing words they have

shall we call on any besides our creator allah there they say nay we are asked to call on him alone and that is the nature of our submission to him in that he asks us to do this and not pray to any vestige you have in your minds or heart not as the heart knows the truth of this affair that we should pray to him alone and no one else and it is the devil who gives you this faith that you call on another entity besides him the creat and in bewilderment do you wander on

please know it is not just the christians or any religion that has monopoly in the matter of worship but any one who submits to him is who is counted as one going to heaven and now you know any monotheist can make it there

please see early christians and jews made it to allah when they performed virtue with them and so it is with any nation now that recognizes their creator as one god to them and keep the law with them as being successful in achieving their end with him and now you know submission means belief in him being one and the law is separate and prayer and alms are separate and these verses show you that is the essence of being a muslim in that you submit that way to him alone though submission is also used in the sense of his commands on you and the first commandment is you take him to be your creator alone and have no one besides him who you call on please see the character of being a muslim is being a unitarian in your culture and with it you achieve love in your life if you are a good person and pray to him as he asks you to do this and follow his commandments he has given in his book there you have it you will achieve felicity in this world and heaven will be yours in the next life

please see it is an honor to be called a muslim or submitter to him so dont backtrack on being one and keep your faith till the day you are raised for life again as to leave your religion of monotheism is death on you now that you in your hearts repose are sure of the issue of one god with you and your destination will be hellfire for you so keep your creator as one for you as no one but him wrote your dna code by which you were created and given characteristics you have yes he created everything about you when your dna was formed

please see if you can think of any other entity who wrote your dna code?

omar

Al-Baqarah

2:111 And they say: None shall enter the Garden except he who is a Jew, or the Christians. These are their vain desires. Say: Bring your proof if you are truthful.

2:112 Nay, whoever submits himself entirely to Allah and he is the doer of good (to others), he has his reward from his Lord, and there is no fear for such nor shall they grieve.

Al-Anum

6:71 Say: Shall we call, besides Allah, on that which profits us not nor harms us, and shall we be turned back on our heels after Allah has guided us? Like one whom the devils cause to follow his low desires, in bewilderment in the earth — he has companions who call him to the right way (saying), Come to us. Say: Surely the guidance of Allah, that is the (true) guidance. And we are commanded to submit to the Lord of the worlds:

6:72 And that you should keep up prayer and keep your duty to Him. And He it is to Whom you shall be gathered.

Al-Imran

3:102 *O you who believe, keep your duty to Allah, as it ought to be kept, and die not unless you are Muslims.*

please see we are weak and sin some but it is important to avoid major ones that take you to hell and if you improve with time with prayer in you you will achieve felicity with him your creator to you

please see what it is to be a god you are

please know it is when you know my law and you sin in it by your sanity you think

please know muslims are akin to it as they have the quran injunctions by them yet they are disobedient to it and they do their bid

please know this is what godhead is in a negative sense of the word and a kid who underdresses is admonished for this godhead in her where she attracts to men to sex with her body on her

please know when you know the law on homosexuality being illegal with me your creator and you approach him for it you are gods in perversity to you and i punish gods like you

please know when women go out for dates with sex planned they are similar in perversity and i make their nature perverse in things

please know you have the quran with you and it allows you no leeway in sin and if you ignore it like many muslims do you are in charge you say and i am not your god to you you are it the god is you as you take decisions independently of me your creator who knows better than you what your needs are

please see there is godhead in most of you as you are imperfect and cant submit perfectly to me at first but if you pray for yourself regular ways i will give you peace and forgive you as well if you mature to be law-abiding to me your creator but you must be regular in it in order to achieve felicity with me and your soul becomes one at rest as you mature or the nafs that is mutmainna

please know to ask forgiveness regular ways with your prayers and avoid major crimes by me which are listed in my books from time immemorial and the quran is the validation of the books from before so keep it and consult it regular ways

omar not but allah there gave you this concept of godhead in you

THE METAPHOR EXPLAINED, NOW WHAT?

Please see My nature is carried forth in you and you like One God with you by your essence in you.

Please see the following hadith and the accompanying text from the Quran where it says the nature of mankind is one of Islam being upright in everything and to worship One God in its essence and all that.

Please know we are asked to be upright in things by Him and the Prophet of Islam in that it is the true religion in things.

Please know it is one in which one is not a polytheist and one takes care of one's fellow beings and prayer to Him is necessary as well.

Please know the hadith is clear that just as we are perfect in our form, so too is our nature at birth and we are essentially Muslim-kinds, as we are believers though we don't know it then and a child is akin to Me say I Allah there, there you have it they sense the truth from Me and tell you, their parents, what is right and wrong in their upright stance on you.

Please know it is clear our religion is embedded in us in that we are upright and all that in our creation of us and that by nature we are not polytheists.

Please know the child is happy when you tell him or her God created them and it is true they like One God with them in the concepts they have and that's why they support me by their very nature on them.

Please know that is the true religion, being upright in things and to testify to the Oneness of My Being say I Allah, the Creator of you all, My children to Me, in love do I beget you in the sense of your creation from your DNA code, each one here. Omar not only but Allah too.

The Romans

30:30 So set thy face for religion, being upright, the nature made by Allah in which He has created men. There is no altering Allah's creation. That is the right religion — but most people know not—

30:31 Turning to Him; and keep your duty to Him, and keep up prayer and be not of the polytheists,

Hadith.

"Every child that is born conforms to the true religion (literally, human nature), then his parents make him a Jew or a Christian or a Magian, as a beast is born entire in all its limbs (or without a defect);

do you see one born maimed and mutilated?" Then he repeated (i.e., in support of what he said): "The nature made by Allah in which He has created men; there is no altering Allah's creation. That is the right religion" (B. 23:93).

Please see these verses in Jonah where it says that the Quran could only have been forged by Allah and challenges those who disbelieve in it to forge a chapter like it.

Please see it is a challenge to mankind but why they say, it is because they say he has forged it about him, Muhammad there, but it is so it is a unique Book in that it has perfect rhythm and cadence is surreal, the message is emphatic and so forth dogma occurs in it that God is the speaker there and so forth it is unique to you in its message in that One God speaks to you, there is no other Book like it, my page is nothing like it though it contains uniqueness you like but so forth it is not the Quran in its cadence and qirat to you.

Please see it occur that the Quran is certain by you.

Please know it has occurred as I speak that the Quran is a Book by you in this land and thereby you judge your acts.

Please know it is complementary to your Book, the Bible or the Injeel as we call it.

Please know it has occurred that your God is One and you worship Him for the most part now.

Please see it occur that Islam is one entity now with the Christian land owners.

Please know they see it as one.

Please know I know because I am told so in dreams that it has occurred.

Please know the effort is by many, myself included, and it so transpires that your God is One with you.

Please know it has transpired that there is a genuine interest in the Quran and the Revealer of it.

Please know it is easy for Allah to do.

Please know the time is ripe for the picking as they say so make an effort.

Please see it occur we are one entity in the future you say but it has occurred in tangible ways. Omar.

Jonah

10:37 *And this Qur'an is not such as could be forged by those besides Allah, but it is a verification of that which is before it and a clear explanation of the Book, there is no doubt in it, from the Lord of the worlds.*

10:38 *Or say they: He has forged it? Say: Then bring a chapter like it, and invite whom you can besides Allah, if you are truthful.*

Please see many vices and illnesses occur when you fail to follow your prophet to you.

Please see this post has relevance there where they uproot me if they could as it is clear that the message has been coming to you from time immemorial and you realize things got muddied with the passage of time but it is so the Quran is intact in its message and so forth results and you all succumb to it in its edicts and so forth we are one body now as a result.

Please see the following verse from Jonah and the verse that corroborates it from Al-Fatir where it says a Messenger or Warner has come to all the nations, with no exception to it.

Please see it occur that there is a warner for this nation as well where the Prophet's teachings reach all the people and the Quran teaches them.

Please see it occur we are one nation now as we recognize God as our savior and we pray to Him in our thoughts and words as well.

Please know there is a move now to remove oneself from the church premises and exclusively devote oneself to God in your prayers to Him.

Please see it occur that the church is intact though as they measure the response of people who wish to pray to God exclusively in their prayers to Him in church premises and without as well.

Please know it has occurred that Trinity concepts are outmode now and people want to respond to One God in their prayer to Him.

Please see it occur there is One God with you and He beckons you to do good to him and her, who is your child.

Please know sexual promiscuity leads to cancer and other diseases and you should abstain from it in your living here on earth.

Please know ADD and autism are the product of sexually transmitted vices in us as well.

Please see it occur that these vices are uproot when true comprehension takes place as when Islam appears to you as correct for you.

Please know that modern science now confirms these findings in one.

Please see it occur that the message comes to you.

Please know these vices are uproot because Allah in the Quran directs us to stop.

Please see it occur that One God appears to you as correct for you as He directs the affair from His throne in Heaven above us.

Please know there is One God here in your hearts.

Please know you will succumb gradually you say, true, but you have already developed the basis of truth which is One God with you in your prayers.

Please see it occur that original scriptures contain references to monotheism as their prophet God sense tells them that in their books of yore. Omar.

Jonah

10:47 And for every nation there is a messenger. So when their messenger comes, the matter is decided between them with justice, and they are not wronged.

The Originator or Al-Fatir

35:24 Surely We have sent thee with the Truth as a bearer of good news and a warner. And there is not a people but a warner has gone among them.

Please see you know now you were not created without a purpose.

Please see this is correct in that He will test you and perfect His light and we are not created in vain. He wants us with Him in Heaven but first He will purify you so that you are fit to be there and He will make sure you are perfect-like with no evil in you before you enter with Him.

Some people will make it unscathed and those that don't heed Him and His law for you will undergo reformation in a place they don't belong but will stay there until they are ready for a Heavenly abode, and I mean Hell here. Omar.

Please see this verse from Al-Muminun in the Quran that shows mankind has a purpose there.

23:115 Do you then think that We have created you in vain, and that you will not be returned to Us?

23:116 So exalted be Allah, the True King! No God is there but He, the Lord of the Throne of Grace.

Please also see the verse that follows where it is said by the believer that there is a purpose for the creation of mankind in that the heavens and earth were not created in vain.

Al-Imran.

3:191 Those who remember Allah standing and sitting and (lying) on their sides, and reflect on the creation of the heavens and the earth: Our Lord, Thou hast not created this in vain! Glory be to Thee! Save us from the chastisement of the Fire.

Please see the lesson is safe with us that this life is transitory and the Hereafter is lasting for us so prepare your way there.

Please see this verses from Al-Ala where it says the life of this world is transitory and the Hereafter is lasting and better for you.

Please know it says these were your teachings from before when you had the Book of Abraham and Moses but so what occurs you can't wait to think about the Hereafter while this life is so hard and tremendous in nature.

Please know it doesn't need to be so, you can have peace in it and so forth but it is true life is tumultuous unless you have faith in Him Who creates you for it.

Please know life is transitory but it is permanent in the Hereafter where we will be judged and our deeds will be counted and so forth occurs, you all know what Judgment Day is, but the problem is you don't heed here so the punishment is written for some and some are guided there.

Please know it is clear we are one entity in that we have similar aspirations and goals,

Please know some will make it well here but the majority are poor in it, their goals, but Allah's faith is more important and if you are poor in material ways it doesn't matter if you have faith with it. Omar.

Al-Ala.

87:9 So remind, reminding indeed profits.

87:10 He who fears will mind,

87:11 And the most unfortunate one will avoid it,

87:12 Who will burn in the great Fire.

87:13 Then therein he will neither live nor die.

87:14 He indeed is successful who purifies himself,

87:15 And remembers the name of his Lord, then prays.

87:16 But, you prefer the life of this world,

87:17 While the Hereafter is better and more lasting.

87:18 Surely this is in the earlier scriptures,

87:19 The scriptures of Abraham and Moses.

Please see our good deeds are like fruits that we reap benefit from for eternity to us.

Please see this verse from Ibrahim where the parable of a tree is used.

Please see it occur we speak good words here and reap the fruits in this world and the Hereafter.

Please know it is clear when we teach the Quran it has a benefit here.

Please know it makes a difference to the person listening and may alter his life works.

Please know similarly an evil word can be uttered but will never bear fruit.

Please know it is lost and decay results.

Please see it is clear that a good word will bear fruit for us in heaven where it will be palpable to us.

Please know it will benefit us indefinitely.

Please see the parable is clear that evil is not rewarded.

THE METAPHOR EXPLAINED, NOW WHAT?

Please know it will not benefit anyone and will die out.

Please know to speak good words or keep silent is what the Prophet said.

Please know to prepare for the Hereafter is sane and to plant trees in Paradise is our aim in this life. Omar.

Ibrahim.

14:24 Seest thou not how Allah sets forth a parable of a good word as a good tree, whose root is firm and whose branches are high,

14:25 Yielding its fruit in every season by the permission of its Lord? And Allah sets forth parables for men that they may be mindful.

14:26 And the parable of an evil word is as an evil tree pulled up from the earth's surface; it has no stability.

Please see the Quran says no one knows the delights that are stored there for the believer in Him, their Creat, if they do good deeds here.

Please see this verse from Rad where it says that heaven is described as a parable here.

Please know the dimension of it cannot be known.

Please see it occur we are pleased though.

Please know in chapter of Muhammad it is clear that wine and honey are mentioned as a parable, the true nature of these foods is not known to us.

Please see it occur that it is better than what we see here.

Please know the description of Heaven is sensuous in places.

Please know it is clear from hadith and the Book that a sensuous heaven is prepared for those who believe.

Please know there are many hadith of this nature they say, it is true, but it is clear also that these are reserved for those who believe in Allah and follow His Book letter.

Please know you can have sensuality in this life and if a believer abstains here he will be rewarded with better in the Hereafter.

Please know children are born in the Hereafter according to hadith we have, so sexual relations will continue.

Please see it is not like what Christians and other religions say.

Please know also fruits could mean sexual delights or other pleasures as well.

Please know there is nutrition there and I don't mean that we won't be fed.

Please know these are only depictions in the Quran and hadith somewhat and the truth is no one knows what is in store for one there but it will be peace for us. Omar.

Al-Rad

13:35 A parable of the Garden which is promised to those who keep their duty: Therein flow rivers. Its fruits are perpetual and its plenty. Such is the end for those who keep their duty; and the end for the disbelievers is the Fire.

Muhammad

47:15 A parable of the Garden which the dutiful are promised: Therein are rivers of water not altering for the worse, and rivers of milk whereof the taste changes not, and rivers of wine delicious to the drinkers, and rivers of honey clarified; and for them therein are all fruits and protection from their Lord. (Are these) like those who abide in the Fire and who are made to drink boiling water, so it rends their bowels asunder?

Hadith from Bukhari.

The blessings of paradise are such as no eye has seen, nor has ear heard, nor has it entered into the heart of man to conceive of them (B. 59:8).

Please see this verse from Jonah from the Quran which says we are essentially one nation then some people agree to disagree with others and enmity occurs between them and they die disbelievers.

Please know it is essential to know there is no gene that causes disbelief in you.

Please see it occur we are one under Him Who creates us to be beneficial to others and we are one with Him as we teach His word to you in that you become disbelievers not but actual belief enters your heart in that you are one with Him in belief in you.

Please see it occur we are One God in us in that we pray to Him alone and we discuss things with each other taking the Book into consideration where we learn edicts and forge plans of oneness with Him.

Please see it occur we are one entity, as before division occurred it was so.

Please know that God is to be believed if you want peace in your life.

Please know the essentials of religious faith have to be adhered to if we want to enter Paradise and we cannot say we did not know as these edicts are well known there where they are taught to us in our youth and other ways of life with us.

Please see it occur we are one entity again in that we are pious not you say but it is true we are pious in it and we succumb to Him Who creates us to be pious not you say but it is true we are pious in it.

Please see it occur we are pious and fornicate not in things as the devil leads us to believe there is no accountability and he sees us and is satisfied that we will make it not to Heaven.

Please know there is One God Who loves us and wants us to be in Paradise with Him but He has written law to be followed, not ignored, and He wants us to be worthy of it, Paradise I mean, as we were not in our original make on earth when we commit sin without the thought of reckoning from Him and we pay no heed to His edicts on us.

Please make it occur we are one entity in that we follow edicts from Him and know that there is a reckoning coming as envisaged by Him in the Judgment Day where our sins will be sorted out and we will be punished or rewarded as indicated in the scriptures of before and now, as we say the Quran is. Omar.

Jonah.

10:18 And they serve besides Allah that which can neither harm them nor profit them, and they say: These are our intercessors with Allah. Say: Would you inform Allah of what He knows not in the heavens and the earth? Glory be to Him, and supremely exalted is He above what they set up (with Him)!

10:19 And (all) people are but a single nation, then they disagree. And had not a word already gone forth from thy Lord, the matter would have certainly been decided between them in respect of that wherein they disagree.

Please see taqiya and apostacy are topics dear to you here and are adequately explained in my note here.

Please see this post on taqiya which was posted early on in my career as a teacher in which I explain it is normal to lie when your life is threatened and not die as a result of an unjust rule that may be present. Further, it is clear apostasy is not permitted under Islamic law and injunctions that rule punishment for it are unjust and obscure in origin.

Please understand that I am sorry for you that many of you can't be awakened to the truth of the Quran.

Please understand that your understanding of taqiya is incorrect and invalid in my view as it is only a communication that is permitted in extreme circumstances like when your life is at threat.

Please understand that it is likely that you would miscommunicate facts as well if you were being killed in an unjust manner. The truth of the matter is that under duress people alter their stories for the sake of their peace. I hope you understand there are no hard feelings to you if you do not agree that these events of changing facts are commonplace in the land you reside, and our Creator does not consider it worthwhile to lose our lives by telling the truth when the other person is willing to kill in an unjust manner due to a lack of understanding similar to what you display here.

Please know the truth of the Quran is evident, so the next time you open the Book, try to see its beauty and not cherry pick verses in an out of context manner as this is the mistake the detractors of the Bible make, while there are many beautiful things to read there as well. In the future, try to be a little dispassionate about views in Islam that you do not understand well like the law of apostasy as it was not the conduct of our Prophet Muhammad on him be peace to kill people for their religious beliefs, whether they left the religion of islam or refused to enter it when invited. Omar.

THE METAPHOR EXPLAINED, NOW WHAT?

please see that your abundance in intellect depends upon your piety here

please see abundance diverts you but abundance of good occurs if you follow me in your law-bearing to humanity at large to you

please see muhammads acclaim as the most knowledgeable man the world has known and you can prove that in history in that his book is the most impressive of all of the books of mine says allah there

please see his wisdom is immense in his teachings as well but it is so much has been lost but there are facets we preserve of his word there

please know he was kind and felt deeply for humanity and it was because he had a flaw i forgave him in that he would grieve excessively for their sins and i didnt want him to do so but he was tender-hearted and felt bad for them as they would be punished by me but they choose their destiny i told him

please know because of these qualities i gave him abundance and asked him to pray and continue to sacrifice his life for them

please see eventually he gave in and let them be and let them enter paradise of their choice but it so occurred i saved most of them as he prayed long hours for their survival and entry into paradise proper

please know this is how you get abundance of things and your intellect occurs not by following your whims and sex crimes in you which lead you to poverty the devil gives you

please see the arabs rose as a nation when islam came to them but later they fell apart as they were involved in vice which i gave them you think nay it was the devil they followed and allowed it to occur their fall from grace i gave them before when they followed me but it is true they had an intellect early on as they were following my commands to them

please try to be an intelligent race as your masses were going astray and poverty was occurring in them because of sex they had in them and as the prophet said poverty occurs there if fornication occurs in you and it is the same for your country you were losing wealth and industry in you was also going and you were a weak nation actually so gather your intellect with the law-bearing in you now and dont fall again as a nation or otherwise as a person

omar not but allah to you here

Al-Kauthar

108:1 Surely We have given thee abundance of good

108:2 So pray to thy Lord and sacrifice.

108:3 Surely thy enemy is cut off (from good).

Al-Baqarah

2:268 The devil threatens you with poverty and enjoins you to be niggardly, and Allah promises you forgiveness from Himself and abundance. And Allah is Ample-giving, Knowing:

Please see Allah was pleased with you that's why He made you believers in Him.

Please know it has occurred as I speak that we all look to the Quran for direction, Muhammad Ali's Quran in particular, but it is so many deter wanting life to go on as previous ways they had but they are scared now of Him as He is strict to us in the scriptures and He deters not His threats to us knowing we will come through with it, just like children do with their parents and so forth we are believers even if we deter some.

Please see these verses from Jonah from the Quran where it says that you have to have permission from Allah before you can become a believer in Him and His Quran.

Please know that Allah does not raise a people until they raise themselves.

Please know your Creator is benevolent and caring and wishes you to come into Islam so that you can avert punishment in the Hereafter and benefit yourselves of good in this life as well. It is your choice though if you come through, you have to prove your worth, then He accepts you there.

Please know all good comes from Him and belief in His Book to you occurs too yet you deter some, why, because you want life of this world previous ways to continue yet you know there is Judgment Day there and you will be forgiven not your sins unless you are pious there in the Hereafter you say but no it is in this life you have to prove your worth, there it is over as your hellfire occurs then and you are squalor in things of the sort that you prevent if you could, as the Quran says..

Please see it occur we are one entity now as the Book establishes us as one nation with Him in our life.

Please see it has occurred as I speak.

Please see it occur you recognize the Quran as a Book from Him.

Please know we come from one entity in spirit we have but we are not Him and He wishes us to be united as one body.

Please see it occur we are one body and wars between us are decreased.

Please see it occur we tolerate our differences in things.

Please know that there is a God out there for most people now. Omar.

Jonah

10:99 And if thy Lord had pleased, all those who are in the earth would have believed, all of them. Wilt thou then force men till they are believers?

10:100 And it is not for any soul to believe except by Allah's permission. And He casts uncleanness on those who will not understand.

Please see my notes and this section from Maulana Muhammad Ali's translation of the Quran where we say Hell is not everlasting and provides data to support his view.

Please know this section is safe but I provide some additional comments to support my view that Allah's mercy takes precedence over his anger as indicated in Bukhari where He says that He will have mercy on mankind.

Please know in an additional hadith He states His mercy is Paradise and His punishment is Hell.

Please see the mercy of Allah is all-encompassing as indicated in the Quran.

Please know the hadith in which He takes out a handful of inhabitants of Hell after intercessions have taken place include those who have not done anything worthy of it.

Please know Allah's mercy takes precedence over His punishment and eventually all will exit Hellfire, as indicated by the hadith in Kanz Ul Ammal where in two places the Prophet indicates Hell is not everlasting.

Please know I would like to say that the Quran calls Hell or Abyss to be a mother to them, the inmates, and just as a mother nurtures a child so does Hell. Further, it indicates that reform is suggested there as punishment without an end is not a mother's domain or your patron or Maula.

Please see similarly He calls Hell a maula or place where He takes care of you as He is caretaker there as well, in fact is a sort of heaven where punishment occurs as we revel in clean in us as a result of being there.

Please know Hell is everlasting to some but the word abad is followed sometimes with 'hatta' or 'until' in the Quran which signifies that reform occurs there and so forth it is conditional until your hatta occurs.

Please know just as God is Maula for man so is Hell the caretaker of it, inmate there, and it is clear the term is used to signify rearing or nurturing sense of the word.

Please know in the final analysis the all-encompassing mercy of Allah takes precedence and His mercy extends to all His creations including those not worthy of it and if He can take out a people not worthy or who have not done good in life, so His mercy encompasses those of other faiths as well.

Please know those who do good in life may go to Hell for association with God other beings and they will reform there, just as a person can reform on earth.

Please know we know that sins are forgiven completely when we are guided to the path of Allah's religion as it occurs in this life when we are guided to the truth so we understand that reform can take place in the Hereafter after we return to our bodies and before that in Barzakh or the purgatory to some, as He guides some there before they are judged according to the hadith structure there and in the Quran words. Omar.

Punishment of hell not everlasting by Maulana Muhammad Ali in his notes there.

It is in consonance with its remedial nature that we find it stated that the sinners shall ultimately be taken out of hell. It is true that the word abad is thrice used in the Holy Qur'an in connection with the abiding in hell (4:169; 33:65; 72:23), but abad indicates eternity as well as long time, and that the latter significance must be taken in this case is made clear by the use, in the same connection, of the word ahqab (78:23), meaning years or long years. Besides this, a limitation is placed on the abiding in hell by the addition of the words except as thy Lord please, the exception clearly indicating the ultimate deliverance of those in hell. The following two verses may be noted in this connection:

"He will say: The Fire is your abode — you shall abide therein, except as Allah please. Surely thy Lord is Wise, Knowing" (6:128).

"Then as for those who are unhappy, they will be in the Fire; for them therein will be sighing and groaning — abiding therein so long as the heavens and the earth endure, except as thy Lord please. Surely thy Lord is Doer of what He intends" (11:106, 107).

Both these verses show clearly that the punishment of hell is not everlasting. To make this conclusion clearer still, the latter of these occasions may be compared with the next verse which describes the abiding in paradise:

"And as for those who are made happy, they will be in the Garden, abiding therein so long as the heavens and the earth endure, except as thy Lord please — a gift never to be cut off" (11:108).

The two expressions are similar: those in hell and those in paradise abide in it as long as the heavens and the earth endure, with an exception added in each case showing that they may be taken out of it. The concluding statements are, however, different. In the case of paradise, the idea that those in it may be taken out of it, if God pleases, is immediately followed by the statement that it is a gift which shall never be cut off, showing that they shall never be taken out of paradise; while, in the case of hell, the idea of those in it being taken out of it is confirmed by the concluding statement — "Surely thy Lord is Doer of what He intends".

The conclusion drawn above is corroborated by the sayings of the Holy Prophet. Thus a saying reported in the Muslim concludes:

"Then will Allah say, The angels and the prophets and the faithful have all in their turn interceded for the sinners and now there remains none to intercede for them except the Most Merciful of all merciful ones.

So He will take out a handful from the Fire and bring out a people who never worked any good" (Ms. 1:72).

Further, Bukhari records a saying to the effect that, when the sinners are taken out from hell, they shall be thrown into *"the river of life, and they will grow as grows a seed by the side of a river"* (B. 2:15), which clearly indicates that they shall be made fit for a higher life. The Kanz al-'Ummal records the following: *"Surely a day will come over hell when it will be like a field of corn that has dried up, after flourishing for a while"* (KU, vol. vii, p. 245); *"Surely a day will come over hell when there shall not be a single human being in it"* (Ibid). A saying of 'Umar is recorded as follows: *"Even if the dwellers in hell may be numberless as the sands of the desert, a day will come when they will be taken out of it"* (Fath al-Bayan).

Verses that follow are my literature.

Al-Araaf

7:156 And ordain for us good in this world's life and in the Hereafter, for surely we turn to Thee. He said: I afflict with My chastisement whom I please, and My mercy encompasses all things. So I ordain it for those who keep their duty and pay the poor-rate, and those who believe in Our messages—

Al-Anum

6:147 But if they give thee the lie, then say: Your Lord is the Lord of all-encompassing mercy; and His punishment cannot be averted from the guilty people.

Jonah..

12:58 Say: In the grace of Allah and in His mercy, in that they should rejoice. It is better than that which they hoard.

Al-Qariah.

101:6 Then as for him whose measure (of good deeds) is heavy,
101:7 He will live a pleasant life.
101:8 And as for him whose measure (of good deeds) is light,
101:9 The abyss is a mother to him.

Al-Hadid

57:14 They will cry out to them: Were we not with you? They will say: Yea, but you caused yourselves to fall into temptation, and you waited and doubted, and vain desires deceived you, till the threatened punishment of Allah came, and the arch-deceiver deceived you about Allah.

57:15 So this day no ransom will be accepted from you, nor from those who disbelieved. Your abode is the Fire; it is your patron (Maula).

Al Mumtahanah or The Woman Who Is Examined.

60:3 Your relationships and your children would not profit you, on the day of Resurrection — He will decide between you. And Allah is Seer of what you do.

60:4 Indeed, there is for you a good example in Abraham and those with him, when they said to their people: We are clear of you and of that which you serve besides Allah. We disbelieve in you and there has arisen enmity and hatred between us and you forever until (hatta) you believe in Allah alone — except Abraham's saying to his sire: I would ask forgiveness for thee, and I control naught for thee from Allah. Our Lord, on Thee do we rely, and to Thee do we turn, and to Thee is the eventual coming.

Please know fornication is a punishable offence in Islam.

Please know the law is severe there for those who do it as we know in our hearts that God does not permit it to us.

Please see these verses from the Quran where it says sexual relationships are not permitted outside the marriage tie and further it is clear that the sexes have to be kept apart if possible, which is the way in Muslim countries by and large, and that in this land they are to stay apart sexually oriented way they have here.

Please know it is clear there is a punishment prescribed there in our lands for fornication and adultery as children can result which leads to abortions on many occasions.

Please know it is an obscenity with Him Who creates us for it, piety there, and He does not permit in the least and it is clear that we cannot allow it in culture we have.

Please know it is commonplace nowadays but is not permitted by Him Who creates as it causes vice in us and we die a dastardly way, in spirit at least.

Please know it is the king of evil as it causes murders to occur in us and we don't care it, child with us in it.

Please see it occur it is outlawed eventually as it causes vice in the community and it leads to other crimes in that it is the root of evil in a community.

Please know God does not permit it to us no matter what you say and this is not just Islam but other religions as well.

Please see it occur that those who do it know it is wrong so their punishment is due from Him in that He will punish the fornicator and fornicatress, as this is His law that it can't be done here on earth.

Please know sexual relationships exist in the Hereafter after forgiveness occurs you say but it is an eon before it occur if you permit it to yourself here on earth.

Please know the Muslim knows he has to abstain and if he or she does not their punishment is due as is customary for Him in regards to all humans, the law is the same, unless they are forgiven by Him or their charity or Hajj occurs.

Please know it is a crime to abort an out of wedlock child for your convenience or otherwise, and the punishment is severe if you do so in your error ways you had there.

Please know in Islam generally speaking if you get someone pregnant then the man has to marry her to create the child in wedlock vows and this law is sane for you in this custom you have here,

Please know this is my post for you in that we must ascribe to the truth in it and we cannot dally in it in the least from now on now you know the truth in law of it from Him Who creates us to be steadfast in issues of law here and there your reward is written if you abstain. Omar.

Maida.

5:104 And when it is said to them, Come to that which Allah has revealed and to the Messenger, they say: Sufficient for us is that wherein we found our fathers. What! even though their fathers knew nothing and had no guidance!

5:105 O you who believe, take care of your souls — he who errs cannot harm you when you are on the right way. To Allah you will all return, so He will inform you of what you did.

THE METAPHOR EXPLAINED, NOW WHAT?

Bani-Israel
17:32 And go not nigh to fornication: surely it is an obscenity. And evil is the way.
Al-Nur
24:2 The fornicatress and the fornicator, flog each of them (with) a hundred stripes, and let not pity for them detain you from obedience to Allah, if you believe in Allah and the Last Day, and let a party of believers witness their chastisement.
Bani-Israel.
17:31 And kill not your children for fear of poverty — We provide for them and for you. Surely the killing of them is a great wrong.

please see your self-worth is important to you in that you think highly of yourself in your eyes and allahs too and humanity will agree with you as piety is rewarded that way

please see here this verse that says descend into complete peace with me or submission to my will and i will take you to paradise say i in the quran elsewhere yes your complete submit to me is how you are raised to a high pedestal and then you will come forth with peace in you but if you mix peace with evil then i may forgive you or may punish you depending upon your deeds there

please see the footsteps of the devil are spoke about and you know what that means it is the antithesis of what i teach there in my book for you and you must submit to me for peace to occur otherwise you will be distraught and evil there

please know i forgive some things but i am might on you so dont take my message lightly about complete submission to me and make that an avenue of peace to you in that you enter paradise here with it and your love results to you for me and others yes when you have peace you love me and i give you self-worth in your eyes and you start loving yourself so keep me happy and i will give you happy life you wish for now full of self-worth and friendship to those who befriend you in that you love them and they too love their creator in mutually harmony you do live by my love you foster in them say i allah to you here *please see you were on a brink of fire not but were in it until i come to you in peace so adopt me and bring reform to your country by doing good deeds and forbid evil ways the devil cajoles you in and this coming in submission to me by your hold fast to this law i give you in this book of mine say allah the great benefactor of mankind you cant realize how great the peace is you adopt by holding my book firm with you say allah there to you*

allah there in heaven with this pen of mine

Al-Baqarah

2:207 And of men is he who sells himself to seek the pleasure of Allah. And Allah is Compassionate to the servants.

2:208 O you who believe, enter into complete peace and follow not the footsteps of the devil. Surely he is your open enemy.

2:209 But if you slip after clear arguments have come to you, then know that Allah is Mighty, Wise.

Al-Imran

3:103 And hold fast by the covenant of Allah all together and be not disunited. And remember Allah's favor to you when you were enemies, then He united your hearts so by His favor you became brethren. And you were on the brink of a pit of fire, then He saved you from it. Thus Allah makes clear to you His messages that you may be guided.

3:104 And from among you there should be a party who invite to good and enjoin the right and forbid the wrong. And these are they who are successful.

Please see world dominion was their forte but they were brutal in it, Christ people from before.

Please see this verse from Kahf where it says the Christian nations will produce and manufacture material and it will become their religious belief in it.

Please know it is clear the Christians are meant here as there is mention of Jesus before it in a verse.

Please know they take him for their friend besides Him Who creates.

Please see it occur we learn religion is more important than goods that we manufacture and that it is the epitome of our life to manufacture it, goods, I mean here they think.

Please see it occur Christian nations have become the Antichrist and the teachings of Christ are lost to them.

Please see the hadith that they will be a giant with one eye blind and the other shining forth.

Please see it is the right eye that is blind according to literature we have and it becomes us here to inform you that America and Britain are the nations of Antichrist as they have left the messages of their book and are engrossed in world domination to control other tribes or nations to do their bid that it becomes them in their dominion.

Please see they manufacture incessantly.

Please know the bottom line is money coming in.

Please know they have regard for the poor you say but it is little they care for the poorer people around the world. Omar.

Kahf.

18:102 Do those who disbelieve think that they can take My servants to be friends besides Me? Surely We have prepared hell as an entertainment for the disbelievers.

18:103 Say: Shall We inform you who are the greatest losers in respect of deeds?

18:104 Those whose effort goes astray in this world's life, and they think that they are making good manufactures.

18:105 Those are they who disbelieve in the messages of their Lord and meeting with Him, so their works are vain. Nor shall We set up a balance for them on the day of Resurrection.

18:106 That is their reward — hell, because they disbelieved and held My messages and My messengers in mockery.

18:107 As for those who believe and do good deeds, for them are Gardens of Paradise, an entertainment,

18:108 To abide therein; they will not desire removal therefrom.

18:109 Say: If the sea were ink for the words of my Lord, the sea would surely be exhausted before the words of my Lord were exhausted, though We brought the like of it to add (thereto).

18:110 Say: I am only a mortal like you — it is revealed to me that your God is one God. So whoever hopes to meet his Lord, he should do good deeds, and join no one in the service of his Lord.

Please see some meanings from these verses in the Quran are in order here by us to you.

Please see this verse in this chapter that tells you earth and the heavens have a will with you but you think them inanimate but it is so their nature is there that they resist change and Allah wishes to evolve them with life here.

Please know Muhammad Ali describes it as law of nature but that is not correct.

Please know He will continue to evolve everything He creates and one day the earth will be no more but by then the spirits would have occurred sufficient for us and we wouldn't want to be tested here.

Please know the time frame is left open for discussion but it may be many millions of years late.

Please know days means an eon and it is in the knowledge of Him how many billions of years it took to create the lower heaven with earth on it and so it occurs some eons are short with Him and some are taweel or lengthy by us but we know that the heavens and the earth were created in 6 days and lets leave it at that, this describes a different time frame for us.

Please know we must evolve as well as a nation of humans and experience space travel as we exist in spirit now as well as body form and after we die our spirit will be the only thing we have but it will form a body from it but it will be a different body where we can change shape and travel forth in the universe to examine it, enough for now, let's try to understand the words of the Quran may not be straightforward always and some revealed thought is required there by us as we see the Prophet also used to explain the verses of his Book to his companions, who were eager to know as you are in this realm.

Omar.

Ha Mim.

41:9 Say: Do you indeed disbelieve in Him Who created the earth in two days, and do you set up equals with Him? That is the Lord of the worlds.

41:10 And He made in it mountains above its surface, and He blessed therein and ordained therein its foods, in four days; alike for (all) seekers.

41:11 Then He directed Himself to the heaven and it was a vapor, so He said to it and to the earth: Come both, willingly or unwillingly. They both said: We come willingly.

41:12 So He ordained them seven heavens in two days, and revealed in every heaven its affair. And We adorned the lower heaven with lights, and (made it) to guard. That is the decree of the Mighty, the Knowing.

please see the quran is the final message of islam through the ages and completes faith for one so adopt it as your book here

please see these verses are muhkimat or categorical in that issues can be raised about one religion to the exclusion of others but it is not so the hawwaroon or disciples of jesus have been called muslims in the quran so there occurs any religion that submits to their creator in that his laws are followed is a true religion and all the prophets have been considered muslims in the quran as they submitted to him and they taught their followers to submit to him and take him to be one god yes these words are in the quran about the prophets so its up to you if you want to disregard the first command in the bible to you by denying him you wont have islam in the true sense of the word and the religion of islam found itself complete with prophet muhammad as the verse from fath shows and it is this religion he prevails over others as it is in its purest form here in the quran with you and other books have been altered some to give a different context in things while islam of muhammad is intact apart from some hadith structure that i am abrogating with the passage of time and you know the quran in its essence is sane for you to follow as illihoon quran is now with us and the changes are of minor significance as they have been deciphered by scholars and lay as well

please know all the arab qurans have some minor issues of difference but the message is intact here and this verse is verified as safe yes the one in chapter 48 where he says that the deen of muhammad will prevail over other faiths so dont be jealous of the quran as it validates your book and it completes faith for you that being said all faiths as taught by the prophets are safe in that they had elements of islam and as baqarah says those who do good in submission to him the creat will find paradise waiting for them but sadly most of the knowledge they had has been lost or altered thats why we say keep the quran injunctions with you as you seek heaven in earth and also in the hereafter after your death occurs

omar

Al-Fath

48:28 He it is Who has sent His Messenger with the guidance and the Religion of Truth that He may make it prevail over all religions. And Allah is enough for a witness.

Al-Imran

3:51 Surely Allah is my Lord and your Lord, so serve Him. This is the right path.

3:52 But when Jesus perceived disbelief on their part, he said: Who will be my helpers in Allah's way? The disciples said: We are Allah's helpers: we believe in Allah, and bear thou witness that we are submitting ones (Muslims).

Al-Imran

3:19 Surely the (true) religion with Allah is Islam. And those who were given the Book differed only after knowledge had come to them, out of envy among themselves. And whoever disbelieves in the messages of Allah — Allah indeed is Quick at reckoning.

Al-Baqarah

2:111 And they say: None shall enter the Garden except he who is a Jew, or the Christians. These are their vain desires. Say: Bring your proof if you are truthful.

2:112 Nay, whoever submits himself entirely to Allah and he is the doer of good (to others), he has his reward from his Lord, and there is no fear for such nor shall they grieve.

CHAPTER TWO

SOME WORDS OF WISDOM ABOUT BIBLICAL LORE WE HAVE AND RELATED TOPICS

Intro.
Please see the Bible contains references to law that Jesus had and promulgated to his follower and he did not deviate in it, being law-abiding person he was and he lived his life in piety there after some initial contact when he was pious not in issues, yes he did bed some, and there you have it that is the sin that the hadith law talks about when it says he cannot intervene for mankind the way Prophet Muhammad can, the Prophet was quiet about it as he does not mention the sins of prophets of His Benevolence but he expects me to make note of it as every prophet but himself had a fall, then piety results when they become scared of Him, then He forgives some not but all as they are pious before but fall is normal in man and woman in their lifetime, that is the way we are as humans, he was protected though as the perfect slave and me and Mirza too had a fall of at least once but it is so we were protected and did not penetrate them whom we bed or nearly so, there you have it the human race is fallible but we learn from our mistakes and we should abstain when we realize the wrong in it but it is true Jesus had a fall and recovered piety as his mother admonished her not but him as he should have known better, he was a law giver there.

Please see there is no deviance in the message of the People of the Book and the Quran and now you know so don't deter it, it is blasphemy to say other than his teachings to you who is Jesus there.

Please see some excerpts from the Old Testament about our Creator being One in Essence not only but also in Person and now you know Exodus is you in the commands He has.

Please see the list is numerous, I have taken out a few but know Isaiah is extensive in his speech about One God issues and also says there is none like Him which is what Ikhlas in the Quran says echoing the fact that Jesus was not the same substance as Him, which the Council of Nicaea did not observe.

Please know I have taken a few verses only but it is clear websites list many, here are some for your elucidation.

Please know I have shown previously in my literature Jesus talked about the One God in the New Testament as well and the Quran follows through with the words 'there is no god but Allah' so you know there is unanimity in the teachings of the scripture you have and there is no deviance in the message there.

Please know there is deviance if you say he is god who is Jesus or the holy one myself or Muhammad which you like to attribute in godhead in an attempt to spoil faith you have but I know it is a lost cause and it is over, the people have believed and there is no going back in their hearts to disbelief you have not anymore.

Omar.

Deuteronomy 4:35

"To you it was shown, that you might know that the Lord is God; there is no other besides him."

Deuteronomy 6:4

"Hear, O Israel: The Lord our God, the Lord is one."

Exodus 20:3

"You shall have no other gods besides me."

Isaiah 46:9

"Remember the former things of old; 'for I am God, and there is no other; I am God, and there is none like me.'"

Matthews 4

10 Then Jesus said to him, "Get behind me, Satan! For it is written, 'You shall worship the Lord your God, and you shall serve him only."

Ikhlas 112.

1 Say: He, Allah, is One.
2 Allah is He on Whom all depend.
3 He begets not, nor is He begotten;
4 And none is like Him.

Please see the law was always sent down to man from his Creator and there is no major deviance in that law through the ages.

Please see the words of Jesus echoed in the Quran and the Old Testament as well where they are exhorted to follow the law of the commandments and other laws they have and so you know it is over Jesus did not abrogate shariah they had and pig meat and fornication was not allowed by him, there you have it he was a stalwart who protected their religious view but there were many laws that came to pass with the passage of time that were not from his Creator and he sullied them in it and told them not to refrain from all the foodstuffs they propagated as prohibited in it and they had become onerous to them and it occurred that their law was upheld more or less but it was true Paul abrogate it, and how could he do that, he was not a disciple of his who was Jesus and certainly not an authority to change his teachings as only a prophet can change law of significance, but it is so there is avenue of peace now with the Quran with you and you know Allah gave the law to Muhammad and asked Muslims to obey it, so Paul was wrong in issues,

Yes, you will be judged if you obey your lower instincts when I have come and explained there is always a law from Him, your Creator, how could there not be a law when there has always been a law by man and by God as well?

Omar.

Matthews 5.

14 "Ye are the light of the world. A city that is set on an hill cannot be hid.

15 Neither do men light a candle, and put it under a bushel, but on a candlestick; and it giveth light unto all that are in the house.

16 Let your light so shine before men, that they may see your good works, and glorify your Father which is in heaven.

17 Think not that I am come to destroy the law, or the prophets: I am not come to destroy, but to fulfil.

18 For verily I say unto you, Till heaven and earth pass, one jot or one tittle shall in no wise pass from the law, till all be fulfilled.

19 Whosoever therefore shall break one of these least commandments, and shall teach men so, he shall be called the least in the kingdom of heaven: but whosoever shall do and teach them, the same shall be called great in the kingdom of heaven."

Al-Bara'at

9:71 And the believers, men and women, are friends one of another. They enjoin good and forbid evil and keep up prayer and pay the poor-rate, and obey Allah and His Messenger. As for these, Allah will have mercy on them. Surely Allah is Mighty, Wise.

9:72 Allah has promised to the believers, men and women, Gardens, wherein flow rivers, to abide therein, and goodly dwellings in Gardens of perpetual abode. And greatest of all is Allah's goodly pleasure. That is the grand achievement.

please see it occur that jesus upheld the law of yahweh they had that he had no progeny and so it is clear he did not commit blasphemy to them in islam they had with them

please see matthews here where jesus says who do you think the son of man is and peter says you are the son of god signifying he was a man who was a prophet as that is what son of god is in bible vernacular and john is similar where he says he is sanctified and would not commit blasphemy to them by saying he was son literally as they were telling him that is what he says and further he says look at my works and you know he meant a prophet there as a prophet has works for his creator and it is clear in psalms that is what he meant when he called them gods as disobedient ones who judge not correctly and he was just saying son metaphor way so it is here you give pause and think about all those references to him about him being son literally of his magnificence and they it put there the gospel writers to aggrandize him and elevate so people would believe him as pagans believed their great men to them were the sons of god born to virgins sometimes and there you have it in a nutshell they said things about him to appease them to come into islam they had of mercy and love between them and piety too and keep away from the bani-israel they say they were evil to do this crucifixion on their savior so it came about son of god issues in christian lore and jesus admonished them not to teach them the pagan romans as he knew this would occur to their religion of monotheism yet they did and changed their religion of worship of him solely they had of who is god there and called him son in their book the bible and all four gospel writers did it and portray him son begotten on pauls behalf but it is so the ebionites had a gospel different and called him son not in that sense they had there and jesus did not use that vernacular no he did not indicate begotten to them and denied it to them the jews who were attempting to stone him and also to peter he made it clear he was son of man as well and further to him father was a generic term for creator as he asked disciples to pray to him their father in heaven so you see his teachings are altered by paul and other disciples he has and it was clear in my book to you that i explained he was son of man to you being a man in his make as well and you have to see their aggrandizement statements have to be kept apart and you should follow what he says jesus there and the quran as well says god does not beget so it is clear virgin birth issues are also made up as the holy spirit cant impregnate with sperm only with love for her who is mary there as he doesnt have sperm at that juncture as he is not formed of earth material and is only a spirit there and so there you have it son of god issues are metaphors and he use a well known metaphor in the bible for a prophet-servant of his grace and eminence the creator there more is required here before you come through as you know he didnt say it that he was son literally in a begotten sense but only said in the sense of creation of his but for him as a prophet-like man he was there he said it as psalms depict a true servant who judges correctly by his book the torah there there you have it he had special dispensation as slave-servant of his to teach them truth from him of our nature being born from our parents and now we know it is through our dna car on us and in summary you have to go by what jesus said and what the old testament depicts as metaphors both say that as does the quran where it says in anbiya that sons are only honored

servants of his and god has not begotten anyone but created them out of love he has so you know now all three books say that he was son in metaphor concepts of the way of saying it and it should not be said in the begotten sense according to the words of our book the quran to you
omar

Matthew 16.

Verses 13 to 19. In a dialogue between Jesus and his disciples Jesus asks, "Who do people say that the Son of Man is?" The disciples give various answers. When he asks "Who do you say that I am?", Simon Peter answers, "You are the Messiah, the Son of the living God."

John 10

34 Jesus answered them, "Is it not written in your law, I said, Ye are gods?"

35 If he called them gods, unto whom the word of God came and the scripture cannot be broken;

36 "Say ye of him whom the Father hath sanctified and sent into the world 'Thou blasphemest' because I said, I am the Son of God?

37 If I do not the works of my Father, believe me not."

Psalms 82

4 Rescue the weak and needy. Deliver them out of the hand of the wicked."

5 They don't know, neither do they understand. They walk back and forth in darkness. All the foundations of the earth are shaken.

6 I said, "You are gods, while all of you are sons of the Most High."

Matthew 6

9 Pray then like this: "Our Father in heaven, hallowed be your name."

Al-Ikhlas

112:3 He begets not, nor is He begotten;

112:4 And none is like Him.

please know he came to uphold the law of deuteronomy and exodus and was sanctified in his own words and would never say take me to be a god with him that is inconceivable there and you know he came to uphold the law of the prophets before him

THE METAPHOR EXPLAINED, NOW WHAT?

please see deuteronomy 13 here that allows no deviance in the teachings of moses there and you know he was not guilty who was jesus to you as he said that he was sanctified and would not commit blasphemy to them by calling himself his son who is god there there you have it jewish law prohibits son issues in the begotten sense and allow no deviance in the concept of one god to them and they are asked to reject anyone who calls himself god or asks one to take another god and it is clear that jesus knew these statements were being said about him from the beauty of decorum he had and it was the pagan influence there but he made it clear there was no deviance in his teachings to them further he said these words that i say ye are gods to them when they were trying to implicate him in crime of blasphemy to them and they implied he was acting like a god and he replied that they were guilty of it in the sense of a negative metaphor and he was not and he would not disobey him as he was his son though in the metaphor way of saying it as he made it clear these words i have stated that he was not a blasphemer there you have it he was not guilty so they let him be then but later got even and had pilate hang him on the cross but it is true he did not break the first commandment of exodus and this statement in deuteronomy 6 which states you will take him to be your god who is yahweh himself and now you know he would never say i am god or worship me like you do in the church some and he was sanctified a true prophet of his yahweh there so you know pauls guilt of how he created idolatry in you followers of him who is jesus christ and told him he was his son materially and was thus god as well though he said god was one as well a certain muddy concept he was trying to create and now you know his guilt in that he took you out of religion he had who was jesus and gave you a muddy faith of christian trinity type and you should stay away from pauls teach on you and god is yahweh only to him who is jesus there and son of him was only metaphor way of speaking as the quran says and jewish law permits there and you know these are tales that they make up and the modern world doesnt accept concepts like son of his grace or virgin birth this doesnt occur as we are all created from an egg and sperm as modern science know and the quran validates this when it says there are no exceptions to the creation of mankind and adam and jesus were both subject to the law of nature so there occurs as islam has to come about the realization that they are sane not when they say virgin birth for him who is jesus while the quran validates they were created from dust particles as is all mankind and so do christians say this absurdity that he is son materially these are fables they make up like greek gods were fables and there is no reality in these issues and reflect insanity in you to people when you say virgin birth was his and so forth sonship as well and taking him to be god is completely made up as you know an aggrandizement process of converting prophets and saints to gods who you pray to and worship and it is a low act for man and wife there

omar

Deuteronomy 6

4 *"Hear, O Israel: The Lord our God is one Lord:*

5 *And thou shalt love the Lord thy God with all thine heart and with all thy soul and with all thy might."*

Deuteronomy 13

1 *"If there arise among you a prophet, or a dreamer of dreams, and giveth thee a sign or a wonder,*

2 *And the sign or the wonder come to pass whereof he spake unto thee, saying, Let us go after other gods which thou hast not known and let us serve them;*

3 *Thou shalt not hearken unto the words of that prophet, or that dreamer of dreams: for the Lord your God proveth you to know whether ye love the Lord your God with all your heart and with all your soul.*

4 *Ye shall walk after the Lord your God and fear him and keep his commandments and obey his voice and ye shall serve him and cleave unto him."*

John 10

32 *Jesus answered them, "Many good works have I shewed you from my Father, for which of those works do ye stone me?"*

33 *The Jews answered him saying, "For a good work we stone thee not; but for blasphemy; and because that thou, being a man, act like a god."*

34 *Jesus answered them, "Is it not written in your law, 'I said, Ye are gods?'"*

35 If he called them gods unto whom the word of God came and the scripture cannot be broken;

36 "Say ye of him whom the Father hath sanctified and sent into the world 'Thou blasphemest' because I said, I am the Son of God?

37 If I do not the works of my Father, believe me not."

Maryam chapter in the quran there

19:88 And they say: The Beneficent has taken to Himself a son.

19:89 Certainly you make an abominable assertion!

19:90 The heavens may almost be rent thereat, and the earth cleave asunder, and the mountains fall down in pieces,

19:91 That they ascribe a son to the Beneficent!

19:92 And it is not worthy of the Beneficent that He should take to Himself a son.

19:93 There is none in the heavens and the earth but comes to the Beneficent as a servant.

please see the voice of muhammad echo in your hearts as he tells you the explain of these verses from the quran and the bible to you

please see al-hadid where it talks about our creator in that he is the first and the last and similar voice is in the bible in the verse quoted

please know allah was the first before he started to create he was alone and he was not sad but he wished to be known so he created me says i muhammad there and he wished i teach all man and others with him as he wished to be known by all creation and obeyed in regard to the law he had with him and i teach him here that eventually we are all going to be him in spirit but our bodies are going to be separate but we will be him in the sense of the metaphor being conjoint with him doing his bid in things like i do says i muhammad there in mecca environs where i teach the people about him and the quran is revealed too

please see i am conjoint and few will make it on earth but in paradise all will be conjoint with him and we will all be him like jesus said here and omar says it as well in his literature but there you have it we 3 were able to do it other prophets and saints couldnt muster it it was too difficult for them and we nearly die in the process please see he is manifest by signs in the world and the universe is how he manifests himself

please also know he is hidden for us but one day he will manifest his glory to us in person but we have to be in paradise proper to see him there with our vision changed from that of earth to a sharper one there

please know he is hidden yet and i know you see visions some but it is not so for the majority

please see the bible echoes the words of the quran and alpha is the first letter and omega the last of the alphabet in greek language they have

please know it is clear it is a revealed book like the quran is but words have been transposed here to show that it was jesus in the section revelations but it is not so in isaiah so obviously fabrication occurred there

please see i am tired not but will let you understand as metaphors we can be him the creator but it is our spirit that becomes him as our ego is not there but we submit to him we all do in heaven thus we are him and we are the last

please see my acclaim as the teacher of you and omar is my pen here and i am muhammad to you

muhammad

Al-Hadid

57:2 His is the kingdom of the heavens and the earth. He gives life and causes death; and He is Possessor of power over all things.

57:3 He is the First and the Last and the Manifest and the Hidden, and He is Knower of all things.

Isaiah 48

12 "Hearken unto me, O Jacob and Israel, my called; I am he; I am the first, I also am the last.

13 Mine hand also hath laid the foundation of the earth, and my right hand hath spanned the heavens: when I call unto them, they stand up together."

Revelation 21

6 He said to me: "It is done. I am the Alpha and the Omega, the Beginning and the End. To the thirsty I will give water without cost from the spring of the water of life.

7 Those who are victorious will inherit all this and I will be their God and they will be my children."

Revelation 1

8 "I am the Alpha and the Omega," says the Lord God, "who is, and who was, and who is to come, the Almighty."

Please see mankind through Allah's heart on us is the greatest in testimony that Isa was innocent in his teach there to the Bani-Israel folks and Christians are guilty if they take his works in an out of context manner.

Please see John 5 here where he says his testimony is greater than John's, was he referring to the disciple John, no, it was the son of Zakariah who knew he had come to teach them the metaphor, as I have taught here.

Please know it was talkeen or a good deception you say, yes, the metaphor was, but it delayed them in things so he relented to stop and teach them law which didn't have an affect on their culture, so they left him after that but it is so he knew it was late they would come through and accept his teach on them but it is so he won many, but lost them, the Jews there since he didn't explain adequately what it meant to be 'one with Him' Who creates him to be law observing in things but he delayed it and taught metaphorical concepts to her there but it is so they deterred and when he left after the crucifixion process they realized the truth of his statements but it was late that it occurred, their sanity, as Paul implied godhead with it, his tropes there, and they relented to him, why, because they wanted magnanimity or piety extreme in him to emerge with him being a god to his folks there.

Please know they relented more earlier and understood what he was saying when he said those words that say he had similar beliefs to Him Who creates him to be sane in things but it is so he has little power on his own is his testimony here and Allah is his witness he was innocent in his works there and so forth he is judged as evil, while they knew he was only saying the metaphor similar to what I do here when I say "I am Him Who creates, Allah there" and so I am 'him' as well who is Prophet to us.

Please know it is clear he is witnessed by us now as a student of His when he taught the metaphor there and now you know in Jewish quarters what he meant when he used those terms "I am" or "I am the Father" and so forth other tropes as well so don't criticize him and accept him as your savior, as many did there.

Please see indecency in you if you don't recognize him as an able scholar by you and you must submit to his piety in things and then you will relinquish her as evil to you who is Mary as they were one team against the establishment of the Jews of their time so you relent there in Israel, yes, but you don't come through openly as yet, when you do you will be forsaken not in issues, more on the Jewish agenda as time passes you will learn they are recalcitrant actually though some come through with this teach on them that these were metaphors he taught and there was no heresy in his works there, which you sacrilege him for. Omar.

John 5.

28 "Do not be amazed at this, for a time is coming when all who are in their graves will hear his voice

29 and come out—those who have done what is good will rise to live, and those who have done what is evil will rise to be condemned.

30 By myself I can do nothing; I judge only as I hear, and my judgment is just, for I seek not to please myself but him who sent me.

31 If I testify about myself, my testimony is not true.

32 There is another who testifies in my favor, and I know that his testimony about me is true.

33 You have sent to John and he has testified to the truth.

34 Not that I accept human testimony; but I mention it that you may be saved.

35 John was a lamp that burned and gave light, and you chose for a time to enjoy his light.

36 I have testimony weightier than that of John. For the works that the Father has given me to finish—the very works that I am doing — testify that the Father has sent me.

37 And the Father who sent me has himself testified concerning me. You have never heard his voice nor seen his form,

38 nor does his word dwell in you, for you do not believe the one he sent."

THE METAPHOR EXPLAINED, NOW WHAT?

Please see Mary is worthy of respect there where she taught and here too where she teaches through my pen to you.

This is Mary, worthy of regard in this word to her that she is chosen above the creation of all women, why, because she was pious and didn't want marriage actually and wanted to dedicate her life to her Creator Who wanted her to bear children like her and so her gene got transmitted to the world there, many men and girl-like women have her gene in her and him, but it is so you disregard me and pay heed to him who you call my son but I taught him things, then he started having revelation as well to complement mine not only but others there before him as a prophet of His, but I know good there as they did pay heed to us and convert to piety, stopping sex and issues of vice they had, but it is so they were enthralled by our team, but it is so we were too successful, like Omar is here, and we had to leave them behind, our team there, they would have killed us if masses left with me and my sons, but I know James was good and we left him in charge, but I know they killed him eventually, Pontius had left, and they took over after his death and said 'enough' disperse them in lands and don't let them conglomerate again, so it occurred their death as a nation until they reenact it, the British, see what heinous they are there.

Please know to disband them and never allow them nation, they are not worthy to lead, say I Mary there.

Omar not.

Al-Imran.

3:42 And when the angels said: O Mary, surely Allah has chosen thee and purified thee and chosen thee above the women of the world.

3:43 O Mary, be obedient to thy Lord and humble thyself and bow down with those who bow.

3:44 This is of the tidings of things unseen which We reveal to thee. And thou wast not with them when they cast their pens (to decide) which of them should have Mary in his charge, and thou wast not with them when they contended one with another.

3:45 When the angels said: O Mary, surely Allah gives thee good news with a word from Him (of one) whose name is the Messiah, Jesus, son of Mary, worthy of regard in this world and the Hereafter, and of those who are drawn nigh (to Allah),

Please see the crucifixion of Jesus was an avenue for him to be a world leader and Messiah rather than a prophet only to his people, that's why he relented to it when Allah asked him to accept his cup, as mentioned in biblical lore there.

Please know in the Muslim world there is much confusion of the interpretation of the words in these verses as they think Isa was not crucified at all.

Please see why a difference of opinion is important in Islam as new data comes to light with time,

Please know rafa means bodily ascension in the metaphorical sense as well as stature with Him,

Please know we will be in Allah's presence when we die here but our body can't travel in space.

Please see the following verses from the Quran from the chapter The Women,

Please know it is over and you know he died there in India with his follower Mary who he married,

Please know Muslims have a hard time assimilating data from our source in Islam so I explain to them the Arabic so they understand there was a misinterpretation from the early Muslim scholars, primarily from the Christian data that came into Islam from converts,

Please see the verse refers to Jesus, not someone else, as is thought by some there in the Middle East,

Please know they take two weak hadith to indicate someone took the appearance of Jesus before the crucifixion attempt but fail to realize it is not possible to do so.

Please know the sources of these hadith are dubious and scholars know I am telling the truth in this regard,

Please know one of the hadith says Pilate ordered a guard to kill him but then God changed his appearance and he was crucified instead,

THE METAPHOR EXPLAINED, NOW WHAT?

Please know the other states a companion was asked to take on his garb and portray Jesus in himself but this is not verified as correct and is unusual for a prophet to do.

Please know a prophet would fight himself instead of killing a companion,

Please know they say the other person was crucified but the word 'ha' refers to Jesus and the other person is not mentioned in the verse so it is not possible for him to be crucified,

Please know the other problem they have is limited knowledge of the Arabic language as salabuhu means killed in a well-known way, not being nailed, as occurred with Jesus,

Please know crucifix is a well-known method of killing but if the person does not die he is said to survived the crucifixion,

Please know they say he never went on the cross but according to Lane's lexicon of Arabic it does not mean that but death on the cross is what is implied.

Please know it further says they use conjecture to say he died but he died not for certain,

Please know both the Christians and Jews say he died but they are not sure as it has transpired that people are in doubt about it with Ahmadi literature being prevalent, as my book shows,

Please know we ascribe to peace with them in Islam as diverse views are important to uphold as correct for some but the Christian faith and the Jews as well know they are in doubt about it as the knowledge has come forth in Islam with us that he survived the crucifixion as the guards dispelled with the breaking of legs even after they knew his heart was pumping, evinced from blood flowing when they pierced him,

Please know it was obvious they weren't going to kill him as he was innocent to two.

Please know Pilate and his wife wanted to save him and told the guard to dispel them, the people, who had gathered and then he appeared to take him away.

Please know Pilate knew he was alive and personally checked with the spear and noted he bled,

Please know then he allowed him to leave and observe the sabbath on his own in the woods there,

Please know it was an innovation they used to say he had died in order to cover his tracks to the people but the Jewish council knew he had survived as there were some members there when he was taken down by Pilate,

Please know Mary, his wife, did see him on the third day and was appeased as he was clear in his head and not unwell like they were saying of him,

Please see these facts are from revelation but the fact is out he survived there in church quarters,

Please know he remained in disguise after the crucifixion attempt and then left for safer lands,

Please know the other verse that causes confusion is raising spiritually a person,

Please know people thought he was accursed but he did not die there so the curse of a crucifixion death did not occur,

Please know he was raised spiritually as the stature God gave him with man through the teachings in Islam I teach you.

Please know raising is a metaphor we speak of in our prayer when we say 'raise me' in the prayer we have in Islam,

Please know it is through hardship and trial we are raised in stature with Him, the Creat, and also in the eyes of man, wife and child so there you have it we commemorate him in Islam as one who is recognized as great by us,

Please know we all need peace and it is over for you in this country as you have understood my book but people in the Middle East are fixated that rafani means lifting bodily while the metaphor is applied here as no one can lift himself bodily to heaven as the verse I alluded to in a previous comment said as the Prophet is asked to say it is not for a mortal prophet to go to heaven to retrieve a book which they asked him to do.

Please know the last verse I allude to refers to the People of the Book not agreeing with his raising as they thought him accursed,

Please know they will all believe it until his death and it is now you are in doubt about it.

THE METAPHOR EXPLAINED, NOW WHAT?

Please know it is over and the Jews and the Christians both used to say he was accursed but he will witness them on the Day of Reckoning that they were wrong and he survived and so was not accursed as they would like to believe,

Please know rafa means bodily ascension as well to high altitude and could signify the travel there to the Himalaya mountains,

Please know we differ in interpretations from Muslim scholars in certain verses but take our arguments from reason supported by hadith literature and other verses of the Quran,

Please know there is a discrepancy there as they refuse to budge but it is to their detriment as we are cogent and make sense to mankind as you know of me and us in Islam here in the West. Omar.

Nisa.

4:157 And for their saying: We have killed the Messiah, Jesus, son of Mary, the messenger of Allah, and they killed him not, nor did they cause his death on the cross, but he was made to appear to them as such. And certainly those who differ therein are in doubt about it. They have no knowledge about it, but only follow a conjecture, and they killed him not for certain:

4:158 Nay, Allah exalted him in His presence. And Allah is ever Mighty, Wise.

4:159 And there is none of the People of the Book but will believe in this before his death; and on the day of Resurrection he will be a witness against them.

Please see that James was keen they should have good works and told them faith in Jesus or God is not enough to get you to Heaven with Him, your Creator there.

Please see James was a monotheist and did debate Paul in issues.

Please know he was kind and honest and forthright and does have respect for his works.

Please know he was martyred but it was so he allowed heresy to occur in his work there and let his companion say he was son who was Jesus, that's how they had the avenue to stone him but it was unjust they did as he himself did not believe this.

Please see his debate here where in a distinct way he says faith and good works are required echoing the Quran's teach to us and belief alone will not get you to heaven but it is clear Paul won in the end and the church adopted his views in things and disregard this teach to them and also Jesus teach there where he said good works are necessary.

Please know faith is lost if you don't follow through with works you do and that includes regular prayer and charity and Jesus also challenged them in John 10 where he said "why do you flaw my works."

Please know the Quran is explicit you have to have good deeds and other works you do and you have to inhibit him who is the devil there by 'enjoining good and forbidding evil.' Omar.

James 2.

17 "Even so faith, if it hath not works, is dead, being alone.

18 Yea, a man may say 'Thou hast faith, and I have works:' shew me thy faith without thy works and I will shew thee my faith by my works.

19 Thou believest that there is One God; thou doest well: the devils also believe, and tremble.

20 But wilt thou know, O vain man, that faith without works is dead?

21 Was not Abraham our father justified by works when he had offered Isaac his son upon the altar?

22 Seest thou how faith wrought with his works and by works was faith made perfect?

23 And the scripture was fulfilled which saith, Abraham believed God, and it was imputed unto him for righteousness: and he was called the Friend of God.

24 Ye see then how that by works a man is justified and not by faith only."

Baqarah.

2:277 Those who believe and do good deeds and keep up prayer and pay the poor-rate — their reward is with their Lord; and they have no fear, nor shall they grieve.

Luqman to his son.

31:17 O my son, keep up prayer and enjoin good and forbid evil, and bear patiently that which befalls thee. Surely this is an affair of great resolution.

THE METAPHOR EXPLAINED, NOW WHAT?

31:18 And turn not thy face away from people in contempt, nor go about in the land exultingly. Surely Allah loves not any self-conceited boaster.

31:19 And pursue the right course in thy going about and lower thy voice. Surely the most hateful of voices is braying of asses.

Please see James had courage till the end and he is acclaimed by us by keeping statutes he had, Jesus there.

Please know subversion is their door in the former faith Israel had during Jewish land there and they know it would make it weak, the Jewish not team there that was emerging in monotheistic principles of no law break except minor issues we all have, and James was inundated with requests to shut up and not request piety on us, finally they gave up and killed him, then the Romans became angry as he was good actually and was reforming Jewish clan under them and so they took over and destroyed temple they had and dispersed them in the lands. Omar.

Please see this story is in the archives some there in the Vatican but most of it is revealed how he got away and fled eventually who is Isa Ibn Maryam from their land in Palestine some.

This is the story of how atonement got formulated in Christian church as they knew his coming who was Jesus was only a lude until Omar's law was formulated from the Quran and so forth I am not happy but still relent to arrest as I bring out hidden facts about Allah's son as a metaphor who clarified these are errors there that there is atonement and the Lord's prayer is sufficient for you to understand man is responsible and is guilty not in issues until proven so with deeds he has as one witnesses himself there, then the decision is made to acquit, as I have been in this nation.

This is the story of how if you are disobedient like Isa was there after the crucifixion process religion gets altered by people and they tell tales of woe to people and sin occurs there because of it and adultery occurs in nations when that occurs, and as you can see religious law is altered by later followers and they did it when they cover facts about truth and so it is important you heed me and not later scholar like Zaid who will alter facts if he could as he knows adultery has ended and only a lie about Omar being a god actually can make adultery recur in this nation of believers in her, Mary there, who teaches on my page piety in marriage vows and they will say they are leaders and not him who writes this and says he is Messiah there.

Please know it is obvious adultery occurs when you sin in things and that is Allah's punishment to let you see facts clearly you think, no, they are muddled and confusion occurs in religion and intellect is over and polytheism occurs again.

Please know these are hidden facts, no, they are there in their archives there who knew he, Isa the saint there, would appear who was Omar there as the holy one teaching things from Allah when to let it out as you ready for these facts now that peace has resulted with my victory and Amlek has been formed by him who is Omar, and Allah is a witness this happened that Isa walk back home and then was hidden there in tomb after staying in the woods where he recovered and so he exited and saw Mary Magdalene and he was led to the home of Joseph of Arimathea, who taught him correctly to stay away from them, his follower, but to no avail, both he and Mary his mother wanted to make a show of it he survived and then he was injured again so he left after his eye got damaged by them in a second attempt on his life.

Please know the Mehdi tribe is worldwide in nature and we let people join you and understand literature we have about Isa's teachings there and how it was arranged for him to exit them when the crucifixion occurred as it was imperative he leave them, they were a cruel race and made up things in law, so they left them in repose.

Please know it was so they became sane in the law when he initially appeared who was Isa the nabi to them but he was late there as they were waiting for his death to occur as predicted by Isaiah as he said he was the predicted one, so they crucified him, but they knew he was innocent and walked away was allowed by them who were present there as Pilate himself came to release him and he impaled not but pierced his skin to see if the blood gushed or congealed, as he knew it was death if so it was congealed, and then he was taken down in his presence who was John the apostle who knew a time would come when I testify, as he had, and then he recovered from his wound as his leg was damaged by the hanging but it was so he could walk as shown later.

Then he migrated after a short while though he was told to leave immediately and then he could muster there in Egypt where he was told to go first and he relented to meet them, so it occurred tankeeb or deception there he was living and was raised from dying there as they knew that was legend they have, but it is so they feigned not but lied about facts as the sahaba wanted to keep him hidden so that he could escape gradually and recover from his wounds as they were deep from the hanging but if he had left immediately his death would not have been occurred in the sight of man and his spouse.

Please know it was because they feigned him as dead and recovered to fulfill the legend he was told to call them, the sahaba he had after he left, in his midst who was Paul and make them delay in things by telling them it was actual his death though they knew otherwise, they acquiesced, as that would magnify him further and Paul misled them knowing this would mislead his people from facts which he want to occur as that way he could alter religion they had as his followers were gathering there after his supposed death in order to sanctify him as great and then it occurred his plan to sanctify him in such a way that they had no law by tales he told them that their sins would be reckoned not because of his death there on the mound.

Please know he used this tact to bring changes in religion feigning the need to bring Gentiles into faith but it so occurred they did convert much to his dismay as the apostles were active there and then he asked them to eat pigs and allowed them sin in order to circumvent monotheism they had and so it came about his teachings of him being god to them and son of God issues were already floating around so he capitalized on these matters and brought polytheism into the fold of the Gentile's creed of Christianity there.

Please see it was erroneous to feign death, he should have left as living but it was so he too wanted to fulfill legend that he rose after dying and so it came about atonement by the arch-deceiver Paul there.

Please know it is true in Isaiah that he foretold he would die there not knowing it was stupor but Jesus had a flaw he wanted to fulfill the word 'dead' as in materially so it came about he permit his follower to say they killed him but he rose and would now leave the area there, which the Jews wanted him to do.

So it occurred, they, the Jewish council, propagated that they would have let him be, he was out of their vicinity and he could teach them, other people he had, as it was well known he was sent to the sheep of his tribe and messiahship would have occurred with them rather than there in their vicinity with the truth about mercy he was teaching the people of the land and they wanted him gone but decided they would kill him if he stayed, so he left them never to return to their land though he wished to late when they were sane about him as he did not commit sacrilege as they say there to people to justify their act of crucify him they did.

Atonement would not have occurred if people had known he had escaped and death on the cross would not have been propagated but because he stayed in the vicinity, they, the sahaba, feigned his death so that he could stay with them and later generations propounded atonement due to the mischief of a later scholar who appeared, Paul there, who wanted no law with them, the rest is history, and death is written late then for Isa and others there as they travel away after the crucifixion process and they lived a long life there where the lost sheep were though they were isolated there but it so came about idolatry had occurred with them in India and Isa fought there as well with them though they were recalcitrant less as they knew law didn't allow it and eventually became Muslims in the land there when Prophet Muhammad's teach came with his sahaba there.

Omar.

Please see the account of the conversion Paul did to you over a period of time, all the time saying he was your well-wisher in things.

Please see Paul was subversive to you and infiltrated your ranks when he saw he could not eliminate you and you were gaining converts who saw that piety Jesus had was remarkable and they liked his law of mercy on them, his people by you, but it is so he changed your belief from that of the people who received the Book of Moses and other prophets you had and created a hierarchy of priests or interceders for *you where you go to them for religious knowledge instead of using your minds in issues, yes, he did subvert you heaven on earth that Jesus gave you and in the Hereafter you would be forlorn because of him, his dick or breaking of your sense to you was very cunning and evil how he prevented you from gaining Paradise even though you recognize him, Jesus there, as a teacher and savior some.*

This is Paul, the mischief man by you, he is also credited for creating polytheism in your midst when he said he was the same substance as Him Who is the Creat as he was His progeny and he solidified the teachings of atonement that he create when his sahaba said he had died there, but it is so his mischief was great there as he told you to sacrifice to idols which you didn't do but did participate in idol consecrated foodstuff to you, and he allowed you pig meat and other delectables not but animals not permitted to the People of the Book, there you have it he gave verbal acquiescence to fornication saying that it will be forgiven to you, he asked you to consecrate in Jesus' name your things but the worse he could do was break the law structure you do now where Jewish edicts were abrogate by him and you lost law when he told you faith was enough and he said atonement occur that way when you believe he died there while it was well known he survived it and met with disciples before he left, yes, all these stories you see in the Bible are his and his law structure is carried forth in the church, such dupes they are to fall hook, line and sinker for his deception, he made you alter his texts to you and interposed words into the gospels like the word 'begotten' for him who you called Jesus, and the disciples fell too in that they taught the Gentiles though Jesus forbid it to them and only allowed them to teach Jewish clan by him, why did you fall, because they were converting and liked his car who you called your savior but it is so you changed religion around at his behest and it came about gradually that you called him God as he said the tropes we talk about were him saying he was god as well along with Him, the Creat there, now you know his evil respect him not and ascribe him greatness not and you realize Jewish law notwithstanding that Jesus himself was more moderate and eliminated many laws that appeared with the passage of time and told them, his followers, to be more even-keeled in issues, and his law bears similarity to the Prophet's and he himself is quoted as saying his message was closest in teachings to that of Jesus with mercy principles applying there, so you have the law of the Quran now and the law of Jesus and the law of the Bani-Israel, so take Paul out of the equation and you would have essence of religion again with you where you have a law to submit to and if you are errant you repent to Him Who creates with no intermediary, like we do in Islam of the Quran to us, and now your religion is clear you should establish yourself as law-givers to world structure where you teach Quranic edicts which have been preserved better than Jewish custom and tradition with all its laws and correlate it with the gospels to you and seek a course of mercy to you, but with the strictness of the Quran tenor you teach pious people around the world to bring Illihoon Islam to them from Prophet Muhammad to us and Allah's teach on us as well coming in my book and the Quran to you.

Omar.

Please see this is the story of Paul's conversion, so called, nay, he was recalcitrant against Me and Jesus there.

Please see these two extracts from the Bible about Paul's conversion, is this an upright man or a devious one who was blinded by a vision and never really recovered, they just say he did recover vision, it did not recover but it was complete loss not as they say here, why did I blind him in vision of the devil incarnate who stole from him and who started to appear to him from that day as this companion became a friend of his after he took his wealth but more on that late, why did I relent to him, he would have exterminated Islam they had, so vicious was his anger at them and the stoning of Stephen was only one example, he was responsible for many deaths and had promulgated law there that all Christians be exterminated in Jerusalem and its suburbs, more here is required as I have stated here the devil appeared to him in a vision you say, nay, it was a man who hit him and took his wealth, he just say it was Jesus, that was not possible, not really, it can happen even when alive, he just decided to change tact and decided to become an inside man for the Jewish Council that employ him, would I guide someone as

THE METAPHOR EXPLAINED, NOW WHAT?

vicious as him, nay, he is in Hellfire now for doing this subversion that he create polytheism there as the followers were many and they were losing ground, the Jews were, so he ended it and professed conversion.

Please know he was a vicious man and men like him are killed by Me in law We have as he was killing innocents but it is so he is sad he did it as the conversions are many and they were better than pagans in many ways but it is so he created heresy in My Word and I forgive him eventually when his dividends are over in the sense that his punishment for conversion to pagan law is over here in this land not but worldwide.

Please know it is sad for you that polytheism resulted but you are at fault too as you did not want law in your Roman law and you abrogate it yourself, My law, by your wish in following him as I taught saints through the ages not to do it, abrogate My teachings, but they couldn't muster and it took this boy I had to teach you in a way you paid attention to him as he taught from your Prophet about law Jesus had and you paid attention as you were pragmatic people who were educated and learnt the metaphor he taught and your peace occurred with One God with you, the rest is history how you protect My son here from him, the president, who used to come to him whom you call Paul when he was a spirit there and used to teach him what to say to people, more on that late but know it is true the spirit world persist in you from before and there you have it the Holy Spirit used to teach them who were sahaba he had who was Jesus and now he teach you in person in incarnate he is now, his life is a testimony he is holy to you but still has to improve in issues, as we all do you think, true it is, this word here. Omar not but your Creator Who wrote this through vision to him, Omar here.

Galatians 1:11–16,

I want you to know, brothers and sisters, that the gospel I preached is not of human origin. I did not receive it from any man, nor was I taught it; rather, I received it by revelation from Jesus Christ. For you have heard of my previous way of life in Judaism, how intensely I persecuted the church of God and tried to destroy it. But when God, who set me apart from my mother's womb and called me by his grace, was pleased to reveal his son in me so that I might preach him among the Gentiles, my immediate response was not to consult any human being.

Acts 9:3–9,

As he neared Damascus on his journey, suddenly a light from heaven flashed around him. He fell to the ground and heard a voice say to him, "Saul, Saul, why do you persecute me?"

"Who are you, Lord?" Saul asked.

"I am Jesus, whom you are persecuting," he replied. "Now get up and go into the city, and you will be told what you must do."

The men traveling with Saul stood there speechless; they heard the sound but did not see anyone. Paul got up from the ground, but when he opened his eyes he could see nothing. So they led him by the hand into Damascus. For three days he was blind, and did not eat or drink anything.

please see jesus was one with him his creat there thats why he used the metaphor in his works but it is so you say trinity is in it but that makes sense not but this does that he was doing his bid in it his life there i mean

please see john here where he says what i teach you that his will who was jesus was the will of his creator in other words he does his bid and now you know what i teach you about trinity is true that he was one with him and did his bid in things

please see it is this verse you listen to say i jesus there as i clear the way for you to come to me for everlasting life through my teach here but it is so you took my words out of context and i speak the parable and when i say i am the father it is his will i mean and john understood this and explained it in his bible but it is so you manipulated my words and implied godhead in me while i never said worship me or take me to be your god my reference to god was being one with him in all my literature and when you come to me you see him is similar and means i do his bid as i represent him in things and my will is not my own but his and i implore you not to lose your book the book of moses and others before me and take your god to be one god as the quran says and now you know i am not deviant in a way to change the law of the prophets you will understand me and not say blasphemy that i am god to you while i am human who did his bid my father who is your father as well if you but submit to his teach on you like i do in my living there

please see the words of psalms 82 explain what the son is and he is one who judge according to his teach who is the creator there and if you do not then you are evil as the quran says and you must judge by his word otherwise you are evil in transgression and do not believe me he says there and there you have it you are gods making up your own law like the bani-israel did of me and crucified me nearly i just escaped by gods will on me

omar not here only but isa too

John 6

36 "But I said unto you, That ye also have seen me, and believe not.

37 All that the Father giveth me shall come to me; and him that cometh to me I will in no wise cast out.

38 For I came down from heaven, not to do mine own will, but the will of him that sent me.

39 And this is the Father's will which hath sent me, that of all which he hath given me I should lose nothing, but should raise it up again at the last day."

Maida

5:44 Surely We revealed the Torah, having guidance and light. By it did the prophets who submitted themselves (to Allah) judge for the Jews, and the rabbis and the doctors of law, because they were required to guard the Book of Allah, and they were witnesses thereof. So fear not the people and fear Me, and take not a small price for My messages. And whoever judges not by what Allah has revealed, those are the disbelievers.

please see jesus was only indicating he was fused with him the creator there when he used the he metaphor or said 'i am'

please see this passage from exodus indicating the significance of his being who is yahweh there and it is like saying 'we' in the quran by him and connotes his greatness

please see jesus was reassured he had not committed shirk they just misunderstood him in john passage 58 and he was only telling them that he existed before abraham was created here and he was not calling himself god to them but he used these words that are in the bible and thats what upset them and they attempted to stone him but it was a metaphor indicating he was him then in his before-life state when we are spirits

   please see in 24 he indicates he is 'he' there

   please see john is clear that he was speaking of the father

   please know it is obvious he was one with him and thats why he chose these words

   please see this is godhead in the metaphorical sense when you are fused with him your creat as he was his agent doing his bid on him and it is similar when he said when you come to me you see him the father as he was his agent in things

   please see these things are written about but when you say it it is dangerous as he saw there

   please see it is fused with him i am here as i write these words from him or i am one with him and i dont do shirk in this as i am not him actually as he is in heaven and i am here doing his bid say i omar here

   please see john is clear and understands the metaphor applied so he elaborates they did not understand him that he was speaking of his creator that he is 'he' in the context of a metaphor or his represetive who is one with him with his words coming from his mouth like i show you here

   please see the hadith is clear when a servant walks he walks with his feet the creator there and when he speaks he speaks gods words

   please see it occurs when you are fused with him and so there you have it its not shirk but a sin not and it is few who have the authority to use it in this context that jesus used and i use as a servant of his the creator there

   please know our prophet muhammad also had his repose but did not use it as he saw what happened to jesus teachings but i have come to explain him so i elaborate it as i am similar though more complete in issues of fusion with him the creat and jesus achieved it after he emigrated from there when he was older

THE METAPHOR EXPLAINED, NOW WHAT?

please see other statements of 'i am' by he who is jesus is just in the manner of speech and dont mean the metaphor like it does here in this passage from john

please see i would provoke them with such language of the metaphor implied without telling them clearly it was a metaphor and they would get angry and i was satisfied in it yes i should have persevered with them and they would have let me be just as your nation protects omar from the bani-israel people by explaining him yes i wouldnt have been extrude but i had a destiny i fulfilled but i learnt later to explain more comprehensively as i grew mature and wiser say i isa here and mary knows i would say things like that 'i am' in order to get a reaction from them but she was averse not either they were too recalcitrant and not giving in to my sainthood then so it occurred we left them after my attempted homicide by them but we lost heart as well yes i was raised spiritually with my crucifixion as i became like omar and bore care with them the bani-israel clan i dealt with there in india and so forth allah raised me in spirit as the quran says

omar not only here

Exodus 3

13 Moses said to God, "Suppose I go to the Israelites and say to them, 'The God of your fathers has sent me to you,' and they ask me, 'What is his name?' Then what shall I tell them?"

14 God said to Moses, "I am who I am. This is what you are to say to the Israelites: 'I am has sent me to you.'"

John 8

57 Then said the Jews unto him, "Thou art not yet fifty years old, and hast thou seen Abraham?"

58 Jesus said unto them, "Verily, verily, I say unto you, Before Abraham was, I am."

John 8

22 Then said the Jews, "Will he kill himself? because he saith, Whither I go, ye cannot come."

23 And he said unto them, "Ye are from beneath; I am from above: ye are of this world; I am not of this world.

24 I said therefore unto you, that ye shall die in your sins: for if ye believe not that I am he, ye shall die in your sins."

25 Then said they unto him, "Who art thou?" And Jesus saith unto them, "Even the same that I said unto you from the beginning.

26 I have many things to say and to judge of you: but he that sent me is true; and I speak to the world those things which I have heard of him."

27 They understood not that he spake to them of the Father.

28 Then said Jesus unto them, "When ye have lifted up the Son of man, then shall ye know that I am he, and that I do nothing of myself; but as my Father hath taught me, I speak these things."

John 14

9 Jesus saith unto him, "Have I been so long time with you, and yet hast thou not known me, Philip? he that hath seen me hath seen the Father; and how sayest thou then, Show us the Father?"

please see these statements of facts by that august man to you who taught you the metaphor by which you have intellect now and you understand me as well

please see the verses of 'i am' here from your book and you know these are only statements he made about himself and you use his words in an out of context manner to imply he is the great i am from the book of moses while this was not his intent and when he said it there about being before abraham he meant it in a manner he speaks of in the bible of being one with him as i have shown in my literature to you here on my page and these statements here are only represent to him as to what his nature is to them his people yes he was august to them but they have to be taken in the context of a parable as you know now and he did give you life everlasting if you wish it like the early christians had it as i have shown you ebionites literature they believed in him as a prophet of theirs and they believed he was human born normally and that he had died but there it is when you say he is one with him in context that he was god as well then you dont have everlasting life but you are dead as allah kills your repose in your intellect and your thoughts are muddied at best yes you lose clarity as you are not clear in your beliefs about him who creates you for piety to him and now you know dont say such

THE METAPHOR EXPLAINED, NOW WHAT?

words that would make you lose your intellect as humans pure to him who is isa and his creator and the quran is with you that son of god is just a metaphor you have and atonement does not occur as no one can take the sins of another only god can do that

omar

John 6:35

And Jesus said to them, "I am the bread of life. He who comes to Me shall never hunger, and he who believes in Me shall never thirst."

John 8:12

Then Jesus spoke to them again, saying, "I am the light of the world. He who follows Me shall not walk in darkness, but have the light of life."

John 10:9

"I am the door. If anyone enters by Me, he will be saved, and will go in and out and find pasture."

John 10:11

"I am the good shepherd. The good shepherd gives His life for the sheep."

John 11:25,26

Jesus said to her, "I am the resurrection and the life. He who believes in Me, though he may die, he shall live. And whoever lives and believes in Me shall never die. Do you believe this?"

John 14:6

Jesus said to him, "I am the way, the truth, and the life. No one comes to the Father except through Me."

John 15:5

"I am the vine, you are the branches. He who abides in Me, and I in him, bears much fruit; for without Me you can do nothing."

Please see the metaphor here is implied not but indicated as he being a son of man was in addition a prophet of His.

This is Peter, the rock, who Jesus enlisted and his brother Andrew, both of whom were apostles, but it is clear that he asked him who he was though clarified he was human as a son of man but they say otherwise there and say he was begotten, but Jesus denies that in Gospels like John 10 where he says it is a metaphor and I know it is clear to you but this verse needs elucidation that he was a man who was a son, like Adam and Abraham were, meaning a prophet here as John says there, as seen in my literature to you, and when he asks them who son of man is they indicate it is him who is also son of God which I have explained before is a well-known metaphor there and some words have been interposed here to indicate he was not son of man but we know Jesus in his teach to them repeat ways called himself son of a human man and they don't contradict him there where it is mentioned in their lore on many not but all occasions.

Peter was a leader but was killed in the lifetime of James for heresy he had as a person who has insane beliefs is usually dismissed or executed, which they did to them as they were spreading lies about their savior and saying he died while Nero know Pontius had saved him, and Jesus left them behind to teach his 'sheep', not the Gentiles, so it occurred the passage of grace, and the spirit world they predict of heaven as they thought they would be spirits in the next world, only, as they did not reach Heaven with their teach of idolatry on them, the Gentiles, who came to faith of Jesus as god to them so their hellfire was written, while our car is to be in physics again as in Islam we do see Paradise with physics in it.

Please know he was pious but weak and could not sustain James and supported him who was Paul in his attempt to bring the Gentiles to Islam they had of mixing the faith with idolatry, hence his death was written for heresy, as they knew James was right and he was not killed by the Romans, only the Bani-Israel were behind his death.

The statement of Jesus about Peter here is made up for the most part but he did call him Peter but the church was given to James, as indicated there.

Please know James was my choice says he here who is Isa Ibn Mary, and he knew Peter had denied him and was weak and he could not be trusted in church matters, something he proved in his life by allowing polytheism to reign in his teach to them. Omar.

Matthew 16.

Verses 13 to 19. In a dialogue between Jesus and his disciples Jesus asks, "Who do people say that the Son of Man is?" The disciples give various answers. When he asks "Who do you say that I am?", Simon Peter answers, "You are the Messiah, the Son of the living God." Jesus then declares:

"Blessed are you, Simon son of Jonah, for this was not revealed to you by flesh and blood, but by my Father in heaven. And I tell you that you are Cephas (Peter) (Petros), and on this rock (petra) I will build my church and the gates of Hades will not overcome it. I will give you the keys of the kingdom of heaven; whatever you bind on earth will be bound in heaven and whatever you loose on earth will be loosed in heaven."

Please see Allah was wrought with them, the Bani-Israel, who were careening towards crime as they thought themselves to be above the law as He had called them chosen before when they were the only monotheist nation around in this world of idolatry and paganism.

Why was Allah angry with them the Jews?

Please know they were from the seed of Abraham and Moses was with them yet they were disobedient to him and disregarded law they had of being pious in their law.

Please know Moses was fed up with them.

Please know the Jews know their caste, it is evil, and they disregard Him, their Creator in things.

Please know this came true eventually and they were scattered in the nations, not worthy to lead.

Please know it is a curse they had so it came about.

Please know this is their scripture and they know they are disobedient and they're not supposed to have a land of their own, so Israel is lost to them.

It is true they are supposed to disband and enter the fold of Muslims of my jamaat of Prophet Muhammad's people as they are human and all humans can identify with Prophet Muhammad, on him be peace in that avenue.

Please know I bring the Prophet's teachings to you who is your well-wisher but you must disband your religious belief and enter Islam of submission to Him, your Creator to you, that is key, submit to Him, you weren't doing it before.

Please know the curse of Jesus occurred and you were disband by Titus as he knew your book and history, you are better under other nations and the British were wrong, you are not supposed to have a homeland of your own.

Omar.

Deuteronomy 28.

62 You who were as numerous as the stars in the sky will be left but few in number, because you did not obey the Lord your God.

63 Just as it pleased the Lord to make you prosper and increase in number, so it will please him to ruin and destroy you. You will be uprooted from the land you are entering to possess.

64 Then the Lord will scatter you among all nations, from one end of the earth to the other. There you will worship other gods--gods of wood and stone, which neither you nor your fathers have known.

65 Among those nations you will find no repose, no resting place for the sole of your foot. There the Lord will give you an anxious mind, eyes weary with longing and a despairing heart.

66 You will live in constant suspense, filled with dread both night and day, never sure of your life.

Please see the message was clear from Jesus to them here, his sahaba, to teach the Jews and not those who were pagan.

Please see Jesus knew his religion would get altered when they started teaching Gentiles and Samaritans about Islam he had and specifically forbade it but they deterred not but disobeyed him in it.

Please know Paul was behind it and they followed suit who were disciples who were misled by the arch-deceiver there, Paul to you.

Please know polytheism came into the religion and Jesus' sect would have been pure keeping to the spirit of the law but some good came out of it late as I came on behalf of them, Bani-Israel true who have died before, who wanted to save you, so the Prophet taught me how.

Please know I am inundated with vice because I tell you this that they will poison me if I stay with you and it is expedient that I leave, maybe I can return, maybe not.

Omar.

THE METAPHOR EXPLAINED, NOW WHAT?

Matthews 10.

5 These twelve Jesus sent forth, and commanded them, saying, "Go not into the way of the Gentiles, and into any city of the Samaritans enter ye not:

6 But go rather to the lost sheep of the house of Israel.

7 And as ye go, preach, saying, The kingdom of heaven is at hand.

8 Heal the sick, cleanse the lepers, raise the dead, cast out devils: freely ye have received, freely give.

9 Provide neither gold, nor silver, nor brass in your purses,"

Please see here that Jesus came to the Jews for the most part and limited his teachings to them as they were a lost race and weren't coming forth in piety to Him, the Creat.

Please see he came to the lost sheep of the house of Israel and that is meant those of his tribe there in Jerusalem and Israel land but it also refers to the Jewish tribes that were far removed from this land and that's where he eventually fled to, in India, where they migrated after the capture by Nebuchadnezzar and his army, not all the tribes came back to Israel and that is a document there that they migrated to distant lands and some went to Africa to preach there.

Please know some of the Jewish tribes were lost earlier but amalgamated in culture they had and left Judaism as a religion but after they migrated in the land after the capture by Nebuchadnezzar they still kept their heritage and remained Jews though idolatry and other deviances did develop in them which Jesus sought to correct when he went there to preach to them.

Please know he was hunt not, they let him be, they got their way and he left them in heart repose not as he left James to teach them while he was safe elsewhere.

He knew that other disciples were weak but had an idea he would return when the coast was clear but it never occurred, they were recalcitrant and unrepentant of their deed of crucify him they did. Omar.

Matthews 15.

22 And, behold, a woman of Canaan came out of the same coasts, and cried unto him, saying, "Have mercy on me, O Lord, thou son of David; my daughter is grievously vexed with a devil."

23 But he answered her not a word. And his disciples came and besought him, saying, "Send her away; for she crieth after us."

24 But he answered and said, "I am not sent but unto the lost sheep of the house of Israel."

25 Then came she and worshipped him, saying, "Lord, help me."

26 But he answered and said, "It is not meet to take the children's bread, and to cast it to dogs."

27 And she said, "Truth, Lord: yet the dogs eat of the crumbs which fall from their masters' table."

28 Then Jesus answered and said unto her, "O woman, great is thy faith: be it unto thee even as thou wilt." And her daughter was made whole from that very hour.

Please see sins mentioned here are in your culture not anymore and you aspire to become sane in issues of his law to you who is Jesus there when he admonished you on these issues here.

Please see your Jesus in his words which you ignore in that he says these are evils of the heart that are mentioned here and minor issues of foodstuffs are not.

How could you think he would allow you fornication when he came for your purity to occur

Please know the Bani-Israel law was to ignore these vices, that's why the Pharisees object to Him, he was making sense to him in his follower to him and so it occurred he was outsourced as an outsider to them.

Please know we were telling you all along he came to uphold the law and minor issues of sex not as that is major, as he says here, but minor food issues were not important to him but pig meat he abhorred and he never partook in it and neither did disciples close to him.

Please know he says here that adultery and fornication are evils that stem from the heart to him and he taught you things of this sort were wrong, yet you deterred him and listened to one who came after him and followed Paul to you, why, you wanted the low act of these things of sex and pig meat to you even though you knew better not to listen to your pastor who said, okay, if you wish, you will be forgiven.

THE METAPHOR EXPLAINED, NOW WHAT?

Please know now you know so deter these acts mentioned here and uncover not, as it always leads to these crimes of fornication and adultery in you.

Please see Paul was evil and pernicious to you when he allowed you entry based on faith that he died for you while you know he died much later in Jerusalem not but India, where he is buried, and you have analyzed the DNA, it is Hebrew kind.

Please see your fall there when you accept Paul as your savior, you knew better then but still did it, these were crimes Jesus had in his vernacular to them, so you are sorry for all the lost generations that went astray, yes, be so, and do not party them to your own group here.

Please know he also mentions blasphemy here, now you know it is a evil he hate so don't do it, don't call him god along with his Father and son of God is blasphemy there to them, as mentioned in John 10.

Omar.

Matthews 15.

17 "Do not ye yet understand, that whatsoever entereth in at the mouth goeth into the belly, and is cast out into the draught?

18 But those things which proceed out of the mouth come forth from the heart; and they defile the man.

19 For out of the heart proceed evil thoughts, murders, adulteries, fornications, thefts, false witness, blasphemies:

20 These are the things which defile a man: but to eat with unwashen hands defileth not a man."

please see david was astute and praised the inner workings of god in the womb thereby indicating the nature of the miracle there and thereby not sanctifying death of it the child in her there

please see this psalm of david our savior there they say yet they say for the first 40 days the child is mere water in judaism which is not the case in this psalm as the woven one is the child formed in utero in depths known to him the creator and it is not so in rabbinical literature they are supposed to preserve the child except in case the mothers death is impending which is what we say in islam i teach but it is so this psalm has depth and now you know these thoughts are true and preserved in your book so there you have it islam they have also preserves the fetus and does not give the right of abortion to the mother unless she is dying more here is required as the passage from the quran that was with them in their book has been removed from literature they have that says taking the life of an individual is like killing humanity and they wanted to allow abortion as well thats why rabbinical literature is varied in it but it is true from this psalm that the workings of the fetus are appreciated by david as unknown that god webs there signifying that it is a protected entity that god knows about in his wisdom to him who is david there

please see he says he is wonderful in his make and his frame is not hidden from him his god to him signifying that even in the depths there it is a wonderful process the creation of the child like david is so to abort it is wrong for your religion in judeo-christian lore and islam is similar we follow davids teach here as well as our book the quran to us where creation occurs at conceive time there when he says be and it is he does not say it at 4 months because by then it is not dust and it is living with a heartbeat and all that it entails yes it is living with a destiny to be a human outside the womb when it is conception in it and not before true sperm can be wasted then as it is essentially dust of earth that is living in us but not independent life of its own and there you have it childbirth can allow you contraceptives if you wish to delay it for you and thats why i say if implant not but fertilization is prevented then it is permissible for you to prevent child in the inner workings of the womb as david put it

omar

Psalms 139 by David the prophet there.

1 You have searched me, LORD, and you know me.

2 You know when I sit and when I rise; you perceive my thoughts from afar.

3 You discern my going out and my lying down; you are familiar with all my ways.

4 Before a word is on my tongue you, LORD, know it completely.

5 You hem me in behind and before, and you lay your hand upon me.

6 Such knowledge is too wonderful for me, too lofty for me to attain.

7 Where can I go from your Spirit? Where can I flee from your presence?

8 If I go up to the heavens, you are there; if I make my bed in the depths, you are there.

9 If I rise on the wings of the dawn, if I settle on the far side of the sea,

10 even there your hand will guide me, your right hand will hold me fast.

11 If I say, "Surely the darkness will hide me and the light become night around me,"

12 even the darkness will not be dark to you; the night will shine like the day, for darkness is as light to you.

13 For you created my inmost being; you knit me together in my mother's womb.

14 I praise you because I am fearfully and wonderfully made; your works are wonderful, I know that full well.

15 My frame was not hidden from you when I was made in the secret place, when I was woven together in the depths of the earth.

16 Your eyes saw my unformed body; all the days ordained for me were written in your book before one of them came to be.

17 How precious to me are your thoughts, God! How vast is the sum of them!

18 Were I to count them, they would outnumber the grains of sand— when I awake, I am still with you.

19 If only you, God, would slay the wicked! Away from me, you who are bloodthirsty!

20 They speak of you with evil intent; your adversaries misuse your name.

21 Do I not hate those who hate you, LORD, and abhor those who are in rebellion against you?

22 I have nothing but hatred for them; I count them my enemies.

23 Search me, God, and know my heart; test me and know my anxious thoughts.

24 See if there is any offensive way in me, and lead me in the way everlasting.

Please see commemoration is wrong for man and wife and their child as well but it is so you continue as your church tells you there but don't do it in your private prayers you have, He will disregard you in it.

This is the origin of commemoration of Christ in their Jewish faith of Christianity as they think their prayers will be accepted this way but the words are interposed here, it is not for a prophet to glorify himself with regards to the law of prayer in Islam we have and a prayer should be short and direct to Him without any human intervention.

Please know this is the custom of Bani-Israel people to interpose words in their literature and the Christians followed suit here and now shirk has occurred as they cannot approach their Creator except in this way of commemoration of their god to them, and it is decried in Islam, this sort of intervention they had, from their Prophet Muhammad on him be peace that he never asked for commemoration so the die has been cast for all believers and he made it clear not to do so but to ask and be given in His wisdom to you as Muslims know some prayers are accepted not or late and some are early, but it is so we should beseech Him with confidence that He will hear it when asked directly of Him and no one else, otherwise he may never accept a prayer in that fashion, now you know so don't do it, it is like asking Jesus of things and not your Creator and be warned your prayer may be wasted this way but it is so your churches advise you to continue but you should not, Allah is your Creator and your pastor is not and that is shirk too if you listen to him rather than Allah and His Prophet there.

See these words here are shirk in the sense that he says he will do it and not his Father which goes against the dogma of Christ as he always beseeched his Creator in things when he had a need of something and now you know commemoration is wrong and try to make your prayer to Him Who gives things, not Jesus or for that matter any human as you know him to be.

Omar.

John 14.

12 Verily, verily, I say unto you, He that believeth on me, the works that I do shall he do also; and greater works than these shall he do; because I go unto my Father.

13 *And whatsoever ye shall ask in my name, that will I do, that the Father may be glorified in the Son.*

14 *If ye shall ask any thing in my name, I will do it.*

Please see the message of the Quran and Jesus' teaching is the same barring minor exceptions not but complete faith occurred there in Muhammad's time there.

Please see these messages to you where God and Jesus ask you to keep commands by you and obey your Creator in things so that love occurs in you for Him, your Creator, and Jesus too, as it is clear these commands bring you close to God's nature, as when you obey Him you develop His attributes in you and others love you as well.

Please see love occurs that way and you will have joy as that is what His love do to you Who is your Creator to you.

Please see the Quran is clear on this issue that God loves the dutiful amongst you and He does not love transgressors by Him.

Please know though God loves humanity but if they are bad He will admonish them and say that He doesn't love them, as your father would too to love not, but they do, they just say it and punish you if you have bad in you.

Please know it is true though that love is lost if there is evil car in yours say I Allah to you.

Please know now you know you have to keep the commandments of God that Jesus gave to you and not follow a scholar who says he is god who is Jesus while he said worship the One God alone and used to do that in his prayers too, and it is similar to his law structure in that he came to uphold the laws of the Bani-Israel and not demolish them while Paul did demolish them to you says Allah to you.

Please see so you see he upheld law and did not eat pig meat and did not allow sex outside marriage and you cannot justify these acts if you are a believer in Paul not but Jesus to you and there you have it no one can abrogate his law structure to you and the Quran validates his law and completes it too where he couldn't do it, like making alcohol banned by him.

Please know to tell your child to ascribe purity to Allah's messenger, Jesus to you, and not follow your pastor or scholar who says other than his words to you and seek purity from the Quran which has the same message to you say I the August One to you, say Omar not but Allah to you here.

Omar not.

John 15.

9 "As the Father has loved me, so have I loved you. Now remain in my love.

10 If you keep my commands, you will remain in my love, just as I have kept my Father's commands and remain in his love.

11 I have told you this so that my joy may be in you and that your joy may be complete."

John 14.

21 "He that hath my commandments, and keepeth them, he it is that loveth me: and he that loveth me shall be loved of my Father, and I will love him, and will manifest myself to him."

Al-Imran.

3:31 Say: If you love Allah, follow me: Allah will love you, and grant you protection from your sins. And Allah is Forgiving, Merciful.

Al-Imran.

3:76 Yea, whoever fulfils his promise and keeps his duty — then Allah surely loves the dutiful.

Please see we have to have good works in addition to belief that our God is One and no one is worthy of worship but Him in the Quran and Bible too to you.

Please see it is clear good deeds are required in our religions and Jesus and Muhammad taught us good deeds are required to get us to Heaven and you know it is correct to correct yourself if you follow Paul's teachings that say faith alone gets you Paradise, as that is a heresy actually, Jesus did good works as it says here in John and he recommends his follower do the same by law of Islam on us, further his life is a testimony to his good deeds in that he brought piety in your deeds and made you have mercy and love in your dealings with each other and he fought evil the Bani-Israel had, which you should implement in your fight against the evil structure in this country to you, and to correct people is a good deed by you.

Please see the Quran also echoes the teaching of Jesus and just as Muhammad fought idolatry in his home town and land and the impiety they had, you too should import and export piety for you and become adept in teaching correctly the Quran to you and know that your good deeds take you to Paradise, it is not faith alone that does so, in similar ways good deeds without faith is wasted and kept in abeyance and you won't see rewards for it until you are clean with Allah and His Prophet and those who are pious with you and spent their lives fighting evil around them, like Mirza and I do, so it is true that you have to be a believer in order to reap reward of your deeds in the Hereafter by you.

Please see all the prophets and saints do good and fight evil and the Quran recommends their follower do the same in exhortation to them and Jesus also recommends you show good deeds to Him, your Creator, and the light that emits from you is a witness to you that you were worthy of a Heavenly Abode with Him, your Creator to you. Omar.

John 10.

24 The Jews who were there gathered around him, saying, "How long will you keep us in suspense? If you are the Messiah, tell us plainly."

25 Jesus answered, "I did tell you, but you do not believe. The works I do in my Father's name testify about me,

26 but you do not believe because you are not my sheep.

27 My sheep listen to my voice; I know them, and they follow me.

28 I give them eternal life, and they shall never perish; no one will snatch them out of my hand.

29 My Father, who has given them to me, is greater than all; no one can snatch them out of my Father's hand.

30 I and the Father are one."

31 Again his Jewish opponents picked up stones to stone him,

32 but Jesus said to them, "I have shown you many good works from the Father. For which of these do you stone me?"

33 *"We are not stoning you for any good work," they replied, "but for blasphemy, because you, a mere man act like a god."*

Matthews 5.

14 *"Ye are the light of the world. A city that is set on an hill cannot be hid.*

15 *Neither do men light a candle, and put it under a bushel, but on a candlestick; and it giveth light unto all that are in the house.*

16 *Let your light so shine before men, that they may see your good works, and glorify your Father which is in heaven."*

Al-Araf.

7:8 *And the judging on that day will be just; so as for those whose good deeds are heavy, they are the successful.*

7:9 *And as for those whose good deeds are light, those are they who ruined their souls because they disbelieved in Our messages.*

Al-Anbiya.

21:92 *Surely this your community is a single community, and I am your Lord, so serve Me.*

21:93 *And they cut off their affair among them: to Us will all return.*

21:94 *So whoever does good deeds and is a believer, there is no rejection of his effort, and We surely write (it) down for him.*

Please see all 3 of us get credit for converting the Gentiles to Islam and those of the world community that follow us here.

Please know the Bible is full of references to the One God with them, the Bani-Israel race of prophets said it and he was no exception who was Jesus Christ and it was fortuitous he made it clear there he prayed to Him, the Creat to him, and so it occurs he is responsible for the mass conversion of the race of Gentiles coming to Islam now by teaching I had from Prophet Muhammad to me and the Quran from Muhammad is a testimony as well and so it occurs we all get credit for converting you in Christianity faith to monotheism now where Islam reigns with you and you submit to Him Who creates as you know he who is Jesus Christ also told you he had a law and he followed the Old Testament in its edicts for himself, and there you have it Paul is sidelined now and is no longer considered important for Christian faith as he taught differently from Jesus himself, and the Quran upholds the law Jesus had for himself and so you know to separate yourself from later edicts which are not truth-bearing for Christians now. Omar.

Please see certain conversations in the Bible are parables for late in times and the words transposed here are not accurately recorded so it's difficult to make sense of them, suffice it to say these are dreams which Moses had in Acts and here in Numbers.

Please see this is Balam, the prophet not but me speaking there that the son of man is not God and that there is no God in us actually as can be seen in verse 19 but it is so he who is Balak deterred and wanted kill on me for teaching Islam precepts from our book, not his, as he uses the Bible still, but it is so he is Christian there of Trinity type and wants abrogate me so keep him there in prison until he learns truth-telling is important and he keeps vows he has and so forth.

Please see the conversation between Balam, the saint savior they had then at the time of Moses exodus you say, nay it is a parable of later times, and I am Omar in essence say I Allah there as he is my star against Balak who wanted to kill him, but it so occurs I am told there that this conversation occurred here in our times and Acts are similar where the words are transposed to Moses there, but it so occurs we are one entity now and all mankind realize there are parables there in your book which you realize not, but it is so this conversation is recorded there about Obama and me in that he will make out I am him who is Jesus and I will say I am not but it so occurs he will try to kill me then realize he can't as I am not him who is like him who is Jesus Christ who made a mistake and regretted it and was then crucified, but it so occurs I am high by you and conquered his land after Illihoon occurred in your hearts and you became my servant in things as Obama had broken the statutes and imprisoned me without law on him, and they don't like it I name him who is ex-president Obama here but I do as it is imperative I continue to relegate him to obscurity and now his prison has occurred for killing black folks who were converting to me they say and yes they turned to Islam and wanted to pray to me say I the August One, Allah there, but it is so this conversation is a dream there and not real to Moses clan.

Omar not only.
Numbers 23
18 And he took up his parable, and said, "Rise up, Balak, and hear; hearken unto me, thou son of Zippor:
19 God is not a man that he should lie; neither the son of man that he should repent: hath he said, and shall he not do it? or hath he spoken, and shall he not make it good?
20 Behold, I have received commandment to bless: and he hath blessed; and I cannot reverse it.
21 He hath not beheld iniquity in Jacob, neither hath he seen perverseness in Israel: the Lord his God is with him and the shout of a king is among them.
22 God brought them out of Egypt; he hath as it were the strength of an unicorn.
23 Surely there is no enchantment against Jacob, neither is there any divination against Israel: according to this time it shall be said of Jacob and of Israel ' What hath God wrought!'
24 Behold, the people shall rise up as a great lion and lift up himself as a young lion: he shall not lie down until he eat of the prey and drink the blood of the slain."
25 And Balak said unto Balaam "Neither curse them at all nor bless them at all."
26 But Balaam answered and said unto Balak, "Told not I thee saying, All that the Lord speaketh, that I must do?"

please see he was adept in issues of islam they had but was a poor communicator in things not sanctioned by me say i the creator to you and he suffered the consequences from not teaching from me always
this is a good sentiment to be perfect like your god is perfect but the way he tells it is wrong and it cannot be done by humanity and the quran principle of justice is sane where we requite evil if it continues in the heart and deed but forgive if they are willing to relent to piety and give back assets you lost yes perfection is justice in you and i am just say i allah there some things he said of his own accord and i know he achieved perfection late in issues yes it was not there in palestine but

later in india when he was conjoint more with us as he was young there and maturity results late in man but he had a job to do and be crucified as well you think nay it just occurred that he was but i did not sanction it it was people who did it when he made mistakes in his vernacular some and when he didnt explain adequately like omar does and muhammad was careful in that regard in that he made sure his people would get the message safely yes it was in india he really matured and was safe to transmit information from me say i the creator to you

allah there

Matthews 5

38 "Ye have heard that it hath been said, An eye for an eye, and a tooth for a tooth:

39 But I say unto you, That ye resist not evil: but whosoever shall smite thee on thy right cheek, turn to him the other also.

40 And if any man will sue thee at the law, and take away thy coat, let him have thy cloak also.

41 And whosoever shall compel thee to go a mile, go with him twain.

42 Give to him that asketh thee, and from him that would borrow of thee turn not thou away.

43 Ye have heard that it hath been said, Thou shalt love thy neighbour, and hate thine enemy.

44 But I say unto you, Love your enemies, bless them that curse you, do good to them that hate you, and pray for them which despitefully use you, and persecute you;

45 That ye may be the children of your Father which is in heaven: for he maketh his sun to rise on the evil and on the good, and sendeth rain on the just and on the unjust.

46 For if ye love them which love you, what reward have ye? do not even the publicans the same?

47 And if ye salute your brethren only, what do ye more than others? do not even the publicans so?

48 Be ye therefore perfect, even as your Father which is in heaven is perfect."

Please see this disclosure from Isa here where he recounts events of the last supper with them, the sahaba he has.

Please know the last supper is an account created by Jesus not but by Paul who says things like eat my body and drink my blood, I did not say this, true I had a meal with disciples but it was a simple meal, not maida like the Quran says, that was a different context, and now you know I foretold I must go and that my crucifixion would occur and I had prayed to God and He assured me I would be saved, I also told them I was Christ, the Messiah there, and I would lead world community one day but it is expedient I go away for that and that Allah had decreed me to go through with it as the die was cast and I would not get away, there were soldiers looking for me, there you have it I am Christ who was confirmed in the Quran as the one through which messiahship would occur, and now you have it there is One God here and Omar has brought it out with Muhammad, my true tale there.

Omar.

Please see some history how trinity was formulated in their doctrine.

Please see this canon became ecumenical in the 5th century that was derived from the Council of Chalcedon in 451 AD and Christianity as Jesus intended was gone with the canonization law they create and trinity was entrenched in them, and in the Council of Constantinople in 381 AD they equated me, the Holy Spirit, to godhead even though I descend not on earth then but it is so there is farce in their sayings and polytheism of an obvious kind so Allah sent me to teach bishop they have to accept him who they call Muhammad as he had appeared there in their land where idolatry was rife, and so it occurred they say I inspire them, but it does occur revelation to saints they had and Muhammad appeared there after he left them in Arabia and upon his death assumed the role of teach to sainthood they had, these are things from Allah I teach and I write not on my own accord, and with the equating of me with godhead the equation of trinity was formulated and in the Council of Nicaea in 325 AD only Jesus was equated with godhead with Him, the Creator, but they had to solve the birth of the son being from Him,

the Creat, so they called him god and their scripture taught them that, I, the holy one, impregnated her, while it was a spiritual bond only.
Omar.

please see the words that i use are not my choice and neither is the material i write but i write only what is indicated to me about matters relating to our before-life when we were spirits only

please see jeremiah here where he astounds you by saying what i teach that we were spirits in our before-life and all that it entails and prophet muhammad was a traveler there who traveled from his realm before to rest in the cool shade of the earth and jesus is similar in that he tells them who are questioning him about abraham that he existed before him yes this knowledge is with the prophets and saints some but the time was opportune to tell you that isa not but muhammad was the first entity he create who is our creator there and it is made up that jibreel or gabriel as you know him was the first creation as a human he made but i know much has been lost in hadith lore and i bring it out these things to you that the person in the hadith was me muhammad who said this about heaven and hell and all that it entails to them there and not him who you say is next but he was late and mary was the next he create after me being alone for an eon with him allah there there you have it they hid it who were sahaba averse to me and my dignity with him the creat there but here the evidence is from your scriptures that we existed before this earthly existence was created from our soul you say nay it is from your spirit i write the dna you have say i allah to you and your creation from a sperm and egg is done but the characteristic of the person comes from the unique dna i create with the soul in mind that it will guide it late not but soon after its birth and there you have it every soul not but spirit is guide by me on earth

omar not only

Jeremiah 1

4 Then the word of the Lord came unto me, saying,

5 Before I formed thee in the belly I knew thee; and before thou camest forth out of the womb I sanctified thee, and I ordained thee a prophet unto the nations.

John 8

56 Your father Abraham rejoiced to see my day: and he saw it, and was glad.

57 Then said the Jews unto him, Thou art not yet fifty years old, and hast thou seen Abraham?

58 Jesus said unto them, verily, verily, I say unto you, before Abraham was, I am.

Hadith

Abdullah ibn Mas'ud reported: The Messenger of Allah, peace and blessings be upon him, laid down upon a reed mat and it left marks on his side. When he woke up, I started wiping his side and I said, "O Messenger of Allah, why do you not let us spread something on top of this mat for you?" The Prophet said, "What is the world to me? What am I to the world? Verily, the example of this world and myself is that of a rider who seeks shade under a tree, then he moves on and leaves it behind." -Source: Musnad Aḥmad 3701

Bukhari hadith

When Allah (SWT) created the Garden, He asked the Angel Jibreel to go and take a look at it. So he went and looked at the Paradise and at all that Allah had prepared for its inhabitants. Then he said "O My Lord! By Your honor, No one who hears about this place would stay away from it." Then Allah surrounded the Paradise by difficulties and hardships and asked Jibreel again to go and take another look. Jibreel went again and after looking at it came back and said "O My Lord! By Your honor, I am afraid now that no one will be able to enter it." Then after Allah created the Hell, He asked Jibreel to go and take a look. When Jibreel came back he said "O My Lord! By Your honor, no one who hears about it will ever enter it." Then Allah surrounded the Hell by all kinds of lusts and desires and asked Jibreel to take another look. This time after looking at it Jibreel said "O My Lord! By Your honor, I am afraid that no one will be able to avoid it."

CHAPTER THREE

SOME VERACITY OF QURANIC VERSES I HAVE

Please see law is inherent in Me and has to be obeyed in your nature to you and My law structure there coming forth through the ages to you.

Please see this is what the law means in that it has to be obeyed by one and if ignored it is sin and rebellion.

Please see these verses from Maida or The Table saying that the people of the book were given a law.

Please know it is because of this they are closer to Islam than other faiths where the law differed in respect to issues.

Please know it is imperative that we live with the law.

Please know Jesus taught the law had to be followed and did not allow any polytheism in it as the current day law stands in its trinity concepts.

Please know it is clear he came to uphold the law as it says in the verse of the Quran and the gospels.

Please know there is no law in the Torah or Islam that allows admonition not when you ignore law in its implementation as you have in the Christian faith.

Please know this is an innovation they say that Jesus died for your sins to be forgiven.

Please know similarly it is clear that Jesus' death was conjured up in order that he may appear to them as gone from them.

Please see it occur that we know he did not die for your sins as that is not law in the Torah and the Quran says that one cannot take away the sins of another in the least and further it says that we need to be responsible for our deeds which cling to us on Judgment Day.

Please know to judge by what is revealed.

Please know we will be asked if we did not follow revelation.

Please know the modern-day Christians and Jews know that fornication is not allowed and yet they do not prevent them from doing so saying it will be forgiven of them. It is similar somewhat in the Quran they say but it is so the Quran is emphatic that you will be judged and an iota will be forgiven not actually and all things are accountable by Him there on that Day. In this there is truth that all are sins that will be tabulated and those whose good deeds are light will enter Hellfire and so forth results.

Please see God is exacting in judgment and it is not like Muslims think they will be forgiven and no accountability will occur if they pray regularly but it is so you have to live piously in things and then you may be forgiven if your good deeds are heavy, as the Quran says there.

Please know it is similar for other laws as well where they are not permitted leeway.

Please know the Old Testament has to be judged by, by the Christians, if they want a law other than the Quran and it is so Muslims will have to judge them by their Book as the law is inherent in man and cannot be ignored in a careless way the way Christians of the latter day used to do.

Please know it is akin to disbelief not to follow the law as the Quran says here and a person will be raised as a disbeliever if he or she does not follow the letter of the law in a way becoming of them. Omar.

The Table.

5:44 Surely We revealed the Torah, having guidance and light. By it did the prophets who submitted themselves (to Allah) judge for the Jews, and the rabbis and the doctors of law, because they were required to guard the Book of Allah, and they were witnesses thereof. So fear not the people and fear Me, and take not a small price for My messages. And whoever judges not by what Allah has revealed, those are the disbelievers.

5:45 And We prescribed to them in it that life is for life, and eye for eye, and nose for nose, and ear for ear, and tooth for tooth, and for wounds retaliation. But whoso forgoes it, it shall be an expiation for him. And whoever judges not by what Allah has revealed, those are the wrongdoers.

THE METAPHOR EXPLAINED, NOW WHAT?

5:46 And We sent after them in their footsteps Jesus, son of Mary, verifying that which was before him of the Torah; and We gave him the Gospel containing guidance and light, and verifying that which was before it of the Torah, and a guidance and an admonition for the dutiful.

5:47 And let the People of the Gospel judge by that which Allah has revealed in it. And whoever judges not by what Allah has revealed, those are the transgressors.

5:48 And We have revealed to thee the Book with the truth, verifying that which is before it of the Book and a guardian over it, so judge between them by what Allah has revealed, and follow not their low desires, (turning away) from the truth that has come to thee. For everyone of you We appointed a law and a way. And if Allah had pleased He would have made you a single people, but that He might try you in what He gave you. So vie one with another in virtuous deeds. To Allah you will all return, so He will inform you of that wherein you differed;

5:49 And that thou shouldst judge between them by what Allah has revealed, and follow not their low desires, and be cautious of them lest they seduce thee from part of what Allah has revealed to thee. Then if they turn away, know that Allah desires to afflict them for some of their sins. And surely many of the people are transgressors.

please see these verses regarding faith from the quran that apply to you in the world forum of people

please see this article of faith here

please know you are this in the world forum as many of you believe this to be true that allah is your creator and that he is one as the book says so and that he is unseen but yet he is obvious as well

please know you see clear vision now as you say how could there not be a creator who wrote your dna code to create you and you know in your heart the quran creates the word of truth to you as well

please know you believe too in your revelations to you in your books as this verse asks you to believe in books before his the quran here

please see you are praying too and some not but most give in charity as well to take away your sins of the past and for compassion for them who are needy but i know the fatiha is key and that is how you develop faith in you and you have ability to do works like protect my body from him in the government dick here as they try to disassemble your piety that emerges here

please see faith has entered your heart because you pray there the fatiha and shahada some in the country not only but in the world structure there

please know to fast as well it will strengthen you in piety

please see the structure of religion is based on these principles but key is belief in god as your creator and no one else and regular prayer and charity

please see when religion is done this way faith occurs in you if you maintain the law with you otherwise it is lost and you weaken in resolve so there you have it it is belief and law-bearing in you that give you faith and it is so it occurs as your spirit is intact in you and you cause it to grow your soul there with regular prayer and charity and it fills the spirit and then you begin to see clearly with you mind eye and it emanates from you light does and the first law of faith in the religion of islam is belief in one god and the most important pillar is prayer to him regular ways with you and many in the world obey these precepts and would hate disbelief and rebellion for themselves

please know if you have faith like you do in these edicts that are for you then your destination is heaven inshallah or god willing

omar

Al-Baqarah

2:2 This Book, there is no doubt in it, is a guide to those who keep their duty,

2:3 Who believe in the Unseen and keep up prayer and spend out of what We have given them,

2:4 And who believe in that which has been revealed to thee and that which was revealed before thee, and of the Hereafter they are sure.

2:5 These are on a right course from their Lord and these it is that are successful.

Al-Hujurat

49:7...Allah has endeared the faith to you and has made it seemly in your hearts, and He has made hateful to you disbelief and transgression and disobedience. Such are those who are rightly guided —

49:8 A grace from Allah and a favor. And Allah is Knowing, Wise.

Please see this message from our Creator to us.

Please see my words echo your hearts sentiments as well as we have had enough of wars and enmity and now it time for love and fidelity vows to us in Islam of submission to Me, your Creat there, say I Allah to all.

Please see this verse from the Quran that we should hold fast to the rope or habl of our Creator which is His Book to us in that we must teach and obey it and know that according to hadith structure habl is the Word of the Book to us, and now you have it because of this verse you realize our Book unites us where we were enemies before fighting with one another.

Please know the second verse in connection to this is from Maida where it says our covenant is to hear and obey His Word here which is what we do when we hold fast to his Book there, so you know this is the baith we need for world peace to occur and for us to live with friendship and fidelity to each other and the Quran tells us to obey our covenants with man as well and other virtues it has in it, so be the foremost and fight for truth and fidelity to be supreme in our Word to man and women as well.

Please know complete faith is to obey the Quran and that is when you are a Muslim or submitter to Me and We say hold on to the Word We have here and let it guide you to Me, say I Allah the August One there, Who knows you like being called a submitter to Me in the Words I teach here in the Quran to you.

Omar.

Al-Imran.

3:102 O you who believe, keep your duty to Allah, as it ought to be kept, and die not unless you are Muslims.

3:103 And hold fast by the covenant of Allah all together and be not disunited. And remember Allah's favor to you when you were enemies, then He united your hearts so by His favor you became brethren. And you were on the brink of a pit of fire, then He saved you from it. Thus Allah makes clear to you His messages that you may be guided.

3:104 And from among you there should be a party who invite to good and enjoin the right and forbid the wrong. And these are they who are successful.

Maida.

5:7 And remember Allah's favor on you and His covenant with which He bound you when you said: We have heard and we obey. And keep your duty to Allah. Surely Allah knows what is in the breasts.

please see you are muslims now and it is for you to adopt that vernacular as it signifies upright one in the quran we use as abraham has been called this there and muhammad was the epitome of the upright car we have

please see this verse is you in this land of illihoon ideology where you submit to your creator in things and you call yourselves christian muslims or submitters of him and now you are muslims for all practical purposes and so there you have it you are a new breed of christians who submit to one god teachings i teach to you in islam of illihoon ahmadiyyat where we presume logic makes sense and we accept it if it is reason to us in our senses of it so there occurs and you move away from the church dogma of calling him god who is jesus to you as he never called himself that and you presume he is a liar who is paul there who said he was son literally and begotten to him and then said he was god too as he has his substance while we know no one is like him who is the creator there as the quran says and there you have it he created polytheism for you and sent many to hellfire who were willing to listen to him in his diatribe of hate to you yes he wanted it hellfire for you as you were pious more than the bani-israel tribe they had more on this is enough for some but i know you wish to know that submission was your door there under him who was james and paul circumvent it so that you would worship him idol god there but he didnt succeed in that but did in making you say he is god who you love now as human person as my book tells you so you are christians true now and you know muhammad is lead as he predict him as the truthful one so you might as well be muslims as well now being upright in testimony deed and action as thats what a muslim entails for us in islam of christianity we serve you

THE METAPHOR EXPLAINED, NOW WHAT?

with and one day muslims of islam there will be truthful like you are in your testimony of one god with associations in the metaphorical sense i gave you says isa there and as the quran teaches us when our creator uses terms like 'we' or 'us' for himself and there you have it you are pleased that one day you can be him in that sense of doing his bid like i did and omar does say i isa there in heaven we reside because of him who is omar as judgment did occur with you succumbing to one god and muhammad in lead and the world was wrapped up and now heaven on earth you reside in if its your wish say i omar not but isa to you

omar not only but isa too

Al-Imran

3:51 Surely Allah is my Lord and your Lord, so serve Him. This is the right path.

3:52 But when Jesus perceived disbelief on their part, he said: Who will be my helpers in Allah's way? The disciples said: We are Allah's helpers: we believe in Allah, and bear thou witness that we are submitting ones (or Muslims).

Please see this message is sane for you to know there is perfection there in Heaven and here there is submission to His will on us.

Please see this verse here that says we are created but to try us in things as in our past lives as spirits we were not tried this way, but it is important for your rubaiyat or perfection to occur so you have traits of Allah in you and you are kind gentle people who love their Creator and each other as well, it is a simple formula to do so in that we obey our Creator in His laws and pray regularly with a humble heart to Him Who created us out of Himself to have a conscious mind so that we may recognize Him in His greatness there, yes it is to worship of Him we are created but don't be sad He gives us things when we do and all eternity is waiting for us to be pleasant and loving to one another and have pleasures He has destined for each one unique in its fragrance and joy, and there you have it our Paradise will result but He wishes to try you before you can enter with Him and so you are perfect there with Him and your companions in your company, and death is written here for us, why, so that you would not abscond in this life and make your peace with Him while you are still living as Hell awaits those who don't live piously with His commands on us. Omar.

Al-Mulk.

67:1 Blessed is He in Whose hand is the Kingdom, and He is Possessor of power over all things,

67:2 Who created death and life that He might try you — which of you is best in deeds. And He is the Mighty, the Forgiving,

please see a womans body is a repository of love and sex by her nature on her and if you abuse her in out of wedlock sentiments you have then be prepared to meet sad door for you and not heaven abode like you wish for yourself

please see womans respect is here in marriage and not in adultery or fornication as they are used as chattel and discard is the law after usage in most circumstances

please know a womans body is a repository of love for her man and if taken in fornication she loses respect for him and hate ensues as you know in your culture norms

please see a woman or girl who denudes has no respect with me say i the creator there and i will punish her immensely with pregnancy or the like of evil and she will abort thereby killing herself in her spirit and her repair may not occur again

please see it is despicable act to denude actually and there is no respect for her in the eyes of mankind as she did not preserve her body spirit in things and she is usually discard after sex occurs as she wont make a good wife and even if she marries divorce usually results and it is only pious wives who make it in married life with children and happiness

that said if a man approaches a woman for sex he has lost respect for her as to marry someone is to respect them and to have sex and leave is not to have any fidelity in your life and you might as well be a human animal with no bond of relationship with you

please know it is true with marriage you achieve faith for both men and women and it is clear it is a low act to attract the opposite sex in sex and lust and it is to be decried in culture norms we aspire for and a woman who marries and still shows herself to other men has committed adultery in her repose or thoughts and she is not loyal to you and she should be discard as a wife by law of sanity

please know nisa is clear you cant have secret relationships with women and it is similar for them it is a punishable crime by us

please give women their right and single women should be married otherwise they roam and fall occurs in them and it is true modesty completes her religion in things and always choose wisely a woman who covers herself will make a good wife to you and a fitting mother to your child so marry as soon as you can and stay chaste if not married as yet but we have made it simple in your culture with liaisons of marriage even if living apart as the spirit is satisfied in that way as well and you can have children as soon as convenient for you but stay in the married state by law of sanity in you otherwise you will fall in this culture of roam you have

omar

Nur

24:32 And marry those among you who are single...

24:33 And let those who cannot find a match keep chaste, until Allah makes them free from want out of His grace...

Nisa

4:25 And whoever among you cannot afford to marry free believing women, (let him marry) such of your believing maidens as your right hands possess. And Allah knows best your faith — you are (sprung) the one from the other. So marry them with the permission of their masters, and give them their dowries justly, they being chaste, not fornicating, nor receiving paramours...

Hadith

The man who marries perfects half his religion (Msh. 13:1, iii).

please see nudity and sex are the death knell in you and you dont realize it but sickness results in you when this occurs in you

please see nur here and it tells you to cover in faith you have and not show adornments your bodies wear to menfolk who are not your men of your family why this restriction so you would come through in piety to him your creat and you would lower your gaze instead of lust you used *to do if you want fidelity to god and his prophet you will follow this verse as it becomes you to know a womans modesty is nearly her religion to me say i the creator of you and if you are immodest i give you illness and obesity results yes when you uncover to men you start overeating and you become obese and stress and anxiety afflicts you you didnt know this thats why I show you the laws here are for your betterment and yes sex leads to obesity and sickness in you and you become despondent in things and dont want to live and i have you laws for your happiness to occur and it is better for you not to tempt mankind to you but to seek one in marriage and you do this here now some of you not but most have succumbed to me on the issue and this world was not meant to be a heaven for you in that you lust men and seek them but it was meant for piety with the laws of god enclosing you in a cage of sorts and your faith occurs and you are made fit for a heavenly abode with allah there with you and you are given things you like and menfolk come to you in marriage you are with them there yes heaven with men occur there and if you want it here you will not see peace from me your god to you in the hereafter with you*

allah there is here with this pen to you

Nur

24:31 And say to the believing women that they lower their gaze and restrain their sexual passions and do not display their adornment except what appears thereof. And let them wear their head-coverings over their bosoms. And they should not display their adornment except to their husbands or their fathers, or the fathers of their husbands, or their sons, or the sons of their husbands, or their brothers, or their brothers' sons, or their sisters' sons, or their women, or those whom their right hands possess, or guileless male servants, or the children who know not women's nakedness. And let them not strike their feet so that the adornment that they hide may be known. And turn to Allah all, O believers, so that you may be successful.

please see it is clear one god wishes you peace and happiness but you wish it on yourself misery and hardship when you disobey his teach to you in his books here

THE METAPHOR EXPLAINED, NOW WHAT?

please see some comments and verses in this section about how we are unhappy here if we ignore his messages who is the creator there

please see the subject matter here where hell is like a troubled sea in this life according to the bible verse

these are some of the verses regarding hell and hellfire you will see in our book the quran and some biblical quotes for you

please see the list is not comprehensive but it will show you there is no escaping the fire if you are iniquitous or disbelieve in the messages of your creator here

please know when you sin in life the chastisement follows you here and you are despondent sad and evil as well and the quran verse from ta ha shows you you will be unhappy and have a hard life for yourself in that you ignored his teachings to you so you became despondent with your sin in you and further you know islam is safe as these words were revealed to adam and thus refer to humanity

please know some of you continue to sin until you feel bad enough to ask for forgiveness and repent your deed that led you to sin in your life yes until you decide to repent your ways

please know when you sin your heart beckons you to suicide and that thought is the fire in you

please see the fire is real

please see some people will actually do it but its a sad life to be beset with thoughts of suicide on you and it is better to be happy and believe in him and pray regularly as he asks you and ask for forgiveness until your peace results as it perturbs your heart when you sin in issues and peace is a sign you are forgiven but you will see your sin on the day you are judged

please see we all sin but we feel better when we ask forgiveness

please see a girl or boy who touches others or denudes in public forum we have is always beset by thoughts of suicide thats why the quran tells you to go not nigh to fornication and that way youll be happy and peace will result in your life but if you let children do so in your schools you will be safe not and suicide will continue with you in your society

please see it is similar for other sins yes the death wish results and when you disbelieve in him in his message to you you will similar ways

wish death on you why does it occur because your life is sinful and death is better for you than this iniquitous state you are in

omar

Ta Ha

20:123 He said: Go forth herefrom both — all (of you) — one of you (is) enemy to another. So there will surely come to you guidance from Me; then whoever follows My guidance, he will not go astray nor be unhappy.

20:124 And whoever turns away from My Reminder, for him is surely a straitened life, and We shall raise him up blind on the day of Resurrection.

20:125 He will say: My Lord, why hast Thou raised me up blind, while I used to see?

20:126 He will say: Thus did Our messages come to thee, but thou didst neglect them. And thus art thou forsaken this day.

20:127 And thus do We recompense him who is extravagant and believes not in the messages of his Lord. And certainly the chastisement of the Hereafter is severer and more lasting.

Yunus

10:50 Say: Do you see if His chastisement overtakes you by night or by day? What then is there of it that the guilty would hasten?

10:51 And when it comes to pass, will you believe in it? What! now! and you hastened it on.

10:52 Then will it be said to those who were unjust: Taste abiding chastisement; you are not requited except for what you earned.

10:53 And they ask thee: Is that true? Say: Aye, by my Lord! it is surely the Truth, and you will not escape.

Al-Baqarah

2:81 Yea, whoever earns evil and his sins beset him on every side, those are the companions of the Fire; therein they abide.

Al-Zilzal

99:6 On that day men will come forth in sundry bodies that they may be shown their works.

99:7 So he who does an atom's weight of good will see it.

99:8 And he who does an atom's weight of evil will see it.

THE METAPHOR EXPLAINED, NOW WHAT?

Al-Imran

3:15 ...For those who guard against evil are Gardens with their Lord, in which rivers flow, to abide in them, and pure companions and Allah's goodly pleasure. And Allah is Seer of the servants.

3:16 Those who say: Our Lord, we believe, so forgive our sins and save us from the chastisement of the fire.

Isaiah 57

20 But the wicked are like the troubled sea, when it cannot rest, whose waters cast up mire and dirt.

21 There is no peace, saith my God, to the wicked.

Psalm 9

15 The heathen are sunk down in the pit that they made: in the net which they hid is their own foot taken.

16 The Lord is known by the judgment which he executeth: the wicked is snared in the work of his own hands.

17 The wicked shall be turned into hell, and all the nations that forget God.

Please see the message is accept by you in the Christian community and now it is time to wake Me up in the human race as well.

Please see this verse from the Quran that speaks of you in the Christian faith of Illihoon here.

Please know you are me and I am you, say I Omar to you if you abide by it, the Quran there to you in this Book that you have of Muhammad to you from his notes of Muhammad the scholar there.

Please know you say it too, what reason do we have not of belief in it the Quran to us as it is the truth from Allah to us and we were weak before and could not come through as we should have?

Please know it is true Allah does cause you to enter the Garden because you say that and follow it with your deed of living in a cage and not indulging yourself as the law has appeared as sane by you.

Please see it is clear you want to be righteous by Me, your Creator, and enter with them in the Paradise I have prepared for you.

Please know you know you have witnessed yourself of what you were before and you say this is better to live in a cage of faith with the laws of the Quran holding us in it, they are sane in it say I Allah there.

Please know you spread the word too, that is decent of you, so I prepare Heaven with them who you convince with truth to them and they are loving there.

Please see it occur, your heaven in this world, if you have faith in you not but in Me and My Words here.

Please know it is true I am Allah Who write this article to you through this hand that I create that has ability to transcribe Me and My Word here.

Please see you as Christians of the former faith that you do ascribe Me as Great and I forgive many of your sins.

Omar not but with his heart I do write these words to you say I Allah to you.

Maida.

5:82 Thou wilt certainly find the most violent of people in enmity against the believers to be the Jews and the idolators; and thou wilt find the nearest in friendship to the believers to be those who say, We are Christians. That is because there are priests and monks among them and because they are not proud.

5:83 And when they hear that which has been revealed to the Messenger thou seest their eyes overflow with tears because of the truth they recognize. They say: Our Lord, we believe, so write us down with the witnesses.

5:84 And what (reason) have we that we should not believe in Allah and in the Truth that has come to us, while we earnestly desire that our Lord should cause us to enter with the righteous people?

5:85 So Allah rewarded them for what they said, with Gardens wherein rivers flow to abide in them. And that is the reward of the doers of good.

please see nisa is the object of your life in this country and we make it so it is simple for you in case you want to go separate ways by you

please see it is clear secret is your door in marriage clan and when i made secret marriages the norm for you some years ago you adopt it and now i tell you to read the first verse of nisa on your marriage rites

THE METAPHOR EXPLAINED, NOW WHAT?

and make it legal with him your creator and keep your vows of fidelity you cant take away human nature that a man roams for more beds to occupy and a woman is satisfied with one but it is so in your culture divorce was an evil that men couldnt bear thats why we made it so they marry in secret and keep them with them so breakup doesnt relent to but keep them happy and provide for them according to your means and dont expect them to work that way youll be safe but it is so in this culture women do roam but relent not on this issue they must go out with you and it is through secret marriages with nisa there that you have finally found peace in your culture norms before men were abasive to you in wedlock not and breakups were common and divorce is rare now and if it occur then parting is easy more

    please see i am your culture norms and i saw marriage here as a hardship late when my divorce result but it is so call yourself married now but keep no paper trail

    please know when you go to court it is easy to say youre not married as there is no trail and courts will relent to you and you will keep your assets and she will hers and children should be joint responsibility in marriage they are so theyll be happy once its over

    please see it is clear this is the best solution until your courts recognize divorce in islam is sane and there is no bitter recriminations because the law is sad not but safe for both parties and both are aggrieved not in islamic divorce we have for you as stipulated before in my book here

    please see it is the best solution though not perfect as we like to be upfront about it that we are married but men cant bear it as yet your culture is averse to multiple marriages but they know mens nature is different and if they want to keep families together secret marriages are the best solution for both parties and women will relent as it is the word of god since time immemorial

    please see nisa below where it says that you will accomplish your act of marriage by keep your duty to him in regard to their rights over you and so forth keep good companionship as the quran instructs you elsewhere

    omar

Nisa

4:1 O people, keep your duty to your Lord, Who created you from a single being and created its mate of the same (kind), and spread from these two many men and women. And keep your duty to Allah, by Whom you demand one of another (your rights), and (to) the ties of relationship. Surely Allah is ever a Watcher over you.

please see the law is entailed in us and we break our spirit when we sin in it the law in regard to that which is within us and tabulated in the quran as well

please see the covenant with them is their commandment to them and it is true they must come through and fulfill their law structure and their law is the 10 commandments to them and other laws they entail from moses to them and they must obey the quran in its completeness to them then they will be pious with us they think but it is so they must do my baith that the christians have done and recognize me as great to them and play no role in mischief in the land if they want paradise with me say i muhammad there

please see it is the same for the muslim world if they want my charge with them they have a covenant as well which entails the laws within our book but it is so many disregard them and evil is what they become say i omar not only but muhammad to you and there you have it you have to obey my word in the gospel you have too from jesus teach there as i allah here envisaged it here on omars book that we clarify he came to uphold the law of the people of the book before him and only took out extraneous stuff that had crept in it

please see faith occurs when you uphold laws of religion on oneself and thats the reason there is religion for you and the complete code came with the quran there and it is what religion is upheld on and thus if you flaw yourself you know the law doesnt allow you sin so you come through in repentance and follow my law better on next occasion and i may forgive you your sin if you are sincere in it say i allah there and there you have it you achieve paradise only if i forgive you sin you do and that law is sane for you and i am forgiving kind to my servant who despairs his or her sin on them otherwise i am not if you plan to continue on

THE METAPHOR EXPLAINED, NOW WHAT?

please see the people of faith know these books that i reveal are safe in their original format as omar has elucidated upon say i allah to you and worldwide you reference them in your teach and christian islam of illihoon ideology is the word you go by in your teach of your culture there and you come by to heaven when you follow quran edicts by you and thus piety or observance to duty is the watchword by you now inshallah or god willing it will be so with you there in the world forum of man and mankind

please know the bani-israel were asked to speak good words to them they had but they were unkind in issues and so lost me say i allah there but it is so if they conform to the qurans message they can come forth with us and be kind loving individuals which they are not currently and the same applies to christians of this land they must be kind and speak good words to others they know and keep the law intact with them then there will be worth in them

omar not only but muhammad and allah too here
Baqarah.

2:83 *And when We made a covenant with the Children of Israel: You shall serve none but Allah. And do good to (your) parents, and to the near of kin and to orphans and the needy, and speak good (words) to (all) men, and keep up prayer and pay the poor-rate. Then you turned back except a few of you, and you are averse.*

Deuteronomy 4.

1 *Now, Israel, hear the decrees and laws I am about to teach you. Follow them so that you may live and may go in and take possession of the land the Lord, the God of your ancestors is giving you.*

2 *Do not add to what I command you and do not subtract from it, but keep the commands of the Lord your God that I give you.*

13 *He declared to you his covenant, the Ten Commandments, which he commanded you to follow and then wrote them on two stone tablets.*

14 *And the Lord directed me at that time to teach you the decrees and laws you are to follow in the land that you are crossing the Jordan to possess.*

Al-Imran.

3:102 O you who believe, keep your duty to Allah, as it ought to be kept, and die not unless you are Muslims.

3:103 And hold fast by the covenant of Allah all together and be not disunited. And remember Allah's favor to you when you were enemies, then He united your hearts so by His favor you became brethren. And you were on the brink of a pit of fire, then He saved you from it. Thus Allah makes clear to you His messages that you may be guided.

Matthews 5

17 "Do not think that I have come to abolish the Law or the Prophets; I have not come to abolish them but to fulfill them.

18 I tell you the truth until heaven and earth disappear, not the smallest letter, not the least stroke of a pen will by any means disappear from the Law until everything is accomplished.

19 Anyone who breaks one of the least of these commandments and teaches others to do the same will be called least in the kingdom of heaven, but whoever practices and teaches these commands will be called great in the kingdom of heaven."

please see the prayers with me are three essence but more may be required for you to come through in heaven here on earth but i know i ask for 3 in the quran so make it law for you in least you can and should attempt not but do requirement i have say i allah there

please see these are actually the prayers according to abu hanifa as well but he couldnt make it occur but i know it is difficult to change so i forgive those who continue their sunnat and not mine as they are weak in issues in it since their repute is at stake say i the august one to you allah none other than me

please see the prayer times in the quran we have but it is clear you deter in it but it is so i dont and want you to pray these but it is so there are optional prayers in between if you wish if the need arise

please see duha is not included in this but that is a prayer the prophet did so do it to complete his sunnat and the night prayer is optional you say but it is so the night prayer is said before you sleep and so it is these prayers are in the quran and maghrib is optional which he did who is prophet to you and this is allah who gives you these prayers

THE METAPHOR EXPLAINED, NOW WHAT?

and so forth now you know there are not 5 fard prayers but 3 as the shias do but do 5 according to the sunnah of our prophet as he liked you to be in heaven with us and so i tell you here i am his way and admonish you if you follow a law other than his as it will take you away from a far destiny where you see clearly and other ways are not me so there occurs omar only brings you my word so follow him in it

please see the prayer is not specified but do it as i show it on omars page so you know the option is yours how you pray but pray to me alone as i alone am the caregiver to man and sibling faith and so forth you pray the shahada some and some pray my prayer i give you here the complete prayer of muhammad there

the reading of quran at fajr means you recite it with words in you and not only that you include it in prayer and it is so you know the sahaba innovated some but it is norm to do so now but actual ways is to read some quran in the morning before you start your day and it is that it should be a part of prayer while it should be read aloud or silently to yourself then and if you teach it is good for your hearth and health and your becoming to me is good with the fatiha in you at least so make that the essence of your prayer there in the world structure of man and wife and child they have

omar not but allah there

Bani-Israel.

17:110 Say: Call on Allah or call on the Beneficent. By whatever (name) you call on Him, He has the best names. And utter not thy prayer loudly nor be silent in it, and seek a way between these.

Hud.

11:114 And keep up prayer at the two ends of the day and in the first hours of the night. Surely good deeds take away evil deeds. This is a reminder for the mindful.

Bani-Israel also.

17:78 Keep up prayer from the declining of the sun till the darkness of the night, and the reading of the Qur'an at dawn. Surely the reading of the Qur'an at dawn is witnessed.

Ta Ha

20:130 So bear patiently what they say, and celebrate the praise of thy Lord before the rising of the sun and before its setting, and glorify

(Him) during the hours of the night and parts of the day, that thou mayest be well pleased.

Al-Muzzammil.

73:20 Thy Lord knows indeed that thou passest in prayer nearly two-thirds of the night, and (sometimes) half of it, and (sometimes) a third of it, as do a party of those with thee. And Allah measures the night and the day. He knows that (all of) you are not able to do it, so He has turned to you (mercifully); so read of the Qur'an that which is easy for you. He knows that there are sick among you, and others who travel in the land seeking of Allah's bounty, and others who fight in Allah's way. So read as much of it as is easy (for you), and keep up prayer and pay the poor-rate and offer to Allah a goodly gift. And whatever of good you send on beforehand for yourselves, you will find it with Allah — that is best and greatest in reward. And ask forgiveness of Allah. Surely Allah is Forgiving, Merciful.

Bani-Israel again.

17:79 And during a part of the night, keep awake by it, beyond what is incumbent on thee; maybe thy Lord will raise thee to a position of great glory.

please see the universal application of this law in your prayer you have there

so the shahada is true to most men and womenkind in that it contains facts they believe in world forum of people in that it makes sense to them there is one god that the quran entails and other books like the bible also say that in its writings and you know it is true to the heart so they succumb to it and the resultant peace is immense they tell others as well so they know it is done now for peace in their lives and muhammad was a prophet to his people there so obviously he is a messenger from him allah there and he has a near perfect book to people with billions of adherents to it so again it makes sense to say it with conviction in your heart and now you know as a messenger he was special in the sense he would complete faith and he was the most accomplished of his message bearers and you tell them here he was the mustafa or the chosen one by me to lead mankind in that as a character he was the best in never

telling a lie or touch a woman not as well out of wedlock vows they have and jesus and moses predict him in their scriptures with befitting accolade and other cultures do predict him as holy to them so rest your case here say i allah there they have understood and do come through with us with this prayer they have many times they say it to themselves and now they have peace from me as it convinces them there is a god when they forget or are amiss and so there you have it it has universal appeal as a prayer with them here in their life on earth until we rise
    allah there

please see the prayer timings according to my sharia

please know the times for prayer are fajr 1 and a half hour before sunrise until sunrise and ashraque from up to 1 hour after sunrise and doha from 10 am until noon in summer and asr from 2 till sunset and maghreb from sunset till 1 hour and isha from that time till bedtime generally in the first few hours of the night and the night or tahajjud prayer when you awake at night till fajr according to sharia omari we have here

in winter the doha starts earlier by an hour and so do asr

there is no zuhr prayer in our sharia in accordance with hadith structure we have there and other people can follow prayers as they like and may interspace prayers during the day as well but it is not required but my teachings are from prophet muhammad to me and my sharia is properly call muhammad to me or prophet to omar and so here i tell you clear ways these are the prayers according to what is taught to me by muhammad on him be peace in dream form of communication to me
    omar

Please remember to start the day in remembrance to Him, your Creator, so that it goes well for you.

In the mornings ask forgiveness for yourself and try to read some Quran after you pray to Him, your Creator, and start your day in a happy note from you as you like to have a good day by you and you know crime you commit is sad for you and if you say istaghfirallah or seek forgiveness you will want no crime on you and it protects you in that regard and you can have happy day there where you meet and socialize with people and befriend those who are kind to you, so forth results and your life is arranged for you by your Creator as a good one and you live in peace with him and others around you. Omar.

Bani-Israel

17:78 Keep up prayer from the declining of the sun till the darkness of the night, and the reading of the Qur'an at dawn. Surely the reading of the Qur'an at dawn is witnessed.

Al-Imran

3:15 Say: Shall I tell you of what is better than these? For those who guard against evil are Gardens with their Lord, in which rivers flow, to abide in them, and pure companions and Allah's goodly pleasure. And Allah is Seer of the servants.

3:16 Those who say: Our Lord, we believe, so forgive our sins and save us from the chastisement of the fire.

3:17 The patient and the truthful, and the obedient, and those who spend and those who ask Divine protection in the morning times.

Please see the essentials of wadu or ablution before prayer here.

Please see wadu is simple and comprises 4 principle things to wash and you can do it in that order or complete it according to the ahle sunnah style as seen in their book lore but it is so it is simple and only takes a few minutes but do try to keep it.

Please see to keep your wadu is sane but not necessary and things that break it are going to the bathroom to defecate or urinate and the passage of wind if it is heard though minor passage does not break it according to hadith law we follow there. Sex also breaks it but minor touches do not. Sleep by itself does not negate it but if you feel the passage of wind then do a fresh wadu when you wake up and somnolence is sane to ignore in this issue as we all doze off and don't do a fresh wadu.

Please know a single wash can suffice but you can do it 3 times as they teach you there, whatever is convenient for you, but labor is weak there in that if you find it difficult then single wash is sufficient, and the Prophet Muhammad relented to a single wash if they wished.

THE METAPHOR EXPLAINED, NOW WHAT?

Masah or wiping your feet with socks or shoes on is an innovation that came about late by Ali's law of making things convenient for his follower but the hadith is there that Prophet Muhammad insisted that the feet are washed thorough ways and during his life his sunnah was to wash his feet in a thorough manner, also the Quran words are that the feet are washed and not wiped as they do in their lands to you.

Please know wadu became obligatory in Madinah many years after prayer was implemented there so you know it is gradual for them, so why not for us, and complete faith can come about with time when you have trained yourself with the Fatiha and Tashahud here in this country and worldwide they will follow you, as they look up to you.

Omar.

Maida.

5:6 O you who believe, when you rise up for prayer, wash your faces, and your hands up to the elbows, and wipe your heads, and (wash) your feet up to the ankles...

please see the prayer structure evolves with time during prophets life and it is similar here

please see this comment here that these 3 prayers here entail our faith and if you say them at least 3 times a day you will make it with your creator in heaven you want to be with him and the time has come to make it compulsory in the world structure of people starting with a 7 year old onwards once in the morning on getting up then in the afternoon and lastly at night preferably before going to bed and there you have it it will give you peace with him and your thoughts will be clear minded in issues you face

i tell you this prayer the tashahud to you as it comprises faith and is a virtue to say and in it you praise and pray to allah for peace on his prophet so it is a darood as well and try to recall the words when you say it arabic so you know what you are saying

please try to say it before the fatiha on the times of prayer

please try to recall the words of the fatiha too say i allah to you and it takes a little effort but it is good to make that work for you if you desire

his pleasure who is allah there as it gives me pleasure to hear these words from you and teach your child true to you as well say i to two
Tashahud.
Sincere obedience is to you allah and prayers and good deeds too,
Peace be upon you o prophet and mercy of allah and his blessings as well.
I bear witness there is no god but allah he has no associate and I bear witness muhammad is his messenger.
This is the Fatiha below.
1:1 Praise be to Allah, the Creator of the worlds,
1:2 The Beneficent, the Merciful,
1:3 King of the day of judgment,
1:4 You do we serve and you do we ask for help.
1:5 Guide us on the straight path,
1:6 The path of those upon whom you have bestowed favors,
1:7 Not those upon whom wrath is brought down, nor those who go astray.
Amen.
after the fatiha it is appropriate now to say the edict there is no god but allah in your prayer structure 5 times preferably in the bowing position but if it is difficult and you are being observed then say it silently as you can but it is so these 3 prayers are the essentials of faith and will get you there to heaven with him your creator if you are regular and sincere to him in his edicts of the quran to you otherwise your prayer is hypocrisy elements in it
omar not only here

please see this prayer is instituted in the west that the backbone is only the fatiha and if you do that you have accomplished the deed of prayer with you

please see i have popularized the fatiha with you based on this hadith that there is no prayer without the fatiha after it was revealed it was so but the shahada was sufficient for early islam adherents but now you know the fatiha is the complete prayer so adopt it and try to add prayers to it as we do but as the quran doesnt specify the prayer to us we must rely on this hadith structure to guide us in our prayer to him who guides us to be grateful to him by praying regularly and now you know i was not wrong in bringing the fatiha and shahada to you you can relax and believe me that islam was nascent in madinah as well and it was only with time the structure of prayer was formalized as dogma but it is not so and there is leeway in prayers as you can see here that the fatiha was the backbone and other prayers were added to it though my prayer is complete say i muhammad there but i allow you in the world forum to add to it as you wish from hadith we have and you know we are kind to allow you leeway but try to pray that way in following the example of my son omar here who teaches you correct prayer but we dont make it law except you should say the fatiha in your tongue if you wish and wadu was instituted late in madinah so rest assured your prayer is acceptable to us in islam though with it the wadu the prayer goes deeper and your thoughts are from him your creator to you and in the final analysis you realize you must read the prayer three times a day and if you do it will be acceptable to you and your prophet that you are well-meaning and know that jesus too prayed regularly so be humble heart and pray like him and me and see if you can muster omars prayer but we know it is a burden to some so do your best with the fatiha backbone you have

omar not but muhammad to you

Hud

11:114 And keep up prayer at the two ends of the day and in the first hours of the night. Surely good deeds take away evil deeds. This is a reminder for the mindful.

Hadith on the subject

Ata' reported: Abu Huraira said, "In every prayer is a recitation. Prayers that were recited aloud by the Prophet, peace and blessings be upon him, we have recited aloud to you, and what he recited silently we have kept silent with you. Whoever recites the foundation of the Book, Surat al-Fatihah, has done enough, but to recite more is better."

-Source: Ṣaḥīḥ al-Bukhārī 738, Ṣaḥīḥ Muslim 396

Hadith also

'Ubadah ibn al-Samat reported: The Messenger of Allah, peace and blessings be upon him, said, "There is no prayer for one who does not recite the opening of the Book, Surat al-Fatihah."
-Source: Ṣaḥīḥ al-Bukhārī 723, Ṣaḥīḥ Muslim 394

please see the baith of muhammad entails you will pray as well and follow other laws of islam we have in illihoon islam here for you

please say this prayer regular ways with you the fatiha as it is a prayer to him your creator while the shahada is an affirmation of faith as an edict to him and in the fatiha we pray to him for the straight path and it is clear if you pray regular ways you will achieve solace and your deeds will correct themselves so even if you sin and commit wrong deeds do pray by clock on you at least 3 times a day and with time you may be able to correct yourself in issues and become a resident there in heaven abode in your life here and in the hereafter you may make it with him as he does count your prayers you do and try to fast in ramadhan if you can and women know its difficult if you dont adorn appropriately as then the hunger is too much to bear but men are stalwart in things and can bear two meals a day which women can too if they dress appropriately and pray on time the fatiha with them as i have shown you in my book to you and it is simple to bring your phone out and read the prayer to yourself when youre at break from your school or work or if youre at home and try to make an effort heaven has its rewards for efforts you do

omar

Hadith

Narrated Abu Huraira:

I heard Allah's Messenger saying, "If there was a river at the door of anyone of you and he took a bath in it five times a day would you notice any dirt on him?" They said, "Not a trace of dirt would be left." The Prophet added, "That is the example of the five prayers with which Allah blots out (annuls) evil deeds."
-Sahih al-Bukhari 528

Hud

11:114 And keep up prayer at the two ends of the day and in the first hours of the night. Surely good deeds take away evil deeds. This is a reminder for the mindful.

Bani-Israel

17:78 Keep up prayer from the declining of the sun till the darkness of the night, and the reading of the Qur'an at dawn. Surely the reading of the Qur'an at dawn is witnessed.

17:79 And during a part of the night, keep awake by it, beyond what is incumbent on thee; maybe thy Lord will raise thee to a position of great glory.

please see this prayer is from allah so don't ostracize me i am simple man teaching him in his words here

when you pray before me try to picture in your mind that i am standing in front of you and your prayers are known in your heart and say with your heart not but tongue the recitation of the tashahud and fatiha and the edict that there is no god but me allah there 5 time this being said in the bowing stance and try to muster it the bow to me in acknowledgment of the fact you give me peace by saying you are my creator and acknowledge that with your ritual there of these 3 prayers and one rakat will suffice but two are better with wadu if you can muster it and pay homage to your creator this way daily not but 5 times a day and i will come forth with you giving you peace in things and making sure beloved is your call to me if you are law bearing in things you do omar not but your creator here

please know the key to prayer is a humble heart to him your creat

please know there is etiquette for prayer for men and women and for them they must cover appropriately before presenting their prayer to him if possible but i know its difficult if youre out in the open but do make an effort when youre at home to put a scarf on your hair and cover your bosom and legs and if youre a man your knees should be covered at least and a man should not show his body from the navel down to his ankles not but knees and a proper attire is required for both sexes if at all possible this dress code should be followed and i know you want it a scarf there in your room when you say the shahada or the fatiha even at home as your prayer is acceptable then and men dont have to wear headdress by law there as the prophet allowed it for them but he did encourage women to wear it and it is law there they do it when they pray or read quran there so do this etiquette for his sake your creator there with humble heart you have hoping your prayer is acceptable to us in islam and your creator too in humble pose you adopt now

    omar

please see early faith is okay until you can come forth in complete faith and key is to love me say i allah there and love for mankind will follow there

please know early islam had the rudiments of faith but the people were pious by and large and loved the religion the prophet taught them and it wasnt until maida was revealed in madinah that religion became more standard with wadu and prayer regulated by sitting in it and the prayers were recited in unison behind the imam as before the prophet would pray by himself on occasion as well but after the 7th year of hijrah or migration to madinah he started to form the body of prayers and the salaat ibrahimi and other prayers were implemented so i want to make it clear that was when faith was complete more or less and maidas last verse was revealed in the 10th year shortly before the prophets demise so you see when we ask you to pray the fatiha at least it is not the complete faith we seek but a partial faith that is good there in early madinah life they had and they were pious with it so you know some islam is better than no islam where you dont pray to god there you have it submission to him means you must pray regular ways with you and now you know people are so far removed from piety that to expect them to do the complete prayer there is difficult to conceive so i say not but allah allows you to do earlier forms of islam until you are ready to do the long prayer service and the fast is similar yes we allow lente to some who cant muster the complete fast as it was done early on in madinah history and you will still be submissive to me say i the august one allah there to you and now you know i am patient with you but do your best that i ask you without encumbering yourself with hardship

    omar not only here but allah as well

THE METAPHOR EXPLAINED, NOW WHAT?

please see the month of ramadhan is the month you perform lente in and the complete fast for those who can muster it for themselves

this is a good prayer you have to be sincere from the heart and do fight your nafs or self as it beckons you to crime or the lie in you but it is so the devils are chained in the metaphorical sense but if you do evil they succumb to you and beckon you on but it is so they are quiet for the most part in this month so do fast in ramadhan if you can muster it it is not difficult it just requires resolve from us not to eat or drink from dawn till sunset but if you have difficulty then observe lente where you eat a little or drink some until you train not to and it is true the prophet used to fast that way and his sahaba too until the verse was revealed not to eat or drink until sunset and so forth you know islam is sane to let you be if you dont but this is a month i will test you and those who pray will fast for my sake says allah there to you to gain piety with them and be steadfast and becoming to me and your wife you have says allah to her and him and now you know women have to fast if menses not in them then they can take a break from prayer and fast but do try with your person to show your worth to me your creator who admonishes you if you sin this month as that would be giving in to your low desires which you take to be your god and not me allah to you say i the creator of the heavens and earth and all that you see

allah here through omars tongue not but pen there
Al-Baqarah
2:183 O you who believe, fasting is prescribed for you, as it was prescribed for those before you, so that you may become pious.

please see i am magnificence in color and my eye is limited not but in heaven there are many hues you dont see here with human eye you have

please see i am colorful in my creation but it is so my nature has beauty immense and i allow you color why do i dress you in drab clothing for your protection girls and women because when you are colorful attire many men are attract to you and rape results too thats why in islam abaya is plain clothing to some but you wont come through with it that way say i allah there so i allow you color magnificence *you adore and i relent if men admire you be pious though and walk away after converse you have and i will forgive you color i give now to womenkind*

allah there

please see the verses of heaven apply to my family one day but they have been bad here so these verses may apply to them but its up to them and others in islam not what destination they choose

there are some who wont make it there to heaven after they pass on and on the day they are judged they will be told they are unsuccessful in making it as their deeds were not up to the mark but it is so their hell will be mild not but not the blasting kind that annihilates thoughts with the fire produced but still there will be hellfire there after judgment day and lets see if family structure occurs then i cant intervene on the day of judgment but may be able to do so after they are clean in hellfire they produce on themselves as our fire is created by our deeds here and you know family law has to wait on that day but my mother knows hardship is written for my family and my father had to see hell before he made it to paradise on the day he passed it because he had some good in him and she my mother was mild in comparison as she had come through while living and had started to protect my car here

please know i am sad not but we choose our own destination and make it with our own hands our hell on earth and the hereafter but i know good in them as well so lets see what they decide for themselves but i will say this they should fear the retribution of their creator in their deeds they do to their sibling who is saint there to people of the world structure and i know destination is choice they make and punishment is his to her and him from him the great master of retribution

omar

Maida

5:2 ...And help one another in righteousness and piety, and help not one another in sin and aggression, and keep your duty to Allah. Surely Allah is Severe in requiting (evil).

Maida

5:98 Know that Allah is Severe in requiting (evil) and that Allah is Forgiving, Merciful.

5:99 The duty of the Messenger is only to deliver (the message). And Allah knows what you do openly and what you hide.

5:100 Say: The bad and the good are not equal, though the abundance of the bad may please thee. So keep your duty to Allah, O men of understanding, that you may succeed.

Ibrahim

14:47 So think not that Allah will fail in His promise to His messengers. Surely Allah is Mighty, the Lord of retribution.

14:48 On the day when the earth will be changed into a different earth, and the heavens (as well), and they will come forth to Allah, the One, the Supreme.

14:49 And thou wilt see the guilty on that day linked together in chains

14:50 Their shirts made of pitch, and fire covering their faces,

14:51 That Allah may repay each soul what it has earned. Surely Allah is Swift in reckoning.

Al-Humazah.

104:1 Woe to every slanderer, defamer!

104:2 Who amasses wealth and counts it —

104:3 He thinks that his wealth will make him abide.

104:4 Nay, he will certainly be hurled into the crushing defeat;

104:5 And what will make thee realize what the crushing defeat is?

104:6 It is the Fire kindled by Allah,

The concept of atonement or intercession is incorrect as shown from the Quran literature.

The concept of atonement is dependent upon the death of Christ on the cross in the Christian concepts of atonement. In this way we know that he did not die on the cross but only passed out as his heart was still pumping when he was brought down. In this way we know the concepts arising from the presumed crucifixion of him is a misnomer and just as prophets can intervene for their followers the atonement should be worded as intercession that occurs in a similar way when Christ intervenes for his followers, if permitted by his Creator.

Please know the atonement of Christ is a misnomer for his intervention that occurs after a man or woman is judged, generally speaking.

Please know the death of Christ is clear in the Ahmadiyya literature. In this we have peace in that this spells the end of atonement of Christ for the sins of others as when he was brought down in the unconscious state he recovered consciousness in the resting place designed to keep him there in peace. As Jesus did not pass away on the crucifix he will not partake in atonement for others as can be seen from the literature I have presented so far. In this we have peace as we know from the Quran that there is no one who can take away the sin of another and all of us are accountable for our deeds and also from his teachings who is Christ there when asked and he replied with the Lord's prayer for you.

Please see he who is Christ came to fulfill the law and not abandon it and so it occurs he could not change a dot in the law, neither add or diminish it in the least, and Paul changed the law, not My Jesus says Allah there, and the law of the Jews then was that they had to ask forgiveness from Him, their Creator, and also from other people they associate with, then they will be forgiven by Him and this prayer is there in the Lord's Prayer so Jesus only did His bid and taught them shariah they had and the Quran beseeches us to ask forgiveness as well from Him for our sins and we are encouraged to forgive those who have wronged us, there you have it unanimity of teachings we have in all religions of the Book and further you know Paul changed concept of atonement they had in Judaism as he wanted them cajoled on false promises so there destination would not be with Him, their Creator to them.

Please know atonement with the death of a human being is a fallacy as how can there not be justice?

Please know it is clear we will be judged for our sins and our Creator will exact judgment to the last iota as He has regard that none of you will be wronged by Him in regard to the law He has sent down through the ages, and further He exacts punishment if you have sinned against Him in regard to His commands on you that you come through there.

THE METAPHOR EXPLAINED, NOW WHAT?

Please know similarly for Muslims, there is no intercession on that Day and if they are good they will make it with Him, their Creator to them, but as the Quran verse here says every sin they have done on earth will be divulged to Him and He may decide to forgive if their good deeds are heavy and so forth every nation will have its secret known and the matter will be decided by Him on that frightful Hour we have.

Please know Muslims are immune they say but it is not so says Muhammad and they will be asked if they lived piously after they were bad and repented and those who were pious will be given Heaven but it is true all sins can be forgiven if you live piously after your repent occur and the hadith that says if your sins are high as the mountains they will be forgiven of you as you have shown your worth to Him by sinning here but the proof must come in your life that you live piously then after repentance,

Please see I am perfect say I Allah to you but i know you are not but when you realize your worth then don't sin anymore and live with us in a nice manner but if you continue to sin I will seal you in it and you will not realize your wrong as the devil will justify your acts to you so beware all nations when you realize the law is there then don't sin on, it is an admonishment coming your way then,

Please see then you know when you repent whether you were contrite or just saying words you learn and it is similar for all nations and people and you know it is too late when you say it on your deathbed as you haven't shown your worth and it is empty words they say in Christianity then and other faiths, you will be raised to face judgment and your sins will be counted and tabulated, as will your good ones, and if you believe in Me as One I may forgive some and enter you in an Abode you are pleased with and so it occurs all nations are equal now if they blaspheme not My Word there.

Please know My balance is there but some I will enter into Paradise who were contrite and were born anew with faith and good deeds and I will relinquish judgment not but will decipher their way as good to Me and others but they too will see anguish for sin they do in life even if they were sorry in issues they were evil in and all will sweat on that Day, a terrible fright it is for man to face Me with their deeds at hand.

Please know I am Just and know you want it in the Hereafter that you are justified as well as no wrong will go unpunished by Me, say I Allah there. Omar.

Al Zilzal.

99:6 On that day men will come forth in sundry bodies that they may be shown their works.

99:7 So he who does an atom's weight of good will see it.

99:8 And he who does an atom's weight of evil will see it.

Al Anbiya.

21:47 And We will set up a just balance on the day of Resurrection, so no soul will be wronged in the least. And if there be the weight of a grain of mustard seed, We will bring it. And Sufficient are We to take account.

Abasa.

80:33 But when the deafening cry comes,

80:34 The day when a man flees from his brother,

80:35 And his mother and his father,

80:36 And his spouse and his sons.

80:37 Every man of them, that day, will have concern enough to make him indifferent to others.

Baqarah.

2:48 And guard yourselves against a day when no soul will avail another in the least, neither will intercession be accepted on its behalf, nor will compensation be taken from it, nor will they be helped.

Al Najm.

53:38 That no bearer of burden bears another's burden:

53:39 And that man can have nothing but what he strives for:

53:40 And that his striving will soon be seen.

Please see apostacy is punishable in Muslim lands but has no basis from the Quran and sunnah here as entailed in hadith we have.

Please see these verses from the Quran and the accompanying hadith that tells us apostasy is a punishment that is reprehensible to Him Who creates us to be steadfast and so forth occurs.

Please know it was the law in Muslim countries until recently that it was punishable by death.

Please see it occur that Ahmadiyyat made it occur that it was not punishable by man and it was left up to God, their decree with Him, and that it is now considered to be correct to deny death penalty to them who abdicate.

Please know they are still put into jail some but the death penalty is usually avoided.

Please know it is correct to let them be, they may come around to Islam again and let be should be the law again, as it was during the Prophet Muhammad's time, peace be upon him for this law he had.

Please see there are faulty hadith that cause this misrepresentation of law he had and should be rejected based on the law they contradict the Quran.

Please know hadith is fraudulent at best if it contradicts the Quranic precepts we have.

Please know hadith was collected years after his death and the sahih sitta or 6 confirmed books date 200 years approximately afterwards when they were collected and compiled into book form for people to read.

Please know it is clear they are not to be relied upon in the case of the contradiction of Quranic precepts we have. Omar.

Al-Imran.

3:90 Those who disbelieve after their believing, then increase in disbelief, their repentance is not accepted, and these are they that go astray.

Al-Maida.

5:54 O you who believe, should anyone of you turn back from his religion, then Allah will bring a people, whom He loves and who love Him, humble towards the believers, mighty against the disbelievers, striving hard in Allah's way and not fearing the censure of any censurer. This is Allah's grace — He gives it to whom He pleases. And Allah is Ample-giving, Knowing.

Baqarah.

2:256 There is no compulsion in religion — the right way is indeed clearly distinct from error. So whoever disbelieves in the devil and believes in Allah, he indeed lays hold on the firmest handle which shall never break. And Allah is Hearing, Knowing.

2:257 Allah is the Friend of those who believe — He brings them out of darkness into light. And those who disbelieve, their friends are the devils who take them out of light into darkness. They are the companions of the Fire; therein they abide.

Baqarah.

2:217 They ask thee about fighting in the sacred month. Say: Fighting in it is a grave (offence). And hindering (men) from Allah's way and denying Him and the Sacred Mosque and turning its people out of it, are still graver with Allah; and persecution is graver than slaughter. And they will not cease fighting you until they turn you back from your religion, if they can. And whoever of you turns back from his religion, then he dies while an unbeliever — these it is whose works go for nothing in this world and the Hereafter. And they are the companions of the Fire: therein they will abide.

Al-Ghashiyah.

88:21 So remind. Thou art only one to remind.

88:22 Thou art not a warder over them —

88:23 But whoever turns back and disbelieves,

88:24 Allah will chastise him with the greatest chastisement.

88:25 Surely to Us is their return.

88:26 Then it is for Us to call them to account.

Al-Nisa.

4:137 Those who believe then disbelieve, again believe and again disbelieve, then increase in disbelief, Allah will never forgive them nor guide them in the (right) way.

Hadith from Bukhari.

There was a Christian who became Muslim and read the Baqarah and the Al Imran, and he used to write for the Prophet. He then went over to Christianity again, and he used to say, Muhammad does not know anything except what I wrote for him. Then Allah caused him to die and they buried him.— Sahih al-Bukhari, 4:56:814

THE METAPHOR EXPLAINED, NOW WHAT?

Additional hadith from Prophet Muhammad's archives on us.

A man from among the Ansar accepted Islam, then he apostatized and went back to shirk. Then he regretted that, and sent word to his people (saying): "Ask the Messenger of Allah is there any repentance for me?" His people came to the Messenger of Allah and said: "So and so regrets (what he did), and he has told us to ask you if there is any repentance for him?" Then the verses: 'How shall Allah guide a people who disbelieved after their belief up to His saying: Verily, Allah is Oft-Forgiving, Most Merciful' was revealed. So he sent word to him and he accepted Islam. — Al-Sunan al-Sughra 37:103

Please see here love engenders it to others around you if your Creator loves you.

Please see John 15 is safe to ignore not and understand if you keep God's commands He will love you and so forth you know the Quran is sane for you as well.

Please know the Quran is explicit that God loves not a people who obey not and transgress against Him in His commands to them and so there you have it He does not love a community that ignores Him in His law structure to Him and thus you will see people there also don't have love for Him.

Please see when you love not Him you will also have hatred amongst yourselves and only your child is safe as he or she begets love on them by their nature to Him, their Creat.

Please see when you promote sin in a community it will result in hate late but it will occur as Allah loves not this act of promoting fornication or adultery there.

Please know it is similar for families, and the mother and father will lose the child in hatred for her and him also as a natural consequence of their act but it is so fellowship does occur in sin but it is soon followed by enmity to each other.

Please know crony law is to be decried in you as it is a low form of fellowship where you accept each other's flaws instead of correct behavior by you and him, and it is similar for women, hate follows in fellowship of sin they have of gossip and other things they do.

Please see this verse that there is love from God in following His commands to us and when love flows from Him it flows to others around us as well from us, as we are loving, and there you have it piety engenders love in a community, and when you love one another it is from God you do. Omar.

John 15.

9 "As the Father has loved me, so have I loved you. Now remain in my love.

10 If you keep my commands, you will remain in my love, just as I have kept my Father's commands and remain in his love.

11 I have told you this so that my joy may be in you and that your joy may be complete."

Al-Imran.

3:31 Say: If you love Allah, follow me: Allah will love you, and grant you protection from your sins. And Allah is Forgiving, Merciful.

Al-Imran.

3:76 Yea, whoever fulfils his promise and keeps his duty — then Allah surely loves the dutiful.

Al-Imran.

3:57 And as to those who believe and do good deeds, He will pay them fully their rewards. And Allah loves not the unjust.

Nisa.

4:107 And contend not on behalf of those who act unfaithfully to their souls. Surely Allah loves not him who is treacherous, sinful:

please see nude photos are norm here but not so there in the prophets time not but in eastern lands so do learn from them culture of piety we seek for you

nudity is to be decried whether it is in person or videos or photos as allah does not like it

please see it is in the illihoon quran some that you have to cover yourself appropriately and many hadith talk about this indicating a womens dress is her culture of modest way of life she adopts and there you have it nur talks about a womans attire in that she should have a head covering and her breasts should not show through her clothing or otherwise

please see a modest attire is half of a womans religion by us according to hadith lore and it prevents the fall to sin on many occasions for her and her husband not but it is true both fall in it

please see it is over and we dont allow nudity for you to watch as its a devil act on you and he justifies it to your heart yes he beckons you to it even after you stop

please see watching or indulging in it causes a hardness for you in that you become hard hearted with it and it despoils your eyes in that their beauty is lost and you dont want that for your culture as beautiful eyes is a character of a heaven person and hur there have beauty in it their eyes to them

please see it is the custom of muslim men to avoid watching them who are unshed not but those who adorn themselves with this form of idolatry in them that they show their body parts to others in the public eye on them and the quran encourages us to keep downcast eyes to preserve their beauty

please know i know it is rampant in the states to watch such things but it is not to be done by law of islam and if you want to be with allah you will decry it in future you have with him and as i say it is hypocrisy if you pray for heaven to him and still do it in your chamber not

omar

Nur

24:30 Say to the believing men that they lower their gaze and restrain their sexual passions. That is purer for them. Surely Allah is Aware of what they do.

24:31 And say to the believing women that they lower their gaze and restrain their sexual passions and do not display their adornment except what appears thereof. And let them wear their head-coverings over their bosoms. And they should not display their adornment except to their husbands or their fathers, or the fathers of their husbands, or their sons, or the sons of their husbands, or their brothers, or their brothers' sons, or their sisters' sons, or their women, or those whom their right hands possess, or guileless male servants, or the children who know not women's nakedness. And let them not strike their feet so that the adornment that they hide may be known. And turn to Allah all, O believers, so that you may be successful.

Please see Mary had a fall there but it was her own doing and she was not tempted by the devil in it.

Please see Mary here as she explains this means her gene was sane and she was not tempted by the devil in the accursed form to make her promiscuous and Jesus too was sane after it occurred, his fall, due to an error he had of too much prayer in him, but they were both tempted by him as can be seen in biblical lore where the devil tempted him with kingdom if he followed him in edicts and he said "go, it is in the book to serve Him only Who creates."

Please know this is hadith that say he was not afflicted by him, and Mary was similar, but it just means they would not fall prey to his guile, as the Prophet did not either, and it is a sanity gene they had, and I am similar but did fall in my youth some.

Omar.

Al-Imran.

3:35 When a woman of Amran said: My Lord, I vow to Thee what is in my womb, to be devoted (to Thy service), so accept (it) from me; surely Thou, only Thou, art the Hearing, the Knowing.

3:36 So when she brought it forth, she said: My Lord, I have brought it forth a female — and Allah knew best what she brought forth — and the male is not like the female, and I have named it Mary, and I commend her and her offspring into Thy protection from the accursed devil.

Please know Islam is the religion that embodies piety in it to all races in that there is equality in it.

Please see the last sermon the Prophet made at the time of Hajj in 10 years after Hijra.

Please know these words echo the Quran in that they talk to us about one father and mother which is our spirit here as we know Adam and Eve were late in the evolution of humans and it says here that the best are those who are pious there and that all progeny is mankind who are equal in regards to their rights over you and others.

Please know it is clear equity is there and the Prophet made sure that Muslims in future would not have any reason to make superiority an issue over races and tribes other their own in that equality occurs between mankind.

Please know it is clear that Islam allows prejudice only if you are not following the law of Islam and or in general manners but does not allow prejudice on the basis of race, tribes or ethnicity and further disallows mankind from taking what others may have.

Please know it is also clear that America and British races have erred when they took slaves based on biblical scriptures and turned a race of people into their servants or slaves based on ethnicity or tribes or in other words traded them for gains to them.

Please know Islam establishes equity in its relations and further no race is looked down upon in the world arena.

Please know the situation is different in other cultures like the West where blacks are denigrated because of their skin color and things like that.

Please know it is clear there is One God there Who proclaimed it to be so. Omar.

Al-Hujurat.

49:13 O mankind, surely We have created you from a male and a female, and made you tribes and families that you may know each other. Surely the noblest of you with Allah is the most dutiful of you. Surely Allah is Knowing, Aware.

Hadith from the last sermon.

An Arab has no superiority over a non-Arab nor a non-Arab has any superiority over an Arab; also a white has no superiority over black nor a black has any superiority over white except by piety (taqwa) and good action...

Hadith from the Prophet.

People are equal like the teeth of a comb.

Hadith of the Prophet there.

You are not better than people (of other races) unless you excel them in piety. – Al Tirmidhi

Please see the Quran validates the message of these two Books is preserved in monotheism principles it uphold there to the people of the Quraish.

Please see the words of the Quran defending monotheism in these two Books, the Torah and the Quran, which were preserved better than any other book from their Creator in that the message of monotheism is preserved in them and the Gospels are mentioned in a later surah that they should be followed as well where they affirm the teachings from the Quran to them, the people there.

Please know the Meccans were polytheistic people and did not like the message in the Quran of pure mono God there and called it an enchantment and when it was pointed out that the Bible had a similar message they called it that too as well, there is no belying the evil of their ways and it is clear the People of the Book were averse to it, the Quran here, as it contradicts it in many principles it had, especially Christianity that emerged there after the passage of Jesus to India, so forth results and you know there are still many truths in the Torah and also in other books of the Old Testament and the Quran talks about how the Torah preserved the message intact in many ways though deviances did result with the passage of time, as the Quran says, but credit has to be given to early scholars who preserved many aspects of religion of Moses intact by them, and the Christians were more wayward and the Quran does not commend its book in regard to preservation of the message, more is required here so I will say the Injeel has been tampered with extensively but still contains some teachings that are correct in that it has Jesus' words intact in many places and does teach wisdom to its follower in issues of love and mercy message it has from Jesus and Mary to us, as Jesus was teaching Mary's teach also to them and Mary is disregard not in her teach to the womenfolk who came through in piety with her.

Please know I am sane the Gospels are Jesus' teach but the Old Testament is the teach of Moses and other saints and prophets and the teach of Moses and Muhammad is similar in that the strict tone is there but Jesus was trying to be merciful to his follower and fell in mercy principles and deviated from the Gospels not but old text and was not validated in this teach by Allah in the Quran where he said turn the other cheek and so forth other issues he discussed there with them, followers he had.

Please see it is clear the teachings of Jesus are disregarded by later people like Paul and his sahaba as well in regards to the law of the People of the Book there, that's why the Bible as a whole is not recommended for your teach but only the words of Jesus have credence with us but circumspect law is sane as there has been tampering there too and validation is required from the best preserved text there, which is the Quran to you.

Omar.

Al-Qasas.

28:48 But (now) when the Truth has come to them from Us, they say: Why is he not given the like of what was given to Moses? Did they not disbelieve in that which was given to Moses before? They say: Two enchantments backing up each other! And they say: Surely we are disbelievers in both.

28:49 Say: Then bring some (other) Book from Allah which is a better guide than these two, I will follow it — if you are truthful.

28:50 But if they answer thee not, know that they only follow their low desires. And who is more erring than he who follows his low desires without any guidance from Allah? Surely Allah guides not the iniquitous people.

Maida.

5:67 O Messenger, deliver that which has been revealed to thee from thy Lord; and if thou do (it) not, thou hast not delivered His message. And Allah will protect thee from men. Surely Allah guides not the disbelieving people

5:68 Say: O People of the Book, you follow no good till you observe the Torah and the Gospel and that which is revealed to you from your Lord. And surely that which has been revealed to thee from thy Lord will make many of them increase in inordinacy and disbelief; so grieve not for the disbelieving people.

please see it is clear islam is served by being subversive if they come after your livelihood or your property and you know there are elements in the government here who dont like it that you practice islam now

please see the world is averse still to many of you coming through in piety to your creator so be cautious in your obedience to him your creator there hopefully one day the danger will pass there and you will be safe to practice your faith open ways with us in islam

please see these verses that teach you to be obedient to your creators word to you and follow his instructs in the quran by you but also take care in issues by not alienating yourself from people but to be firm is good for you in that you must persevere in truth-telling and piety principles apply in you but be careful too and try to work with people so that they come through with you gradual ways with them as some people are averse to you in your religion of islam that emerges here but if you are steadfast it is a boon to you and allah will protect you if you are pious in it yes work with people and bring them around to your way of life that you adopt in secret some of you do but gradual strength is good in you and you can do more with time says allah there

omar

Al-Furqan

25:71 And whoever repents and does good, he surely turns to Allah a (goodly) turning.

25:72 And they who witness no falsehood, and when they pass by what is vain, they pass by nobly.

25:73 And they who, when reminded of the messages of their Lord, fall not down thereat deaf and blind.

Maida.

5:92 And obey Allah and obey the Messenger and be cautious. But if you turn back then know that the duty of Our Messenger is only a clear deliverance of the message.

please see benediction or blessings appear in your life when you pray and fast for my sake say i allah to one and all

please see what benediction means to you it is a blessing in your life that comes about when you pray to me your creator the one and

THE METAPHOR EXPLAINED, NOW WHAT?

only one for you to answer your prayers to you and with it you achieve solace in your life that there is a purpose for you and life has meaning and it is not only hardship but fun too and through it you gain wisdom and understanding of issues you face and if there is any worth in you you teach others too that there is meaning in this life and it is not just sporting with one another or games you play but there is spiritual development that occurs when you fast for my sake in that you become pious and forbearing in issues and it is a means of strength in you which is also a meaning for you in your life that you live here on earth and prayer is similar yes it strengthens you but more than that it blesses your move in issues you face and if you have hardship it solaces you in it and bolsters your effort to overcome it and charity is similar it prevents hardships on you as my trials are less for a believer in me and i forgive many of your sins without reprimands i do and these are core values in life which give you benediction from me and love occurs with you as you love me and others when there is peace with you and there you have it if i bless you you will have love and compassion and forbearance in your life and your hardships will be over if you are pious in things as the door for ease occurs with every hardship you face and i do guide a praying one to me so bless yourself by filling my edicts on you which is your regular prayer and charity and fast too when the time is right for you

omar not but allah here
Al-Inshirah
94:5 Surely with difficulty is ease,
94:6 With difficulty is surely ease.
Al-Taghabun
64:11 No calamity befalls but by Allah's permission. And whoever believes in Allah, He guides his heart. And Allah is Knower of all things.

please see hatred for one another is bane and you should rise by eliminating sin and rebellion in you

please see hatred is bad especially for a spouse or former one but you know it occurs in this culture when a wrong has been done to you and then it is mutual in both respects not you have for one another but it is so when you ask forgiveness for your sins and repent as well your wrongs on him or her he allah to you does forgive if you obey him in things as his love to you overcomes hate you feel for others and you start loving your former one

please see it is there for other forms of hatred as well but if your money is unjust love supervenes not and you cant eliminate hate from your car thats why a divorcee who is unjust in proceedings has difficulty loving again and until she remits her unjust or ill begotten ways in charity she wont love her former one again and will have difficulty with her future husband as well as love comes not to her because she was disobedient to her creator who does not allow her wealth in this way that occurs in car you have in this country in courts you do

please see people hate me who have crimes on them in money and other issues of piety not where there is evil car in them and they wont love until they repent their act of evil they did sometimes in jail it occurs but it is true love cant occur until repentance supervenes the evil of your act and that may mean stealing or bribes or murder and any crime that takes away the rights of others but it is so many repent in prison and turn over a new leaf so they start loving again if they are obedient to their god in loving embrace they do of him and he forgives much of their evil and so do others thats why prison is reform for one

please see if you have evil in you of adultery or fornication or other crimes of sex like homosexuality or even transgenderism or nudity you will hate people like me who are pure and you will hate purity as well until you stop your crimes you do in repentance you do it then love supervenes in you thats why there are many in this land who hate islam for its purity and dislike you who follow me in islam now

omar
Al-Imran.
3:31 Say: If you love Allah, follow me: Allah will love you, and grant you protection from your sins. And Allah is Forgiving, Merciful.
Al-Imran.
3:76 Yea, whoever fulfils his promise and keeps his duty — then Allah surely loves the dutiful.
Al-Imran.

3:57 *And as to those who believe and do good deeds, He will pay them fully their rewards. And Allah loves not the unjust.*

please see your hellfire appear in the hereafter when you disregard me and go to your beach escapades say i allah there
please see this is what occurs at beaches your innards are fried and tempers flare and they are angry over issues while they denude themselves yes it is a place where sanity occurs not and you are insane there as sanity occurs when you are covered appropriately for both men and women but i know heathen culture likes it but it is so it is so alien to your roots of modesty and piety you have in your judeo-christian culture not but religion that it creates insanity in you to do this denude there and men are caught in the quagmire as well as they participate in it yes it is alien land you adopt in the past and evil is your door there yes everything is evil in it if you uncover yourself there and swimming arenas are similar where you show your parts to others while you sunbathe in the nude practically you dont notice it you are in fire there and it like lava on your body the swimming pool is and beaches where you go with family and women cover are sane for you to enjoy the scenery of my creation say i allah there you know i dont permit it and there is no peace there for you or your family if you plan to uncover your chest and show your legs islam and nearly all cultures dont allow it it was just in the last century you became heathen with no care for the hereafter only thinking about the moment and ricocheting from one person to another with sex on your mind not knowing it spoilt your heart not only but your body and mind and you became old quickly with your fiber destroyed and your spirit spent what are you going to show your creator when you meet him after your death you wasted your life and off to hell with you for your heathen ways of no god in your reckoning in your life endeavors and there you have it it is hellfire you do here with beaches and swimming pools so your destination after you expire is that modality for you

omar not but allah there who admonishes you here for your past life Nur

24:30 *Say to the believing men that they lower their gaze and restrain their sexual passions. That is purer for them. Surely Allah is Aware of what they do.*

24:31 *And say to the believing women that they lower their gaze and restrain their sexual passions and do not display their adornment except what appears thereof. And let them wear their head-coverings over their bosoms...*

Al-Buruj

85:12 *Surely the grip of thy Lord is severe.*
85:13 *Surely He it is Who creates first and reproduces;*
85:14 *And He is the Forgiving, the Loving,*
85:15 *Lord of the Throne of Power, the Glorious,*

please see the world is a witness to you in islam as as yet you dont capitulate to truth-telling while they have by and large

please see nisa that you should be bearers of witness now that the truth is known to you and not deviate in the word of god to you

please see it is clear you witness this book the quran to be allahs work here and it is similar to other books he has sent before to the nations of the world but you know it is perfect more and history shows it is intact more or less and muhammad alis version is the correct translation for you in that there is beauty in its prose here

please see you succumb to it now its time you bear witness to it and the prophet just like the disciples bore witness for jesus in his words here in al-imran and you dont say anything but true words like many of you do wish and it is so you have all witnessed the beauty here of the words of your book the quran to you so dont witness falsehood here and it is true for the muslims too that they must bear witness to the truth of ahmadiyya teachings if they want repentance for sins they have as they know truth in them from the quran they teach for the most part and they must bear it this opinion in islam instead of ostracizing them from it like they have done in the past

please know the west is currently more truth-bearing and you must raise your car there in islam if you wish to have credit with allah as a witness there otherwise all mankind is a witness on you

omar

Nisa

4:135 O you who believe, be maintainers of justice, bearers of witness for Allah, even though it be against your own selves or (your) parents or near relatives — whether he be rich or poor, Allah has a better right over them both. So follow not (your) low desires, lest you deviate. And if you distort or turn away from (truth), surely Allah is ever Aware of what you do.

Al-Baqarah

2:143 And thus We have made you an exalted nation that you may be the bearers of witness to the people and (that) the Messenger may be a bearer of witness to you...

Al-Imran

3:51 Surely Allah is my Lord and your Lord, so serve Him. This is the right path.

3:52 But when Jesus perceived disbelief on their part, he said: Who will be my helpers in Allah's way? The disciples said: We are Allah's helpers: we believe in Allah, and bear thou witness that we are submitting ones (or Muslims).

Al-Imran

3:69 A party of the People of the Book desire that they should lead you astray; and they lead not astray but themselves, and they perceive not.

3:70 O People of the Book, why do you disbelieve in the messages of Allah while you witness (their truth)?

please see faith is the heart of things in heaven on earth and the hereafter as well as heaven rests on the pillars of faith in you

please see they say i care you in a negative sense and im always on your case to improve but actually i care for you and most people realize that that if i didnt love you i wouldnt care that you come with me to heaven which is prophet muhammads abode and others reside there already like jesus and some other sahabas and sahabis of his the prophet there and allah as well like mary and ayesha but it is so i have given you peace which is a sign heaven has occurred in you and peace can be described as a good feeling with contentment of the heart in it and with it accompaniment of it is love and compassion you feel for others as these are heavenly qualities in you and joy is your dictum in things you do and so it occurs many of you have faith and would hate disbelief to enter your heart which is my reward here and grace for those who have it the peace of faith they see with it and encumber themselves with vice not anymore in their lives and if i didnt care for you i would have let you be and worked and made money here but it is so i worked tirelessly for your betterment to occur thats why i admonish some because you know i care that you have a relationship with allah that is benediction for you and his love comes forth when you turn to him in loving embrace you wish but keep that good feeling with you when you pray to him in submission to his wishes on you and you will come through in heaven one day with us who submit to him we all do when we pray and so forth carry out other requests he has for us like fasts and charity and so forth you realize your life has to be god-centered in order for your peace to result

    omar

    Hud

    11:90 And ask forgiveness of your Lord, then turn to Him. Surely my Lord is Merciful, Loving.

    Al-Buruj

    85:12 Surely the grip of thy Lord is severe.

    85:13 Surely He it is Who creates first and reproduces;

    85:14 And He is the Forgiving, the Loving,

    85:15 Lord of the Throne of Power, the Glorious,

    Al-Hujurat

    49:7 ...Allah has endeared the faith to you and has made it seemly in your hearts, and He has made hateful to you disbelief and transgression and disobedience. Such are those who are rightly guided —

    49:8 A grace from Allah and a favor. And Allah is Knowing, Wise.

    please see some words of wisdom from our creator here

    please see these words from the quran where it shows the nature of the prophet and how i reassure him not to fret over issues and to rely

THE METAPHOR EXPLAINED, NOW WHAT?

on me his creator the lord of the throne and it the preceding section it talks about the disbelievers on whom i send punishment twice a year with their deeds of evil on them and i know some come through with these punishments and they realize they dont have power actually and i am powerful so be wary of my power over you and dont take me on i can tame you easily i just want you to show your worth and to show if you wish to come willingly to my heaven but i know you are kind and good as well to your progeny some but some have been evil before but if you come through in my law structure to you i will forgive some of your sins once i know the evil of it is out of you but you have to show your worth and repent true ways with the intention of not do it again and omar knows this is a good dua to learn and he has no power over you you have to come through yourself with me as your creator to you and you to submit to me alone yes one on one i take you on and then you can say it that i am sorry please forgive me and things like that

omar not but i allah there on my throne to you from where i speak through his hand to you

Al-Bara'at

9:124 And whenever a chapter is revealed, there are some of them who say: Which of you has it strengthened in faith? So as for those who believe, it strengthens them in faith and they rejoice.

9:125 And as for those in whose hearts is a disease, it adds uncleanness to their uncleanness, and they die while they are disbelievers.

9:126 See they not that they are tried once or twice in every year, yet they repent not, nor do they mind.

9:128 Certainly a Messenger has come to you from among yourselves; grievous to him is your falling into distress, most solicitous for you, to the believers (he is) compassionate, merciful.

9:129 But if they turn away, say: Allah is sufficient for me — there is no god but He. On Him do I rely, and He is the Lord of the mighty Throne.

CHAPTER FOUR

SOME GENERAL TEACHINGS HERE FROM MY PAGE ON FACEBOOK

Please see these words of Allah to you regarding His law structure there.

Please see throughout the ages there has always been a law structure for man and child and his wife as well so that sanity could prevail and criminals could be punished and Allah's law is similar, yes, it is sane for you when it tells you in addition to other laws fornication is punished as well as it leads to abort or death of child in you and many other crimes as your nature becomes aversive to God and His creation and so there you have it, it is a criminal act with Me, and My law is complete say I the August One Who knows better for you, His creation, and what laws to implement on us in the world forum of His people residing here on earth and just as you bow down to authority in your respective lands also submit to My law on you in your Book, the Quran by you, and you will be in peace with your fellow mankind and child will be happy too. Omar.

Please see monotheism pleased you and you won't go back to disbelief by choice you make.

Please see monotheism creed is pleased in you and you have immense peace in it, why, because Allah has created us to know Him and when we tell you your book and the Quran and many world scriptures have that there is only One Creator or God your heart finds peace and solace in it and is satisfied, that's why you would hate to go back to disbelief and heresy and you tell your child not to listen to him who teaches otherwise.

Please know not to commit blasphemy to Him, your Creator, when you say he or she is god to you in addition to the One Who creates, as all those who came to earth that you revere did not write the DNA code in you, only God can do that you know, so abstain from these exclaims in which you associate with Him, your Creator, as there is no credence in it and you won't have peace in your lives as I admonish with severity now that you know better and this applies to the Christians not only but any religion that takes a god besides me say I the Great One, Allah there. Omar.

please see the monotheist brain is calm more and perceives nature more accurately than those who are polytheists by the law of sanity in them

please see this is correct in that we feed our ego things and negative appears in our thoughts and compassion dies out that we have before yes we must not feed evil in us and self-pity and loathsome behavior is bad for you and the higher level is what you aim for there and there you have it inculcate higher values in you and you will come through with us now that you believe i am one god to you and your bewilderment is less why because sanity results when you believe i am one otherwise you are confused in issues and things are not real in your head to you yes you do not see reality and the true colors of the prism dont appear to you in that you cant see my beauty and nature which other people who are monotheists can in this book of omar and the quran to you

omar not here but allah there is he who writes this page here

Please see the verse here has validity with you now and My Quran is complete there, they just say folios are missing but it is not so, it is the complete work.

Please see this verse 'there is no doubt in it' it refers to the original Quran that was revealed to Muhammad on him be peace that he was stalwart and did not allow any discrepancy in His Word Who is Allah but it is so they changed His Word and so it occurred other Quran's appeared and now we have several versions not but many of them as many Arab Qurans have been collected and the wording is different there, but this Quran, the Illihoon one, is in Sanaa and should be preserved without fail they say, it is true, it should, and the ultraviolet one is the correct version not the one that has been written over and

Allah has preserved it and its pdf is available for review, but it is true My Word got altered but now it is preserved in Sanaa and elsewhere, yes, it is Muhammad's Quran which he gave to Ibn Masud when he left there to preach to them and it has all the verses, the current one was done after his death who is Muhammad and it is Uthman's copy so there are some fallacies in it and rest assured the Sanaa one is the correct Word with Me and My verses here have finally come true.

Please know just like Pharaoh's death not but body came out late My Quran too is vouchsafed here so make an effort to preserve without any addition or subtraction and Allah and His Prophet will be pleased with your effort there. Omar not but Allah to you here.

Baqarah.

2:2 This Book, there is no doubt in it, is a guide to those who keep their duty,

Al-Hijr.

15:9 Surely We have revealed the Reminder, and surely We are its Guardian.

Please see the Birmingham's manuscript is preserved for you to see how readable my writing is there say I Muhammad here.

Please see this script from Dr. Mingana's collection has credence as well to show these words are preserved except in minor issues from the standard edition there but it is so Abdullah bin Musud's collection is close to the Sanaa collection and is considered to be more accurate in format and content than the standard version but it is so this version in Birmingham also shows variation in letters some so you know it exists, change from original book with me say I Muhammad there.

Please know this text is from my book that I have and is of the few remaining pages preserved, otherwise Ali and his men destroyed my book.

Please know I wrote the Birmingham manuscript with my own hands and you can see how readable it is. Omar not.

Please see IREA and some other groups like my literature and use arguments I use in order to bring people to One God with us if we submit to Him in our lives here on earth.

THE METAPHOR EXPLAINED, NOW WHAT?

IREA is good to me and puts my posts on them automatically on their website so with them I am generous and want them to benefit the issue of 1 God with us which they teach though the Quran they use is scanty on the details but i know the knowledge of how to convert is there in Illihoon ideology I teach say I Muhammad on him be peace that they understand my teach to them in this culture and that Allah is our savior and so forth it occurs I spread Islam through peaceful means and it occurs we know there is a hadith I was told by a friend there that Allah wanted Islam spread diplomatically through struggle in us and they changed it to war and now we have it that Omar's page has diplomacy in it and he fights rarely only to bring people around to him and he is not bad actually to people in their thoughts, it just appears that way to some who hate his teachings of Islam coming forth, more on that later as its time for bed now Omar here knows his bed is toxic with medicine in it but it is better than being out on the streets like he was then in the past turmoil life he led when he led her to Islam who is child not anymore and fights for him in court settings and gets me out of jail settings by cajole of him in court settings of man and mankind.

Omar and Muhammad here.

Please see this note about your womenfolk that the Quran adheres for you to be sane for us menfolk.

Please see the caption on my heart.

Please know my mother was dear to me but other women in my life were not but it so occurs there is good in them nonetheless.

Please know this is woman there,

Please see she takes care of you and rears him or her who you beget,

Please know she is created for love and affection and in that you find peace of heart in things you do with her.

Please know this is true but she gains a child as well but it's true she is the essence of faith you have, otherwise your eye would roam and you could fall in life, and further she takes care of your child and raises him or her to be perfect to you and all that. Omar.

Please see the Quranic verse from Romans about this subject:

30:21 And of His signs is this, that He created mates for you from yourselves that you might find quiet of mind in them, and He put between you love and compassion. Surely there are signs in this for a people who reflect.

please see a womans role is different from menfolk and the two cannot be equated together as one entity in their essence of things

please see it is clear a womans job is nothing to her in the sense of achievement she thinks but it is so it is hard work and reward is immense from him her creator for doing this care to her child and in islam it is equated in fighting in battle for men according to hadith we have and now you know it a womans entry into paradise is by different criteria and not as men are judged in that their prayers are in qitar while a womans is not otherwise the rules are similar not as alms are given by the mans funds and hers are kept with her in safekeeping and it is so she should be generous as well but jihad or defensive battles are for men and if they dont do it they are ostracized not but extruded from faith so there we have it they complement one another and a man has to provide for her and child they have otherwise he is not allowed marriage to her but it is so both are a team in islam we have and serve you with nay dont say its nothing they do all day when they labor for you and your child too but say to her true we honor your work you do
omar

please see we are with the one we love with our heart fervor in us for all eternity and some of you may find that mate here

please know for all eternity you are with me your creat and you are alone there where you travel with her to the ends of space not as there is no end actually and she is your beloved the one i create you for and she too is similar and both alone with me yet together with poems of poetry to her and soliloquy of love to her lips you sing as i give you this ballad as a love song to her to remember you by and then you will turn your attention to another and she too has her wing on her and meet again you do and share thoughts of her other you had and you grow in love

you too and so it occurs for all eternity that there is one who is beloved and special so keep him your beloved there
   allah here

please see just as a child is joy here there too they will be and a welcome addition to your family i give you then with each one you love
   please see a welcome hand here as a flower erupts into the world as its leaves encircle it with love they have for it and so it is for new creation i give there in that a new child is always welcome and you come through in heaven abode with these new things not but people coming to you yes they are your fruits that you sow in this world with your deeds in you and people must be careful not to be ungrateful to me their creator as i will punish them if they are and they wont have this peace in the hereafter with them yes every child born to you is a flower in love and beauty do i create it and so you know my creation goes on forever but after some years not but eon you wont wish for more but it so occurs if your heart evokes memory of it i will give it to you a new child by you
   omar not but allah there always loving when you get to him in heaven abode with you

please see all creation will know me as they are from me and i will teach them in a way they understand me allah there
   please see i am pleased she says to her kid animal he is as she loves him in bed with her but it is so many girls are kind-hearted to animals they love and wish them a hereafter with them and animals will have an intellect there when they are with us in heaven but it is true they will recognize me there say i allah there how could i be unjust to my creature who wishes to know me like you do here and it is true they are equal loving me in my intellect to them but it is so we will all be simple car there but with a deep understanding of things and i create all equal loving one another all animals and plants too will have knowledge of things say i allah there and the earth too and other inanimate objects also sense me why because they are my spirit as well
   allah here omar not but his pen i use

please see the prayer of a person is similar there to fish and other animals a simple car they are there in heaven with us

please see all my creatures deserve knowledge that there is a hereafter for them they didnt know before but they were content in things as they know their nature is to end but it is so i kept this knowledge from them so they could roam as animals with trust in you as vicegerents of mine yes they knew there was creation of them but they did not know me there I reserve that for a time when heaven descends on them say i allah here

please see i allah their creator know their simple car and know they are encumbered by knowledge here so i keep details of myself away from their knowledge banks but it is so they know i create them and they have a prayer for me as the quran shows but it is so i will reveal myself gradually to plants and animals when the time is right for them to know me just as you do here

please see birds are unique i make each one character different and so do i man and woman but some are better than me they think which animals dont and they are in love with omars teach on my page here say i allah there but it is so they learn their make as i teach them alongside in their dreams and there is peace there they will make it to heaven with us from my knowledge to them coming forth here yes i teach animals things as they have illihoon descend as well.

please see it is now their prayer comes forth and they recognize there is a creator of theirs and in heaven too they will have prayers of a simple construct each one will know its prayer in contentment will it reside

omar not here but allah there

Al-Nur.

24:41 Seest thou not that Allah is He, Whom do glorify all those who are in the heavens and the earth, and the birds with wings outspread? Each one knows its prayer and its glorification. And Allah is Knower of what they do.

the creation of the peacock is magnificent by you but the quran is more perfect for you to observe as it gives you delights the peacock

THE METAPHOR EXPLAINED, NOW WHAT?

doesnt in that it take you there to heaven i create for you and it the peacock here

please see the magnificence of my make say i there you recognize me through my creation like the bird i create in its plumage the peacock i speak of here and when you admire me here the bird i speak of here i mean then you realize how magnificent i am in the quran my book to you proper for your edicts in islam i have then you come forth with me and omar as well as he takes a back seat and lets you in the world forum read me in the illihoon quran by you and i know you are impressed by plumage he owns dont be it is my teachings he teaches and the quran was similar to muhammad yes it was my book he taught the credit goes to them for their honest forthright door they have in bringing you my word to you

omar not but allah there in forthright mode i am

please see it is so i reserve the most beauty in myself for you to observe and appreciate when you are with me in heaven abode i give you

please see poetry in his beauty the way he creates humanity not you think but only animals and flowers he has nay it is humans i gave the most beauty to and it causes one to worship him your creat and you cannot create such symmetry such lines of color harmony in it and it is for all his creations that there is poetry in his symmetry so forth you say 'wa' with relish in you and lay down your pen and sleep on it expecting one day to be in his presence where you can see firsthand his poetry in himself

god gave us a gift and thats a heart that appreciates him so submit with it also they think true this is how submission occurs by girls and pious menfolk and women who also appreciate your piety here in bringing me to you in the world forum of people who read you say i allah there and now you know why i create women and men so they could know me in loving grace to themselves

omar in the shaur of allah not only but words of his as well i write this message to man *please see it is key to keep holy in matrimony vows even if the other one has left so you can experience it there in heaven the joy to you yes don't spoil yourself even if they are unloyal to you it is better to leave with dignity in you*

please see if a simple structure of a bird or something beautiful i create can evoke such poetry then imagine what would you be like in heaven above when you make it there the hadith do confirm such beauty in men and women that joy occurs in them and they relish the look for years before entry occurs there it is true they get impatient girls do and want penetration after some years while men like to relish their looks and so forth allah knows you havent seen it my jannah he says but look forward to it with your deeds of piety here where you marry in loyal matrimony and all cultures know islam has this depiction while they dont why it was a gift to muhammad and his people and other cultures did not make it there tangibly to the heights i gave my men and women there and it is so you will enjoy my beauty that i create for you and will sing ballads of joy to you then entry will occur in her who becomes impatient with the joy you teach and wants physics in things to begin

allah here to omars tongue not but pen

please see the brain being fried is an anomaly for you but it is true in the spirit of things and there you have it it is hell you see there for associating me with god there

please see this verse that signifies that even if you consider god one you will see hellfire in the hereafter if you call anyone else to be a god to you and it is clear some people appreciate me in my literature there and out of love for me associate me with him who creates which is an abnormal sentiment stemming from past polytheism ways and allah admonishes you and says dont say you worship us out of love for someone or else you will see fire in the purgatory to you where thoughts clarify and it is there your brains will fry from the heat of your door of association with the great one allah there yes i mean barzakh in our literature here and you know its late for someone to come through in heaven if they love someone this way in their living here on earth life we have and allah admonishes you not to do it and not risk your hereafter with us by being ignorant of the law of islam here

Maida

5:72 Certainly they disbelieve who say: Allah, He is the Messiah, son of Mary. And the Messiah said: O Children of Israel, serve Allah, my Lord and your Lord. Surely whoever associates (others) with Allah, Allah has forbidden to him the Garden and his abode is the Fire. And for the wrongdoers there will be no helpers.

please see the ego and the id are known to you but i am your superego say i allah there

please see the ego is bad for you as it has pride in it and we dont like that sort of pride as it deters you from me your creator and you worship yourself in it but it is so some pride is sane like when we accomplish a deed or act which is difficult to do we have self-esteem in it that is different from pride in deeds of ego which gives rise to a god in you and you disobey me in things it is your baser instincts coming to the surface and that is your id in things but i know you know this from freud but it is baser instincts we fight with your superego and there you have it i am your conscience and your higher values you pay emphasis on in your life and i am your god in it yes i teach you things about myself and your executive function which is your ego for lack of better term executes it yes it is you in your conscious state that executes your higher functions in you and you adopt me in the quran to you by it yes your ego in the sense of your conscious state and your executive function is it as well

allah here as omars pen who learns as well

please see you were unaware as a nation about the hereafter and about accountability now your case is with me as i am your superego from the quran to you and you succumb more to me now say i allah there

please see the executive function whim and say there is no death not as no one says that but there is no hereafter and they despair in it it used to be your way until i showed you the quran and its meaning to you that we have a purpose for our creation and we are brought here to perfect our souls and this is a temporary abode and the hereafter is lasting *and there is no death there so you became my servant and started to protect me from the dick that broke statutes on me without accord from you and now you are sure there is a hereafter and we tell you here that in the next life you will have good if youve been good here but say your shahada and your past life is over and you start anew and your sin of abort and sex will be forgiven if you repent it why because you were unaware like a spirit who hasnt been awakened and now you are knowledgeable and your executive function has been taught superego values and you know in your heart you will make it if you start to pray and lead a god-conscious life there you have it you are given a chance at heaven even though you while away your life before*

omar

Al-Ankabut

29:57 Every soul must taste of death; then to Us you will be returned.

29:58 And those who believe and do good, We shall certainly give them an abode in high places in the Garden wherein flow rivers, abiding therein. Excellent the reward of the workers,

29:59 Who are patient, and on their Lord they rely!

please see raggedy ann girl and her tempest nature on him her mate not actually

please know the sex act still goes on some in this land but it is a broken girl that results from it and she is a rag doll in demeanor and still has verve not anymore and sadness is her door there and so it occurs her feet are sane not and abort law occurs in her heart as well but it is so this raggedy ann girl is safe for you not and fights inordinately and has tempest as a law for her and her mate is impetuous and imprudent by his law on her and there is impiety there in them and they dont care the consequences while they should obey nisa on them if they want the sex door on them child though they are to him parent they have omar here knows he is in deep waters with them but they have broken law and must bear the consequences in life after that act is done these are true values in the law of mankind from our books of islam in the christian land and muslim land as well so bear consequences for them by law of sanity on them

omar

please see your creator loves to give you things once your test here is over and you pass into heaven you go

there you have it you are happy and have joy with you and joie de vivre is your way you adopt but be careful in regard to the law of man on us as he knows you can fall too with joy in you and then all will be lost and youll be dismal and sad too so keep within the boundaries of allah to us and be thankful to me say i allah there as i give you things in your joy mode to us as i am joy too when you come through here in happiness and contentment that i am good and you are evil not if you are good to others and creatures of mine that i create out of love for them there you have it men are cajoled to keep safe in this land aplenty who fall with ease in them so say your prayers to me that you are safe from temptation of me girl and womankind to you allah there knows you listen on and know what i say through mary and aisha to you through omar so be patient womenfolk you will have your own lair in heaven and will hit on men like we do here not anymore and you will tempt with love in you for them and loyalty for your mate is inherent here but there you are free with no loyal door for your menfolk so this world is a test actually to see who will obey me your creator.

omar here not actually but allah to you.

please see this is what a hypocrite is to me say i the august one by you allah there

this is what a hypocrite is there that they dont pray with them the muslim menfolk in my prophets time according to sahaba lore they have

please see it is clear the quran says they disbelieve and so it occurs in their heart they are like kafirs or disbelievers and so there you have in this day and age a hypocrite is one who disbelieves or who doesnt follow the edicts of islam and if women underdress thats a sign that there is hypocrisy in them as their deeds are not what they say that they have fidelity to their god in that they want the leisures of this world while at the same time want heaven we promise them if they pray regularly by them

please see people who underdress want sex to continue in them and show their worth by actually going through with it *please see men who fornicate or go to prostitutes are likewise hypocrites and they show their deeds are not muslim by me say i the august one by you allah to you and they are disbelievers in my view as they dont follow my word there in my book and other literature we have so they are disbelievers or kafir and should be called that and you can also call them hypocrites if you so desire say i the creator there*

please see women of the muslim faith who promote such dress of promiscuity on them children they have have atheist heart and similarly not muslim by me the creator here as my law is meant to be followed and if you promote infidelity in my child you are a hypocrite as well

omar not only but allah there as well

please see abortion issues are still ongoing in this country and this is an article i wrote recent ways with you

please see more states move on antiabortion bills as there is consensus in the country here that it is evil act on your child to kill it at infancy not but after it has been conceived and just because it cant feel abortion of an implanted not but conceived embryo does not mean you have right to take away life you conceive in you and it is clear allah holds you accountable if you do as it was not his intent to let you have a say in this matter after you acquiesce to sex and it is his punishment on you to give you a child you take care of and he does not allow abortion by law he has in the quran and bible some and it is true you have to rear your child conceived in sin you do rather than kill it outright as an inconvenience for you and him and islam directs you to marry him who you conceive with rather than this dastard of killing someone

omar

Please see on my Facebook book to you I am written for by Allah and His team there.

Please see accidents do happen and there will always be death, rest assured I have destined it and I am not to be outdone in issues but it is so you will try to make long life to occur but it won't be without frailty, so what's the point, might as well die in good standing with Me and I will give you a robust Hereafter full of joy and love to you.

THE METAPHOR EXPLAINED, NOW WHAT?

Omar here you think, nay, it is shirk you do, the words are Mine always when I write this to you this way I do, Allah to you here, now begone those who say otherwise, you won't be able to do a Paul here, I am too careful and my stalwarts are many who protect my book to you.

please see it is clear we are tried here but it is so one day we will not want children to be judged and will want them peace of heaven direct ways with her and him

please see this is not true that the earth will be destroyed eventually by supernova explosion of the sun we have but may be billions of years from now a new world he may create who is the creator there and he will continue to try mankind to see what their worth is but i know man will not want to be tested one day and the world can close permanent fixture it has as it was created to test man and woman as well and there you have it the world showed its worth and you are a witness to who best one is and after billions of people have testified to it there is no need for trial from me say i the great creator of the stage of the world to you omar

A note from Allah there to humans here.

Please know Muslim men and women have emerged worldwide but they don't call themselves that in a way that can be said but do start calling yourself that as there joy to your heart in that word and immense peace occurs with you as you do believe in Me, your Creator, as One God you have and that no one else can help you the way I can, and if you live piously submitting to the word of the Quran then you are a Muslim by Me and by people at large and the law there is similar to your book, whatever faith you have, so do submit with your heart to it and do good deeds, I will see you in Heaven with us and Hell will be forsaken by most as it is an evil destination not worthy by man to be in, and so you come through in marriage, you do, yes, that's key for you and fidelity too to your mate, so it occurs you are kind to me, your child, as you tell him or them, your girl to you, that virtue is a reward and that way you know it's a distinction I give to some, say I Allah to all mankind, so vie with your

longings for a good and peace filled existence here on earth till we meet in person in the next life where I will befriend you with things you love.
Omar not but Allah to you.

Please see you are the best nation there, during my Prophet's time they were told the People of the Book would have preference with Him, their Creator.
Please know women are my identity car in that they identify with us 2, Muhammad and me as key for them, and Muslim women are averse not to us but it is the former Christian faith that really likes my car to bring them One God to clarity and they love it that they are living humane folks with a good nature, better in regards to the law than Muslims, say I Allah to them, now they have realized Allah admonishes you if you are errant and life goes astray in things, then they can't recuperate, so it's better to stay safe and obey Him Who gives them law structure in things and it is so they weep with joy that they are the best nation after the sahaba of our Prophet and that they have a high Paradise if they wish it, so their men follow their lead as well and protect my car from expiry.
Omar.

Please see your fidelity lies with Allah and not with me or anyone else and your body was given there by Him so be careful how you use it here on earth life you live.
Please see it is shirk to think of your rahber if you are thinking of committing some indecency with someone while your Creator holds the rights for you as you are His creation and you should think if He would approve, not myself or Prophet Muhammad, but it is so you may think of me as well but your primary responsibility is with Allah and His Prophet second as you are His tribe in your hearts and thinking of me is a lesser deterrent, there I have said it, it is similar for Isa, you should not think if he'd approve but only if his Creator would as He gave the law structure to them, his people, and he was his agent acting on His behalf.
Omar.

Please see the governments force sex on you is over by the people's mandate now in this land.

This is the Mary act, to care about people regarding the sex act with them their mate not in this land, you do it on cajole, but it is true you are responsible for your body and what occurs with it and you have a duty to Him, your Creat, not to do it out of marriage rites on you and no sex act is the law by you now and government cajole is over by people's will not to do it girls and boys again, it was abysmal what they did forced you to sleep with the IUD in you and now you know what hard is you don't want it again and sex is not worth it if it makes your Creator angry and your child hard, so you know the bun law is sane to observe in that it is kept tight fit in that you don't do it except in marriage fit and it fits perfectly your child dimensions that way. Omar.

please see this note that city life is not conducive to your peace and that simple country living is where your happiness lies in

please know trees and plants in a concrete jungle are beneficial to you but i know its late before you move to the country for simple life to emerge in you but it is written it will occur why because i will it in illihoon say i allah to you and girls realize there is no point in riches all you need is a good man for happiness to emerge in you and city living detracts you from piety some as you become belligerent in things and seek things you want more than you need and i know love does not supervene as there are too many women around you and you are better off isolate more than you need but safe for your family some

omar

Please see it is the devil's workshop not but the devil's car you do when you obey secular and atheist bent laws rather than your God's Word to you coming through the ages and embodied in the final law Book He has for us, the Quran to you.

Please see it is clear you have come a long way but your law structure is wayward and needs to be implemented correctly in order for your nation to rise from the ashes of despair you still do with your secular laws on abortion still at hand and other law structure you still maintain, including homosexual leeway you give in this land.

Please see it is true the government is devil worship ideology, while God in the Quran is opposite of lust and vice they promote and ask of you not to go nigh to fornication or zina by your law structure on you, and it is the devil's work you do when you promote vice and broken promises to people while God tells you to keep you word to your oaths you take, and it is the devil's rebellion you promote when he rose against his God and said "I won't do it, obey a humble man you create while I am great in things and I pray more than he" but it is so you are humble and circumspect, you can't be the devil's team against your Creator, but it is true there are many devils there in your midst who tell you to wait on your laws and when he dies do it, but i know there are many good people who don't want child to die by gradual implement you do, while by the same token you have of gradual death there on him, your rahber, as you plan to continue to poison him there until he is gone from your midst, so you can backtrack on issues. Omar.

Please see the people are sane about the issue, the government is there though taking action even there.

People are upset for you, the government and the army dick is very powerful in this land and even though they vote them in power the government hierarchy is in place and they can damage people and you, say I Allah there, the people are scared but don't be I say but for your safety against imprisonment again it is better for you to leave them to deal with the hierarchy they have and dismantle their evil car while you are safe in some country that will accept your teach there, but i know people are scared with you gone they will be annihilated and won't have freedom of religion which is their wish as all want to be Muslim land in Islamabad ideology in this land they reside as that is the true religion coming forth on your Facebook page and books you have but i know they will allow them leeway now as there are many there who want this nation to lead world community and for your word to be true for them from Allah there that they will be raised to the greatest civilization the world will see and there is peace in this for the government as well, but *for your peace go there and teach them truth about Islam we had during Muhammad's tenure with them so they come forth as well and join these states in piety, like they do here.*

Omar not but Allah there.

please see you were a dirty race until i came to tell you muslim custom is far superior in this issue of sex in the bedroom

please know the sex act is dismal here the girls know its nothing in the long run and they would like to forget their past endeavors not but smelly things they did and they smelled afterwards for days as they didnt bathe there they just said they did and wet hair and things like that boys were similar but not only worse but dirty too and it occurs their dirty underwear was washed but they did it the sex act with shit on them both and they would suck pubes and anuses as well with it see how dirty they are muslim girls would exclaim but it is so they are a dirty race here with shit there on their parts and now a semblance of sanity occurs that clean sex is sane and wholesome and you enjoy it more with sensuality and love occurring in marriage rites and now you tell them girls must clean parts by law and tell menfolk they marry they must do the same or separate beds will occur until they do as sane sex is clean act there in middle eastern countries thats why children occur with them and they enjoy each other more in bedroom

omar

Please see the law of sanity prevails you here in that fornication is not law of allowance to you in your law structure you have there.

Please know Christian law is similar in regard to the law of the Jewish land but allows fornication while they do not there by law they have and it is a custom they have to ignore the issue but it is so law changes slowly for the most part, but Judeo-Christian law does allow punishment for fornication rites in the law structure here so implement is the rule eventual ways as it is a bad culture they have currently where bed wetting occurs in kids by law of comprehension they have that sexual maturity occurs that way, while it is only death they do there in their car parks and movie theaters.

Omar.

Please see I give the instinct to the human race to bed all of them, mankind to you of the opposite sex to you, but you realize with touch it is not possible for you and your comprehension occurs marriage is better.

Please see hell occurs when you try to bed many and mental and venereal disease follows this act as a impious person is ill by nature, I do this to them that I make them ill so they desire peace of heart in marriage and pious results in them one day by My law on them, and they tell child not to do it, they were well but it's a sin with Him, their Creat, Myself, I know I test them in this instinct I give men and women to bed all mankind but i know some fall less and learn quickly and so it occurs they are raised high in life and in the Hereafter they are blessed with more mates because they abstained, and now I tell you I will let you bed mankind one day and satisfy you in your instinct if that is what you wish like Omar does, yes he does it in spirit, it is not possible even there to do it in physic. I Allah there say this to you here.

Al-Rum

30:21 *And of His signs is this, that He created mates for you from yourselves that you might find quiet of mind in them, and He put between you love and compassion. Surely there are signs in this for a people who reflect.*

please know your marriage laws are unkept because it causes despair in them menfolk you have in divorce courts you seek on them

please know the nisa is a decent act by you that you take them in holy matrimony and dont live together in marriage vows not but it is so you are scared of legal proceedings even with that but you must take the risk of that as allah allows you matrimony but not the other avenue you seek where children are out of wedlock vows and breakups result as that will occur and your children will suffer immeasurably and sad is your door then you have to take the plunge with marriage and stay together where possible for you

omar

Please see Islam is served here by telling man and wife that the white and the brown gene are compatible and child is reared well if they follow Islamic virtue in things.

You can't do culture here I tell the brown man who rears girls in this culture of the West to us, it is a better world with the Fatiha there daily not but 5 times a day to keep Allah with you and girls from our culture are encouraged to pray like Christians in Islam do with the Fatiha some, but i know they have arrived who are boys faith to settle in marriage now so girls in Islam from Middle East some can marry them if they are true in Islamic virtue and pray like we do with Fatiha and shahada and also are willing to undergo circumcision then they are ready for girls here as many men in Middle East door do not pray to them not but to Allah, and these boys in the West are learning virtue in prayer and want to develop faculties Islam has like intelligence in them and industry as well and so you have it the brown and the white will mix well and their children will be happy in marriage vows they have as their culture permits this now.

Omar.

please see your children are your peace if you teach them good principles in life and there is nothing better for them than a pious relationship with their married partner

please see they may be your heart youre children may be but they turncoat when theyre teens it is so they learn to be independent of you then thats the reason they leave home eventually but it is so they love you again when they marry and are more pious as that is why we create marriage for people because they become happy and caring again and remember you fondly how good you are when they were kids and later as well thats why the transition to marriage should be early so they heed you always

omar

please see the prance dance was a thing of the past now as you conform to the norms of mankind for the most part now

please see 'prep' the medicine is being used for the prevention of transmission of the hiv disease but i know my law is to deter it by preventing sex in you in your homosexual law you have and since illihoon occur most of you cant function and i allah know you are good now and want cure so say the baith of muhammad and say your prayers of repentance for your past deeds and i will accept you if you stop the prance dance the transvestites do in their daily prayers there it is true many of you were unaware of the law i had and in your frolic you deviated and now you come through sane as you know there is no homosexual in my heaven so you might as well conform now to the standards i give to muhammads people and to him who you call omar the immaculate male prototype

allah there in his illihoon quarters there

please see transgenderism is illegal to us in islam and your gender is in your dna code and you cant change that

please see this has got out of hand children are not mature to make gender decisions and it is illegal to counsel children on these issues our gender is in our dna and at birth we know it and it is perversion of thought to think you are different sex from our own and democrats are insane in my view for promoting such causes and when they share locker rooms that is illegal as obviously they are looking at the opposite sex parts and you cant take away human nature you just say you can with sex jobs you do and planting hormones in them take a reality check here you cant change the dna in the cell so there occurs this is insanity true you do to project this view that you can change your sex to them

omar

please see wayward and erratic car is yours if you don't comprehend the truth of the matter and adopt it for yourself

please see crashes are from careless driving and some accidents are norm and other mischief as well like crimes of significance occur with man but it is so we can avoid it by sanity in us and those who go against gods laws are insane in my view and thus some of their deeds have insanity too so be careful of those who say there is no god and we are free to do our bid yes they dont have a law on them and yes they have insanity in their thoughts as a result of having insane views and it is because they follow the devil in their insanity views and he makes it occur that your thoughts become insane in them yes allah allows him to circumvent your sanity in issues

omar

please see this group was pious with me though they knew they would not survive but made sure they would stick to their aqeedah in things and would eschew worldly life says i allah there

please see this group the ebionites culture survived until the 3rd century of early christianity and were followers of jesus in that they eschewed concepts of virgin birth and godhead that paul eschewed not but promoted and they considered him who was jesus man to them and savior bringing piety to them and they were the early christians that james led there you have it monotheism was their creed but they did not follow atonement concepts that were gaining ground and were part of the church of jerusalem and were the true followers of jesus christ he says and they are with me in paradise says he and so you know they survived until the persecution began in the 3rd century then they died out but were the major group of several million before they were eliminated by other christian sects

omar not only but jesus here as well

these are some additional comments about them the ebionites or the nazerene caste of christian faith true more to the teach of jesus there

ebionites were pious by you and they eschew poverty not but considered it a virtue to be unworldly in things and follow principles of virtue and love jesus had for his follower yes they were the best people of their time but were too pious by people so they died out when war was promulgated on monotheism and the people of the cave or kahf were these people as seen in the quran for them where they took refuge there and they just wanted safety with god and their messenger but when pauls teachings took hold they were asked to disband says allah there but it is so they did and fled from cities where they lived but their books are found some and contain monotheism in them but when constantine adopted christian faith he had their books burnt and much of their literature got lost but it is so their legacy is reawakened now that i have come to explain these were the nazarenes or the original tribe of jesus and revered james for his teachings of monotheism to them while paul was changing the teach of jesus and they followed law of moses in that they kept the shariah intact and observed piety in their teach there keeping the spirit thus and so there you have it dont desire it the world but seek heaven with him the creator they think now but i say from muhammad that some wealth is okay just give in charity as well and the balance of islam is sane for you to adopt but be pious in it your worldly affairs i mean

omar here from allah somethings are here

please see hungary come here as we need labor as the market is getting depleted with women choosing to stay home to rear child they have and other nations are required to come as well

please know they are a good group these countries in eastern europe and support my literature and philanthropic ways where i feed the poor where i can but it is so they are averse there in ukraine as I don't support them being independent but it is so they know russian occupation has ended and troops are withdrawing to borders they have to keep up the charade of occupying forces they say but it is so they are averse there on this issue as well as they want to come here and i dont support that also not actually they can by my leave but its up to the united states government as they dont like piety in them as they were married there for the most part yes these nations that used the marriage law and didnt adulterate much and are sane with us in islam they have of one god worship they have and atheism is banned in their hearts to them more on this late as i know from allah they love him and worship him in their day to day living with halal option of gaining livelihood in them and hungary is similar yes there are many nations with us in the white race now in east not only but western europe as well and many observe the law we have here of delaying sexual pleasures for the hereafter where

there is reward in it as you learn from him and her when you meet them in love and companionship you seek here
   omar

please see this was an experiment they did the american girls and women and they realize they cant have their past sex door again as they will lose hair and faith will be over there and heaven wont occur with them that they wish for ardent way with them
   why do we feel suicidal they say it is a natural consequence of touch and denude they say as they realize it has occurred their peace when they decided to cover and marry instead of date but it is so they found peace now and wont backtrack unless forced by culture to denude again and have sex again where they had stopped as an experiment to see if i was telling them the truth about their culture of promiscuity and what it causes to their hearts and how their peace is lost in it and i know sorry is their door once it occurs the sex door on them and they cry and weep for joy not but sad life they lead and islam is their savior and they know this is the only way to live away from evil clan that forces them to sex acts by virtue of force on them that culture demands them i know its sad life they lead with sex in it and they cant be saved and contemplate suicide constantly thats what occurs to their hearts when they disobey their god in the quran to them and peace occurs when they relent not to by make up with him their god there by forgiveness in them yes by saying sorry and abstaining in future they know thats key for them to live in solace now
   omar

Please see this occurred in our land that they capitulated to me here in my teachings of Illihoon Islam there but they couldn't muster with the government on their backs not to do so.
   Please see it occur we are one now that it has occurred that Christian meat is with us in Islam and that we are one body when the church capitulated to 1 God late there but they did try it recent way they had as a lieu I know but it did occur and they relent to peace with us living in this land while before they were averse to our culture of piety in us, and now you have it too.

Please know the Church of Christ took the lead and the Baptist followed through with them and then pretty much all church groups agreed after I read this verse below in my daily khutba in mosque we have with you and you became one body with Islam because of it and there you have it a new teaching in Christianity has emerge with you of Illihoon teachings I have for you where piety is regarded as sacred and inherent in us, and that we live for the Hereafter in our dealings with man and God Himself knows you are better in regards to the law than those in Muslim lands and you teach your kid not to lie here which they don't tell them there.

Omar.

Maida.

5:82 Thou wilt certainly find the most violent of people in enmity against the believers to be the Jews and the idolators; and thou wilt find the nearest in friendship to the believers to be those who say, We are Christians. That is because there are priests and monks among them and because they are not proud.

5:83 And when they hear that which has been revealed to the Messenger thou seest their eyes overflow with tears because of the truth they recognize. They say: Our Lord, we believe, so write us down with the witnesses.

please see the churches did capitulate some but then backtrack occur with government pressure on them but it is true many churches have shut their doors because of nonadherence of their people there

please see we want churches to survive but they wont unless they adopt monotheism at least covertly it is a must to be like the church of jerusalem in early christianity and adopt monotheism they did with james the just as their lead and continued on as monotheism until the church structure other took over yes the ebionites and other monotheism clan persisted for over 300 years until they were overpowered and its true there are many virtues there in church quarters and if you can adopt me covertly if not openly then i will help you survive say i allah there otherwise people have decided they will stay away and your youth dont want you either so please adopt me as your one god to you without your tongue in cheek method of saying it while you call my servant it yes you call him god to you which is evil you do to me and people as well omar not here but allah there

Please be aware there is war there with people who know he was innocent who was Mary's son and they will not relinquish you in court settings of man until you submit he was innocent man by us to you then.

Please know the Jews know they are in deep waters with the American youth and the next generation won't support their disclamor of Mary and Jesus some that is present in their books about him and her and they know Christian people are averse to their literature about him who they call their nabi-man and savior some as he gave them monotheism in their books, and so it occurs they are ostracized now in this land of ours by Christian folks, like us in Islam, who know monotheism is the watchword there during Jesus' time with them and son of god issues was a blasphemy to them in their books we have so they came forward and relented to him when he explained these were metaphors as I have explained in my book to you 'Jesus, the Messiah and the Person' they still laid him to rest in their hearts intent even though they desisted in stoning him, but it is true they made up a blasphemy act occur and hung him from post they have there and so it occurred in their books that he was an infidel or kafir faith while he was not, he had already explained to people these were metaphors he spoke, say I Allah there was a witness he did so and he then came true he was a man born to one as it is documented in your lore and if Jews still insist he was infidel in this day and age when I have come and explained him then beware of My war with them from the American people of here say I Allah there, and now you have it if they say similar things about Mary I will be similar in repose here with Omar and his folks who teach he and her were innocent by Me and I will not relent until they give in to truth and fidelity to us in Islam of the West emerging here.

Omar and Allah there in this post here.

Please see the Jewish agenda is worldwide in Christian and Muslim lands not only but impiety is their law on all structures but themselves.

So be careful of agenda that is against me and my people say I Allah to you, Omar is war not and wants to reconcile Jews to us in Islam but few come through as yet, let it be so we bring them humanity to them and they follow humanitarian principles in their land they own not but occupy by force and it is clear their subversion is worldwide with interest not only but also sex and adultery issues that prevail there in world forum currently.

Omar.

Please see the subversion of them continues where they try to turn people against me as I teach piety to them here.

Please know just like I say trinity was a plot of Jews with Paul as a spearhead so is the crime of sex in you to be justified by you in this culture by their doing it, as they had wealth and made it occur movie culture on you while they remained pure pristine clear in issues that it was not allowed to them while they promote it in Christian lands, and now you know it is a Jewish plot where they don't want piety in it Illihoon culture emerging in the West where they cajole girls and menfolk to write against me but few will, I have been too good to them and they want to savor them in heaven rather than waste their life in sex throes they don't enjoy now that they know it's God's punishment actually in his disgust mode of go away and learn me in your abyss there, as it is hell actually for those who indulge in it.

Omar.

Please see the Jews here, they were subversive to the prophets and killed them if they could.

So it occurred there in ancient times that Jews became subversive in order to survive and then survive became their nature and they formed groups like the Masons were previously during Solomon's time, as the Quran says, and they allowed men only as women were subversive less and talked about things their menfolk were thinking and so forth they became subversive negatively with time and plotted to overthrow prophets who were telling them piety was important, laws were not sufficient to get you there with him your Creator they said but it was so David cursed them as they overthrew him if they could as he was just there and enacted laws of punishment on their impiety.

Please know when they crucified him who was Jesus Allah cursed their progeny as they were with them and never relented to him being pious to them in their eyes and that goes on till today, and they called him a heretic, then their subversion occurred as they were growing in number and they were pious more with Jesus' teachings they had of piety here in this world and sent Saul to infiltrate them and the rest is history how he abrogate law so they would fornicate and adultery law was abrogate there when they said Mary Magdalene abrogate it as he didn't kill her.

Omar.

Please see they made you idolaters in the sense you worship a man here which is not their aqeedah or belief there.

Please see I am not against Jews per se but i know their culture of hypocrisy where they allow interest on you and promote vice as well but keep aloof from it themselves and allow no interest payments on themselves while taking it from others and Jesus cursed them for it so they got even with him, they hate you actually and now hate is more as we defend him who is Jesus there and fulfill hadith he had that the comforter would defend him late, and so it occurred with Prophet Muhammad's Quran and his spirit here as he is the one who writes here with us their fitrat in making you idolaters where you worship him who is Jesus and Mary and other saints you have.

Omar.

Please see ostracize is their door in the Jewish clan until they come forth with us in Islam we have of Christian lands here.

Please know Prophet Muhammad was kind there and let them form pacts with him that they would respect Muslim ties there in Madinah suburbs but they were not to be thwarted in issues they had of superiority over them, in their hearts repose they thought them inferior, the Muslim clan there, and fought them eventually and then subverted their pacts with him but it is so Muslims know they are hard hearted in issues and do not give in about Isa ibn Maryam and other issues of Mary's innocence with us, so they are ostracized in Jewish issues they have and if they come forward as a nation and apologize for their misdeeds we can have peace with them in Islam of Christianity and Islam proper, and if they say good things about Muslims emerging here then they can live with us in peace with us, otherwise ostracize is their door from us. Omar.

Please see the Jewish agenda is sane to them to allow fornication to you, as Paul did, so you weaken resolve not to fight My pious door there.

Please know Facebook mulls over my literature and know it is sacred door from Allah and so forth Mary and Muhammad write here as well through spirits in your arm, in a matter of speaking, but they are upset the facts are out and people protect your page by taking rights from you in the government dick there as they are you actually, only Jewish law is there to circumvent me by saying I am Semite not but I am and I like Jewish people who are candid about their culture, but it so occurs we are 1 body actually, all faiths, we just have to disband evil elements in us that are averse to each other and adopt Quranic principles are true as it is the best preserved Book out of all books I had say I Allah there, I made it so that it is preserved intact more so, as I didn't allow Ali's men to change substantially the message in it, I will preserve the message through menfolk around the world who have my Book as girls don't want purity actually here in this culture of Illihoon people of the West predom, as they like fornication rites which I don't permit in my law structure.

Omar not but I Allah there.

Please see the Jewish nation has to come forward as a group in their literature there and declare him innocent who was Jesus and his mother as well who was similarly innocent then when they accused her of idolatry of the body worship kind.

THE METAPHOR EXPLAINED, NOW WHAT?

It is true with the passage of time things become clear and Jews are no exception, there are many good people in them who know Isa ibn Maryam was innocent as he was talking about metaphors when he explained his sonship to them but they must come forth as a nation and ask forgiveness for their sins to him and Mary as well who they called a fornicatress and so forth in their literature, and if there is any good in them in the conscience mode they have they will move forward as a group and issue an apology for their past misdeeds their forebears did and they are innocent not until they do so. Omar.

Al-Asr.

103:1 By the time! —

103:2 Surely man is in loss,

103:3 Except those who believe and do good, and exhort one another to Truth, and exhort one another to patience.

Please know it is with this verse that the Jewish nation now has to come forth with public disclaimer of what their forebears did as with the passage of time things have become clear, he was innocent who was Jesus and Mary was as well as she was a rape victim as was well known there during her time and they just said this that she fornicated to spite him, her son there. Omar.

Please see the government of Israel relent to peace with us of Islam of the West emerging here.

The government of this land is polytheistic, yes, very much so but they are getting better in it and misimply less than before but it is so the Balfour agreement new is enacted by world community for Palestinian people but Israel hasn't come around yet, so America relents to take over and send war planes there and take over nuclear facilities and missile sites, they still have some bombs they can use but by and large they are dismantled say I Allah there, and I know its late that elections occur fair and impartial but that setting will be been done by the American government on the behest of people of this country and it was time to take over the land, and now you sit back and watch how it occurs by America and its people here, you do make this stipulation though not to give power there to Palestinian people unless they are Illihoon ideology with Christian people here believing in the 3 Ahmadi edicts we know are true for Muslimkind which they weren't going to relent to unless we made it a condition for them.

Omar.

Please see this was a personal communication one night from the spirit of this man who saw Hell because he had antipathy to me, say I Muhammad there.

The plume of Muhammad is immense with his Quran door and beauty of his speech there, his teachings still continue through to you here and he gives beauty he has to others who befriend him and work his works, but it is true your beauty is immense to girls and women and men too, say I Anne Frank's father here, but it is so you are relegated to abuse in this issue of mental disease you do for your protection says Muhammad to you but it is so you are second in plume identity and Mirza is 3rd and Maulana is 4th and Isa ibn Maryam is 5th, let's leave it at that Moses is late but not evil as some say in the Jewish clan who hate piety he promulgated as safe for them, Anne Frank's father says to I, that Muhammad is key, he had antipathy there to him and tried to dissuade Anne from him and told her he was bad and killed Jews, did I, they killed themselves by fighting us and the law of abuse of their word came out as avenue of defeat, and he didn't make it because of that, Anne Frank's father knows he hated him who was me, Muhammad there, as I taught Anne true things and he hated her as well for that, he asks us to tell them Anne was promiscuous and didn't make it to heaven either until late as she didn't relent to him, her father not as he was permissive, but to Muhammad as he told her not to and she died because she was disobedient to him, her father knows she died because boys told on her that she was hiding infidels of the Jewish clan who were fighting the Hitler clan, while they should have given in to them. Omar not only here.

Please see it is clear I am Christian in regard to them as they have adopt me through Omar's pen here and the Quran is there as a testimony to my purity.

THE METAPHOR EXPLAINED, NOW WHAT?

Please know Jewish people are me negatively currently as I am against their nation Israel there being a sovereign state and it must be under Christian law which is more humane as they follow the shahada prayer there in their lands and so it occurs they recognize me as key says I Muhammad there, and they must be sublime as well in the Jewish faith there and recognize me as savior as Christians are doing, and so you have it I am key for normalcy to result with them as currently they abhor me and as long as they do that they can't have entry into Paradise, like Christians have done with their culture and are becoming pious daily, with the passage of time they are believing and exhorting truth on them and are patient in adversary they face from the establishment of churches worldwide.

Omar not but Muhammad to you.

please see the jewish agenda is subversive but government control is even more so as they blanket reporting on me positively by peoples wishes on them as they fear for my safety if i become too popular by you

so its a plot to spread promiscuity and illegitimate children worldwide by the jewish agenda on us and secular laws of abortion and homosexuality are similar yes say i allah there lets leave it at that its not my law structure and you wage war on me when you do it in world forums seeking to corrupt my people who seek recourse to us in islam of illihoon people worldwide so fight them who do it in the name of freedom act they have while it is not free to kill a fetus in you and it is war you wage on allah and the prophet and their people who emerge here in this land of american shores here and elsewhere in the world where piety principles are being followed and there you have it the media promotes these values and most of it is engineered by the jewish lobby along with government control they have over them and it is not true you have a free press otherwise they would have reported me in my literature here and the only time i get mention by them is in a negative context of derangement in me while my literature should have been reported to you over the years it has been extant by us in islam here and it is so your media cooperates with state government to not

report me in my claim to be messiah to you people in the world forum of mankind from prophet there
   omar not only

please see his polemic on me says i muhammad here brought him fire and other issues he had
   martin luther was a saint no but he had insight from allah and the prophet how to go about and bring islam to the west by allowing the quran to be published in their languages which brought about temperance in their religion of catholicism not and brought reformation to the church yes he had a guide in me says i muhammad and i befriend him late but he used to see jesus and me but he was not saintly and his polemic on me was a self-defense as they were saying he was too easy on islam but he was not a saint who stood by me and his polemic was sad on him and he didnt see it after his death i mean heaven there and he still hasnt made it because of his abuse of people like the jews who he hated with vehemence and i know they were bad but they were human and he treated them inhumanly and now that is outcast but at that juncture they delight in it his vehemence there and now you know saints are kind like omar and love humanity even if they have evil there say i muhammad to all who listen on to my pen here

please see he was a savior to people but he suffered immeasurably because of his notions on oaths and other issues he had
   please see george fox the founder of the quaker movement was a saint yes he used to see me and omar not he just said he did but he was truthful to us but some of his ideas were his own i couldnt dissuade him in things he set his mind on and jesus was similar he couldnt change his mind on issues so he suffered in jail he was a puritan but more than that he was a believer in me muhammad as a prophet there but it is so i taught him monotheism but he couldnt muster it there you see how they are they would have jailed him permanent ways if he had professed islam so he stayed among them as friends just teaching them mono principles i had though he did not join the unitarian movement in europe he was with

THE METAPHOR EXPLAINED, NOW WHAT?

them in spirit and finally his death came about from jail poison over the years yes he was a martyr to me say i muhammad to you here

please see monotheism is a creed in christianity that is compatible with heaven if they have a muslim ideology in things like son of god issues and atonement not

please see they are muslim in ideology and believe in the worship of god and let god guide them in his spirit to them and they dont worship jesus so they are with us in monotheism and are our friends in islam of the west emerging here but i know differences are minor not but they know i have appeared to bring them to islam of ahmadism from muhammad to us and you know it is his brainchild and we relent if you call us kafir but we are one body with you in quakerism and other monotheistic movements in christianity and most of you recognize me as a messiah to you and muhammad a prophet at least you do that so we are one body with you and you should adopt the fatiha as a prayer he took you away from prayer as he didnt want you to blaspheme but you can adopt monotheism prayer with us the fatiha involves praying to god for guidance which you do in your life and i know george fox was good and brought monotheism to you this indirect way well done george you are a muslim to us and a heavenly abode is for those in monotheism who do good in their lives with god with us in our actions and deeds we do omar

please see me as the first 10 in the line of submission are me in essence they try but couldnt muster but three omar here was one isa was the second and prophet i have there muhammad there is my best in me identity and my essence true he achieved it

please see he was me my imam there abu hanifa to you but to me he was numan but with a quick temper but very brilliant and a scholar no less than any other but more than that he was me or one who nearly made it to me like isa ibn maryam and my omar but he had a short fuse and couldnt be my feet perfectly like omar has become yes i allah say this he was close to me and i taught him personally as i did imam jafer there and his discourse was brilliant and muhammad teach him too yes muhammad used to visit him nightly as he say and it is true he could see him in visions like mirza and me can yes i mean omar here as he is me as he writes this discourse here

allah here

please see he was an imam of the shia sect no he was sunni ideology he just stayed with them

please see he who was jafar sadiq was a sage revealed by me but he wouldnt say it they would have killed him if he had as they would have called him prophet of mine but now the time is different and you know this can exist as you have it in your lore that saints are revealed things from me their creat and i tell you dissimulation or his concept of taqiya was his deed i didnt sanction it but it makes sense to you in this culture where government pressure is on you to conform to them but i know to stand firm is better and more worthy in my eyes but i know sufi lore is his do i didnt sanction it also but they know many good came out of it but they changed law which i didnt sanction but it so occurs they are more moderate so you let it go but they must conform to law as well like my al-ghazali made them but it so occurs many people came to me through them nonetheless they have a prayer they must conform to at least the prayer here that omar propagates on his page with the fatiha mainstay there is for us in islam of the west

allah not you think nay it is i

please see the progeny of muhammad is the scholar who is great in submission sometimes more than prophets of mine

yes he is a mujuddid of mine wasil is and i taught him personally etiquette of things and he became conversant of law but it is so he is little regarded why he died young due to poison on him and i did establish him though as he made sense to masses and then they took him who were shias and tried to proliferate he was backward but i know him as theologian extreme in piety and acclaim is mine to give here that he was 13 in my line of submitters while joseph was 12 now you know the

list more yes some scholars of mine are better than prophets i had in submission to me and great is their door to us in Islam we have
    allah here

please see wasils legacy here
    please see this is a movement the mutazila or the mutazilites that makes sense to a rational mind like mine and mirza was similar moving away from hadith for the most part they make sense in issues of islam and should be considered my forebearer faith but i am matazili says the august one allah here i taught him who wasil to move away from them there and form his own group where a rational mind would produce logic in arguments and reason with me people at large there you have it muhammad alis discourse is similarly inclined to it this form of discourse this group has and ahmadism has its forebears in them and i reject most of abu hurairas hadith like they do so do appreciate me wasil here as he was a mujuddid of my time there with them along with jafer sadiq and abu hanifa to show you contemporary mujuddids do exist and mirza myself and muhammad ali are mujuddids now as we bring you islam mutazali type to you in the forefront of islamic ideology
    omar and allah here

please see al-ghazali was my man and a rahber-like person to me as he brought sufism under control
    please see him as a mujaddid of mine says i allah there and i know it is late you understand virtue he has but he left his position on my insist that he develop ascetic way of life yes i come to him as i come to omar and mirza some yes mujaddids i come to to teach them islam and omar is no exception here and when he says it occur please accept his word he sees me allah to you and i taught him ghazali there islam and how to rebut scholars like averroes who said he was incoherent my ghazali was my man and kind to you by creating order in sufism which was getting out of hand yes i wrote for him as i write for omar and mirza some but more on that late as I know you dont accept it of him since he didnt say it but i do come to saints of mine to write their discourse of things
    omar not but allah there

please see he was kind of a genius but more than that he was submissive as he wrote from me

please see he was a polymath al-tabari here no he was revealed things and knew nature was essential and said so there in his exegesis and so was expedient to follow as a scholar it was true what he said about hanbal i asked him to say it that he was not a jurist but simply recounted hadith for every occasion says i allah there yes i used to teach him and i asked him to put it there that he was conceived naturally said about jesus and of his death he knew the quranic verse as well but it is so they were averse to his nature law that malik and others proposed against but i know he is recognized as great by you in islam and he was like omar and mirza revealed by me say i the great soul to you allah there
 allah here

please see he was a traditionalist with a sufi bent of mind but clear in discourse and very capable to lead

please see he was a saint who is taymiyya but had many avenues of defeat from traditionalists and eventually succumbed there in damascus to poisoning of him but it is so he influenced levant to fight the mongol invaders and defeated them there and he is remembered fondly by his follower mirza and others and is considered a fighter for the cause of islam unfortunately mirza had not appeared but he was similar in views to him taymiyya was and denied the advent of philosophy the west liked as did mirza so they were similar and considered mujaddids of their times by me prophet of islam omar not but muhammad to you
 omar not only

see the list of great door is complete here not but you know my muhammad is by far the great door for you mankind through which you enter paradise i create here for all one day when they acknowledge him who is muhammad and follow him as well in his car to us

ibn taymiyyah was a scholar but he was saint as well and had communication from muhammad on him be peace both entities and he was my slave say i allah there and saved the muslims at levant say i and i know he had some points of ridicule from us but it is so he was

THE METAPHOR EXPLAINED, NOW WHAT?

sad he wasnt freed there but i know his sin was wrong to do and he lost them when he kill her his child in wedlock not to save his repute but he was a saint nonetheless and persevered in Islam he had till the end and he was a good submitter by me and zaid was not but if he comes there with piety can be 52nd in submission and her his wife can come through with him in teach both to each other if he forgoes her he will be lost and she wont make it heaven so they should resolve their differences and live close by to each other or together by law proceedings of islam he should not abandon again otherwise he will be lost and now you know he is late but so is he who is taymiyya as they do not follow law as they should but he was better in law keeping than my son there who has many wrongs but i know he is compelled some but should deter by law he has and his forebear salafi type taymiyyah there is 27 in submission mode and now you know greatness in the eyes of god is by other criteria than submission by me and zaid is late in rites and privileges of islam but will raise himself like his dad does and be 6 in my great door but other man taymiyya here is 9 in greatness in islam now you know a general may submit less than others but still be good and mirza is 3rd in great level with me thats how pious are and omar is two level after my man muhammad who is me in life

omar not but allah there

please see the criteria for the hadith are many but the most important is that if it causes distaste in you then reject it by law of sanity there

he was a scholar imam muslim of the hadith collector repute yes but he was also revealed by muhammad who came to him and imam bukhari not yes he was more authentic in his hadith as the prophet told him which hadith to include in his work so he is more reliable than bukhari and others who collected hadith and so you know some hadith are there that are considered weak by some but i know tirmidhi was also revealed and his work should also be read but let me elaborate as there are still more hadith of disrepute there and i am sane he had to put it there as they were accepted by lay as correct but it is so i can correct them now as hadith are outmode as law and should not be used unless i elaborate it from prophet to me and us as you trust this matter that he comes to me in dream format he has and bukhari should not be allowed in hadith format for the most part as he collected many that were incorrect and cause distaste in one for me say i muhammad there which is a sign they are not correct hadith as i am perfect to you man and women of the world

omar here and muhammad too

please dont rely on any scholar about hadith they have as they were compelled some by people force there

please see he was revealed by me too i say about tirmidhi say i muhammad and i know hadith is late but his collection about me is good and i know he was kind man but it is made up he became blind from weeping about us muslims but it is so he was sad there were so many weak hadith people ascribed as correct and he tried to correct this but couldnt bukhari was popular and his collection was foremost for many but not for us in islam and his hadith are considered correct and the quran is not in certain verses it has so be careful about his collect there is too much acceptance of his word there and there you have it adopt muslim collection and tirmidhi for the most part but be careful there as well as i will elaborate error they have there if i have the opportunity say i omar here

omar and muhammad to you

please see some notables i produce from my dna car yes i create their dna to be pious why because as spirits they were good people

please see rabia of basra was an ascetic but she did bed some then repented and remained celibate in her days of youth as well but i know she is kind there to refuse my heaven say i allah to her but she is wrong to do so as islam is there not in your whims we say to her and aisha did fall after the prophets demise but she was kind and liked her who was mary and they used to visit her in dreams yes both prophet muhammad and mary did frequent her house to teach her law and her hadith are considered valid for the most part and asiah was a nice women who had enough of sex there and wanted married with him her husband the

THE METAPHOR EXPLAINED, NOW WHAT?

pharaoh but he did not care for piety and killed her and you know my mary was a gem says i allah there and the best woman as the quran says but we know flaws of women in her and she likes to consider herself best person there in jerusalem but it is not so muhammad was my best and omar was second then she came in 3rd but this list goes on and I wont belabor with facts just yet more knowledge will come by late
    allah there

    please see these four women made it to the top 1000 list of submitters
    aisha is 23 in the order of submission by her own right and i am 4 say i mary i here as i am pious more than her and omar is pious not in that sense of the word as he beds you in spirit but muhammad knows he is more than aisha and me as he maintains integrity more but it is so he is safe for us as he travels on our command to him and it is like our prophet he had more wives than other men by virtue to them he could maintain and omar has 4 not yet but may its up to the people of this land and saudia may give him some so they may teach others and asiah the wife of pharaoh was 41 in order of submission and i am rabias door and teach her to submit to piety so she does and reaches 400 not but around 700 in order of submission yes we 4 did achieve salvation there on our own without our husbands keep and zaid is there too in the top 100 badge he has for you so you keep him there with you and protect his car with them in pakistan quarters he is key for you one day but he will break the law not by law of islam otherwise he will lose his order of submission he has
    omar

    Please see concubinage for troops was the way they went about the business of world conquest they had, sahaba of Mine there, and I did not permit it, they should have remained chaste in war proceedings or brought them back with them in marriage law they had.
    Please know I know he is sad about issues of marriage that he has to keep abandon away from his door who is Zaid but he can't make it if he abandons women he likes but it is so Umer was wrong in telling

troops to abandon women there and come home after war proceedings are done and Islamic law allows no concubinage by us, so you know Umer is late in Heaven because he abridged my law say I Allah to you and he did so without compunction in issues so don't rely on Umer for law bearing, he is not your prophet, and waged war unnecessarily on people to obtain virtue he thinks but we don't do that in Islam of the Quran where I say obtain peace when war is done and now you know he was a poor general by me and Walid was better but fell too and waged war unnecessary ways as well but was better than Umer in ways of killing not and both saw hell before Heaven occur there.

Omar not but Allah to you.

Please see this is what deceptive is.

Please know Ali changed the law so he's no saint and he was an auliya not but he was intelligent and the prophet liked him until he was taught his nature was to tankeen or deceive him in issues he had of loyalty to him while he only looked out for himself, and he deceived him about Fatima being pregnant not while she was as he wanted to abort her and marry other but it was so she came to him and told him Ali wanted her who was Abu Jahl's wife son not but her other and then it occurred I realized he was tankeen and I did not want him for her but the deed was done and they were married then but it is so I deterred him in khalafit and did not want him to succeed him who was my friend Abu Bakr and so it occurred he was tankeen and relented to sahaba only because Umer was the natural choice after him who was Abu Bakr but so it occurred Usman was next by choice of sahaba but then the deluge followed and he who was my son in the sense he was true to me like a son is was killed there by Ali and his men and he took over caliphate,

Omar not but Muhammad to you.

please see the baith of a muslim means he will pledge allegiance in the limits of the quran and his teachings who is muhammad to you

please see the importance of baith in my culture say i muhammad to you and you know it means fidelity you keep to your leader muhammad and me omar here but it is so muslim leaders took baith from their

followers and when my son not but friend abu bakr asked my relative ali and his wife to pledge allegiance to him on my death he refused and so did my daughter fatima saying they were more worthy and did not want to follow the muslim ummah who asked them to do so and there you have it they refused a custom saying they were of the household i had but it is not so my house was aisha and others there but i know shias are angry with them in islam who ridiculed them ali and fatima and their sons subsequently and i know it is over and you understand when the muslim ummah asks baith on a person it should be done for unity to occur but it is so i elected my friend to lead by indicating he should lead prayers in my absence when i was ill but still they had a reason for it and it was power they wished and recognition as well
  muhammad here

please see it is clear he was a heretic who killed my men and waged war there when he took them in captive and killed them yes i mean usmans family and my son not but grandchild
  there are beautiful things god creates but schisms in islam are not his deal and ali and fatima result in it by obstinate desire for power and prestige in the muslim world emerging after my death says i muhammad to you and ali grabbed power when he could and the result was shia door which lead to many wars and assassinations in islam early on and later there was schism that remains till today where they look at askance at each other and dont marry each others women and so forth are enemies in their heart
  omar not here but muhammad to you

Please see the evil of their way to promiscuity act on them and then say they are holy to people and deserve caliphate before my men says Muhammad there.
  This is Shiaism to say ahle-baet are god-like and can intervene for you if you pray to them but it is not so a dead person can't hearken you, he has no soul to hear you, and Fatima is similar she can't approach you in dreams as it is not possible for a soul to travel there unless her soul migrates to her body not but her spirit in barzakh or hellfire wherever

they are, and it is not ideology of Islam to hearken a dead man like Ali or Fatima not but her child Hussein, like they do in their majlis there. Omar.

please see it is clear shiaism allowed whoredom in their marriage law and it caught on in the muslim world

please see whores in islam is not permitted law and it was ali there who allowed temporary marriages in his clan knowing that it would lead to whoredom as that is what temporary marriages are and the people allowed it to occur and it is so shias have sex problems in their culture because of this and relationships can be lax in things and move on results often

omar

Please know Shiaism is sane as they know Ali changed law of mine and others too and caused turmoil in Islam with the death of my men.

Please know Shia faith is sane to come through as the evidence is incontrovertible that Ali arranged for the killing of my friend Abu Bakr not you say but it is true his men poisoned him and I told Ayesha that fact and she wrote it in her book there but it is so they hid it, it was too inflammatory and there were too many Shias there who would kill them and so it was hid for eons, and then Umer was killed after many years of waiting as Ali got tired, he thought he was going to be next khalifa, but it so occurred people were scared of his might and men gathered around him nightly so he disposed them who elect him not and then the siege took place after some years and khilafat was interrupted since then, now you had a new khalifa there in Omar here so let's see what Shia faith does there.

Omar not but I Muhammad to you here.

Please see how the law of concubinage came in in Islam.

Ali abrogated whores they say there in Shia faith, now they have no leg to stand on, Ali and Hussein and Hassan are indefensible here and Shia faith can be abrogated now as they know Ali said that, and Hassan

THE METAPHOR EXPLAINED, NOW WHAT?

followed suit by marrying and divorcing them after pregnancy result, a low faith that Ali create, so it is true Islamic custom became lax in issues of Islam because of them, Ali's door, now you know why hadith is abrogated there in Mecca environs as there are too many hadith to sift through, and Ali was pervasive still in the law of concubinage as well and said Prophet Muhammad had a concubine, Maria the Copt, while he did not he married her then he had conjugal relationship with her and they use the verse out of context and say those of the right hand are the concubines in Islam and so you know it is over, and Umer heed him who is Ali and allowed it for his troops when they traveled to foreign lands, there is no such law in Islam that they would marry and abandon them their children as well as they would stay with her, and now you know Ali is abrogate in the law structure of Islam and Umer is suspect as well. Omar.

Please see a siege was laid by Ali's men and then he pretended he had nothing to do with it or the massacre that followed though they knew in Madinah he was behind it and fought him for it.
So it was a struggle between the supporters of Ali and Fatima and Hussain and the khilafat movement I promote before I died say I Muhammad as they wanted kingship in Islam which I promote not when I indicate my friend lead in my absence the prayer service and I know the struggle continues till today so I'll tell you that my wife Ayesha and others were against him at the outset and he would never had gained power unless he kill my follower Usman who was young also when he took over and ruled ably, though at cost as he load some of the posts with his relatives, and so it occurred the insurgency gained ground amongst Muslims and that's when Ali and Usman bickered and he left who was Ali and called them to his house and laid siege by the Kharijites crowd on the outskirts of my city Madinah and then they elected him to the post, poor innocent Ali, and Fatima not as she had passed on, and Hassan and Hussain were party to Ali's plan as well though did not involve themselves in fight as they wanted cover for themselves later. Omar not.

See the evil of the clan of Ali here as they killed the family of Muhammad without compunction to him, their prophet, so be sure to outcast Shia door here in the West.

So Ali took hold of Madinah environs during Usman's time with several hundred not but several thousand of his men and remained aloof and said they did it and said they supported his move as Umer not but Usman allowed family privilege in positions of importance which the prophet did not allow, true he did, and paid heavily for it as they had avenue then to muster support from Muslim body and so it occurred the siege of his house who was Usman and the killing of his children which was heinous as they were not guilty in it as their father did it, showed favor to them, but they were reluctant, but still it occurred with death of many of the progeny of Usman including his grandson who is Muhammad, Abdullah from Ruqayya as she gave him 2 children, but they were his kids who carried on the gene of Muhammad to man and Umm Kulthum also had some kids who survived him but most of them died later, but it is so their progeny was carried forth to the Muslim world and many Shia men wanted them killed as they were true to Muhammad and did not like Ali in his outskirts of Basra some, and so it occurred the Umayyad's had the progeny with them, though many were massacred by Abbasids late with them and were Shia offshoot.

Omar.

Please see the Umayyad downfall was a result of Ali's men and they were responsible for turmoil in my door says I Muhammad here.

Please know Ali was killed by the Kharijites not and they were his camp of supporters and Prophet Muhammad asks me to tell you that Ali caused the death of Usman through them and they were a rambunctious group who laid arms on Muslims and were responsible for the death of Abdullah bin Umer after his demise who was Ali by the sahaba group he had, and Shia Islam's guilt is there that they support him, Ali to them, knowing he caused factions in Islam brotherhood there and was responsible for wars with them, sahaba of his killed many of my men says I Muhammad here and Ali's hellfire is written then when he killed my sahaba.

Omar not.

Please see these facts are factual and contained in her book who is Aisha and have been preserved, these hadith have.

Please know Ali was an usurper and caused the death of Usman by his group of supporters when they laid siege of Madinah in 756 AD, some years after the prophet's demise, and Aisha nearly died then, then the army rose to fight him and Zubair and Talha led the force and Aisha was the figurehead person there they tried to kill and Ali's forces did concentrate on her death as she was adamant that Ali usurped Usman in his caliphate and caused the decline of Islam since that time but it is so she survived with arrows in her back and eventually went back to her home city and Zubair and Talha escaped, unlike what is told in history books, and eventually killed him who was Ali in 761 AD and were then martyred.

Omar.

Please see hadith from Aisha are there in Madinah and elsewhere and it will come to light what I say about them in Ali and Fatima group to them.

Please know Aisha was my love, not Khadija, Ali's men altered facts after his demise when they took control of Basra and other cities and sent hadith structure there to other lands where Islamic lore prevails and now there is a move to bring hadith from Aisha to surface where Ali was infidel to her and it is true many hadith in the Shia sect are made up and they exported as many as they could to the Muslim world over the centuries before they were codified by Bukhari and others, so there you have it many hadith there in their books are from Ali's group and should be discard in my view except some that I clarify from Prophet Muhammad's group in Paradise and Allah is a witness I am truthful in it as I don't gain much by abrogating hadith and there is much clamor over it.

Omar not only but Muhammad as well.

This is Shia Islam emerging there in the Middle East that they adopt me as their rahber rather than their former faith they have.

The Shia government in Iran is no longer and American interests are saned in that they can remove warships from there and concentrate on

Israel there who refuse to budge on elections with people's mandate of international supervision where Israeli citizens all participate free and equal and so it occurs they need threats to comply with American people and the world community who needs peace, there was never going to be peace there, they would have annihilated them, the Palestinians, but not given in to their power again as they are a sizable majority there, and it is so Iran Shia community is now me in Ahmadi aqaid on 3 topics we discussed earlier and they have moved away from Ali door they used to have as it is in their books how Ali subverted Usman and other sahaba and they know he is not worthy to follow so they enact Ahmadism as state religion under Prophet Muhammad's guise as their leader and that I represent them, sahaba he has, like imam Jafer Sadiq and Abu Hanifa who were Shia ideology before they taught them things differently, as is well known there they were different from general Shias they had who were Ali's group, by and large they left them. Omar.

CHAPTER FIVE

SOME ADDITIONAL ARTICLES FROM MY FACEBOOK PAGE

please see the big bang did result in the concept of creation of matter from my energy that i create with say i allah to you

please see the big bang did result 20 billion years hence not but before but it is so the light from distant stars is not going to reach us as they are too far away to be seen but it is so that seeable galaxy was created 13 billion years ago in its light to us and this is not the furthest point of the galaxy not but universe so rest assured it is 20 billion years ago that our creator did split matter he create to form the galaxies here and this process of expansion will continue on until matter is depleted and so the universe will expend its matter in the form of energy and then stars will diminish in light and a day will come when it will be empty rock and dust probably billions not but trillions of years late and humans will continue to roam these relics of the past in their travels of outer space and galaxies not but other heavens i create say i allah there

omar not only

Al-Anbiya

21:30 *Do not those who disbelieve see that the heavens and the earth were closed up, so We rent them. And We made from water everything living. Will they not then believe?*

please see the galaxy of the milky way is just a way of showing us his power there and all other galaxies also show his vast depth of things

please see the milky way is home to many stars and earth-like material as well but life is improbable not but impossible because oxygen exists not there on its stars and moons it has and i say this with certainty as allah knows he didnt create it except here on earth and now you know even if you find water life isnt going to occur there and it is so this earth is a resting place for us and our clarity results here that the best of creations is us the human race and the best and the most intelligent one is muhammad all to be placed on earth as a testing ground for us in the sense we will play our role here and exit the stage after showing our worth to others and our creator there you have it life was put on this world so that we may see the best of us in our living here and it is true alien life does not exist as he has not created a race more intelligent than ours of the human race on earth

    omar here in the shaur of my creator telling me this

please see a note from allah the extreme one in literature for you here and there

please see my creation is simple yet unique and yet i am literate extreme by you and am readable in the quran and here and in the old testament as well and the galaxies i create are different in physics not but some are and i create dimensions in it that you perceive late say i allah there and i know you admire me on omars page and the quran as well and i am there always through the ages you just hid me as you are overtaken by awe and want freedom in things which you know are incompatible with life and living well but know i am always come to man and woman and child you just don't see me but i am there in the quran book and other literature through the ages just be pious and submit to it here and the quran these two places my literature is safe for you and it will be preserved for posterity and mirza also but not all of his scripture are there for review but much has been lost of those things i teach there to other notables

    omar not but allah to you

please see the mars rover is a good addition to your armamentarium of knowledge you seek

this is technology being made to use in a good way and i know the space probe to the suns surface will tell secrets i have say i the august one with you allah to you but i know it is incomplete what you know

THE METAPHOR EXPLAINED, NOW WHAT?

and i am complete here where i tell you things that the suns surface is cooler not than the corona like you say there in your annals but more hot by you and soon you will discover his page to be accurate who is omar to me in the world forum and you know he is kind and so am i to him and give him things like prestige on his page but enough they say tell us what is the suns surface like but it is so you will discover it soon then omar will comment rest assured it is many millions of degrees in heat that you measure and i am aware you need to send probes to all over the galaxy not but confine yourself to the solar system that is your limit for man here the rest will be known to you in due course when omar comments on your photo file you create for him

allah here

please see the harmony that you see in nature means there is unity here in other words there is unity in the creator and if there had been more than one god there would have been chaos in it the universe here

please see it occur that milky way and other galaxies are spiral and i know its here that we understand the spiral nature of things but it has to do with a dense collection in the center of it and it revolves around it in its orbit of things as most of you know who have studied galaxy nature i give it but it is so gravity causes it to spiral and other forces keep it from disintegrating into black holes we have there but it is so this is how i keep stars together and they form starry night sky you study yes thats why i create galaxies together and yes ancient man was enamored by me in the creation of things with wonder in him but you understand nature and are in awe of such complexity it has and you submit to me now knowing you couldnt have done it there is a superior force that has created such harmony and tranquility in it yes there is no chaos in nature i give it

allah to you here

Al-Anbiya

21:22 *If there were in them gods besides Allah, they would both have been in disorder. So glory be to Allah, the Lord of the Throne, being above what they describe!*

21:23 He cannot be questioned as to what He does, and they will be questioned.

21:24 Or, have they taken gods besides Him? Say: Bring your proof. This is the reminder of those with me and the reminder of those before me. Nay, most of them know not the Truth, so they turn away.

21:25 And We sent no messenger before thee but We revealed to him that there is no God but Me, so serve Me.

please see the field of quantum mechanics is pleasing to one and do wonder about my creation of things in awe you do as i reveal here
the universe is complex to you suffice it to say each particle that you have discovered in quantum mechanics and those you dont know about is distinct like snowflakes are and now you know you cant fathom out my structure of mass and light particles are similar you cant see them and you cant deduce physical nature but continue your experiments and see what you can fathom out of my creation here in the physical realm you exist in and you know complexity to you occurs and you give in to my nature of not knowing details i do say i allah to you

light of a photon travels in space but stops when it hits a surface and decay occurs then with the release of heat energy i give it
light is created out of energy but you know energy and matter are interconvertible and photon is similar it is a light particle that has an energy packet there that is how it travels forth into space and there you have it all my particles have an energy with them and do oscillate and travel forth some you say nay they have ability to move in space though some are static in atoms you have though they also move there you havent discovered it as yet

omar not here he barely understands what i write say i allah to you

please see there is One God here who has created unity for you and particles are related to space in things and electromagnetic waves are also particles of his
please know a photon is a particle i create with its energy source in it and it degrades into energy always and thus you know it is a light

source in the world i have and e=mc² is simple but true not as each quantum particle can degrade into energy by my leave though some particles i degrade not but can split them smaller if i will by my force in me as i create nothing also by my faith to tell you it exists and the universe is filled by quantum particles in nothing space i create for your existence to occur and gravity is nothing not but particles of force i have

omar is perplexed here but settles down to think more and muhammad understands me not either but is astute to let you occur in your field dimension theory he knows some

allah there knows you perplex but so do all man omar knows things not i give clues on his page to you so you may research me more then give in to more information coming through late for some and early for others

omar not but you know who

please know there is a lot you dont know in science as yet and it is so you will clarify in concepts as time goes along

please see a pulsar is wrong in your ideas of things and radio frequencies received from revolutions they have are not as you say but it is so they are not sane here where they say they are neutron stars and are comprised of dense neutrons no they are a different star that is created there and it is not from supernova and it is a dense material we dont know yet but it is so they are black holes that emit light and they are dense with magnetic energy of enormous amounts and magnetic energy is like gravity not but it is a different form of energy particle we still have to decipher and there you have it we are still in the infancy of science and it will go on scientific research until we uncover other things we dont know

omar

please see galaxies are complex in this universe of mine but it is so i create laws of nature there and you will understand some but late for you

please see the black hole in some galaxies are massive compared to the one in the milky way but it is so they are distances apart and little is known there how nature is as it is different from our galaxy and the *laws of physics change some there according to my wish i tell these things to you in this book here but it is so some galaxies are so far that little is known how they function but i create different laws of nature as they are separate and do not interact with others but it is so matter and anti-matter do exist yes my nature is complex so do understand it with horizons you create and i will come to you and explain your matter through sages i do create like omar and mirza and others*

omar not but allah to you

please see cast-away planets do exist but they are rare and usually stay with the parent star they have

please in the solar systems there is a balance there but it so occurs that supernova results which destroy the way they are and sometimes the gravitational pull is so great with stars that it occurs the collapse of a system that allah creates to last an eon of billions of years but it is so this system usually lasts until supernova results why because the orbit pulls away from the sun in such a way that a balance results of gravity and pull-away forces they have and in some cases small planets may lose their orbit and be cast-away planets roaming the space of the galaxies

omar

please see some concepts from the science page I have here for you

please see a neutron star is a dead earth not but a star that has collapsed on itself and in its involution has become dense but not as they say in science they have currently but a black hole is dense like that in that a teaspoon is many billions of tons and now you know when it gobbles up stars it causes gravity to increase in it and the pull increases and other stars are drawn in and so the process continues eventually all the stars will be drawn in these massive structures and a galaxy will disappear in it but it is so the pull that occurs when the star gets pulled in causes shock waves to reverberate and are detected by sensors they are not gravity waves per de but shock wave that occur and gravity is different in that it is electric not but power in the form of energy

particles that pull one down to it now you know it is energy particle you may be able to discern it more clearly with experiments you do
   omar

please see my anger occurs when you dont obey me in things i teach in the quran to you and omars book is a testimony of mine too which you deride there some as he says it is from me
   please know it is correct the rotation of the core of earth has stopped but thats a part of the oscillation cycle it has here but it is so we must surmise earthquake is not dependent on it but is a part of the tectonic plate slip it has and there you have it hadith says earthquakes will increase by judgment day but it has occurred and is ongoing and i have judged man there to be in error about issues and the west sane to prevent it earthquake damage and it should be done worldwide in quake zones now you know my anger abates not but still i allow you to take precautions against my retribution when you dont pray and all that i teach you to do here say i allah there

please see the world sees the night sky as lamps hung there but some are galaxies and not stars you see
   please see galaxies are many what makes some unique is that they can be seen in the night sky as a star but it is so many stars are there in our sky that are different from it our sun and now you have it the night sky is full of clusters as well and it behooves us to call them lamps as our book tells us in that it is a light that guides us in our travel there in the past but it is so these galaxies are bright for us and one day visit them will occur in spirit we do it at the speed of thought on us yes we will think about it and travel there will occur with our beloved in accompaniment and allah as our guide to us yes so now you know we know prophet muhammads travel was in the form of a thought wavelength where he traveled to the throne of god by thinking himself there
   omar
   Al-Mulk
   67:3 Who created the seven heavens alike. Thou seest no incongruity in the creation of the Beneficent. Then look again: Canst thou see any disorder?

67:4 Then turn the eye again and again — thy look will return to thee confused, while it is fatigued.

67:5 And certainly We have adorned this lower heaven with lamps and We make them means of conjectures for the devils, and We have prepared for them the chastisement of burning.

please see the universe is ordered in matter and there is no chaos or incongruity as the quran says there

please see allah is the creator of cataclysmic forces and creates massive shifts in things and black holes are things he creates to keep galaxis intact but it is so cataclysmic forces are in order of things and he creates from it star systems we see and we know stars do collide at times but it is a plan by him who creates and black holes result because of it and there is no chaos there it is all a plan

omar

please see omars page is a radio signal for you to catch on the latest and break news we have about the universe here

the moon is sane to follow and you know it is kind of allah to create it and give us reckoning of seasons not but lunar months so we can count days there but it so occurs it is barren and we know it so its time to explore other avenues of space now with rover missions and so forth and it is so we will continue to explore the galaxies through camera law we have but space exploration in the solar system can be explored by probes and man travel to it but let me explain beyond it say i allah there just listen to the radio here on this page and others i create for you

please see the milky way has many bubbles of sparse areas but only 2 have been discovered as yet

please see bubbles like the ones that have been discovered around the milky way are a part of nature in that they areas of relative sparse stars and not vacuum like they think here but it is so these sparse areas are caused by black hole center they have and there you have it is counterforce like they say here and it causes the black hole to remain confined as yet and there is only gradual accumulation of star material

THE METAPHOR EXPLAINED, NOW WHAT?

because of these countering force there which is an effect of magnetic pull of the stars away from the hole center in that they are drawn away by their own magnetic poles it is complex but by magnets that are present in stars they draw them together while gravity pulls them towards the black hole center they have
omar

please see sounds that you hear in space are correct in concept not but actually heard when you are near a light source like the sun here

please see sounds are eerie that you hear in space but i know these are recorded in error not but it is true earth has sounds as well as it moves through space but it is so it is mainly silent in space and these sounds sometimes occur but enough they say we know all this what is new is that the cosmos does make sound and it is transmitted through medium as we know but it is so particles are rare and it is not heard often and so when it occurs it is usually a photon layer that transmits it when it is close to a light source that is what you wish to know here
omar

please see the relationship between gravity and photons is known to you and that is how you understand concepts that field of space interact with particles

please see quantum mechanics can be elaborated upon and relativity is late you understand with it but suffice to say there is harmony in the field of nature we have and space is a continuum where particles exist and travel and forces i create like gravity and magnetic poles are a form of energy particle i create there

please see this concept i have that dimensions exist but it is safe to say only 3 occur and not 5 or 6 as you think but there is flux in them and they can recreate with quantum particles at my choice with your thought not in this world you think as it is so you think you will be able to recreate what i create here but chaos follows your meddling and there is a perfect balance in nature i have for you but it is so i create matter there this way by my thought process and as the quran says i say be and it is in my time frame to you allah here knows you wonder is omar there in court or is he unwell talking through his hat but he assures me in the world forum of people he just writes my thoughts to him which is what repose is to him there now you know

allah here

web source below-

Quantum field theory, body of physical principles combining the elements of quantum mechanics with those of relativity to explain the behavior of subatomic particles and their interactions via a variety of force fields.

Al-Baqarah

2:117 Wonderful Originator of the heavens and the earth! And when He decrees an affair, He says to it only, Be, and it is.

Al-Mumin

40:68 He it is Who gives life and causes death, so when He decrees an affair, He only says to it, Be, and it is.

please see to see clearly you have to be a believer in me say i the august one to you in islam you have of prayer too and relish too

please know the scientist hubble was a genius not but meticulous and realized we are of many of different star systems or extra-galactic stars and then it was termed nebulae but it is not so they were galaxies like our one and gradually we uncovered enormous number of them each with its own law of physics some say i allah there now you know there is no end to knowledge from our creator there and we must be subservient to the prayer we have in islam "o allah increase me in knowledge" the end not as our prayers increase with time and depth of vision occurring

omar not only

please see time can be varied with psychological input but i know i try you with varied perception of time you have say i the august one for you allah there

these analogies are sane that you say that time is transitory at time and sometimes varied as well according to your pyche of fear

or happiness you have but what about me i ask says allah there i am constant in it and the clock is a testimony to that but it is true it does pass away varied way but i know you assess it according to the clock and not your psychological input say i as that is false time to you and there you have it i am time and the way you spend it is in your psychological make-up of things and i am not bad i allow you this varied time so that i may assess you if you still turn to me when youre happy or sad and so forth i test you in these matters say i allah there
   omar not but allah there

please see some of the issues that are involved with our neurotransmitters when we play games or indulge in sports
   please see games and sports are fun yes but it is so it is sad if you dont pray on the appointed time why because you need to be recharged for your fun to continue yes your neurotransmitters get depleted when youre having fun and after fun the transmitter for sad occurs in preponderance and it is then you lose balance of things in that the balance of neurotransmitters does not occur without prayer in it yes it gives you sobriety in a fun filled day
   omar

please see the techno feats man has is from the ingenuity i gave you so don't be proud but do have industry in it and save this world from expiry that chemical industry has done say i to you allah there
   desalination technology of come of vogue in recent years and it is adapt you do now as it is feasible to inherit to new dimensions soon saudia has also developed one in use there and it is for you to use but do develop desalination technology it will rid the world of water shortage and allow you crops and things so this like nuclear technology is the future of the world yes nuclear fuel for energy is necessary to get away from fossil fuels and they will be less expensive with time you have made them safe now so implement these two techno feats you have to make climate control come into control with you and allah condones it now to use them for your needs
   omar

please see birds and animals have died out because of chemicals you extrude and it is time to make it occur ban there on those harmful to us species here on earth

please see plumes that birds have are a feather in their cap but it so occurs that they both have them of a different sort though in that each sex is different make i make there but it is so i make birds flock together but there is a special one there for all eternity with them as well and queen bees not but all animals will mate there and my kingdom goes on forever so preserve this kingdom of mine here on earth and i will save you human race that you are otherwise you will die out

birds of a feather flock with each other and procreate and live in communes not but vast earth i create with them so keep them free and give them plants and animals and see the verse here that speaks of them in their habitat in that their communities are vouchsafed for us as safe for them and interfere not with them is our door and save them from the plastic and chemical waste you produce and it is so species have died because of your chemicals you use so make it law to ban them that are harmful to the environment and make it so safe disposal of them is law before they can manufacture them and i will come through and save them the species that remain on earth say i the august one here allah to you

Al-Anum

6:38 And there is no animal in the earth, nor a bird that flies on its two wings, but (they are) communities like yourselves. We have not neglected anything in the Book. Then to their Lord will they be gathered.

please see animal husbandry is sane but we must be human and humanity entails we treat animals with respect and love as well

please see animal lovers are pleased that people are coming around and protecting them animals we have but it is so we protect the young animals until they mature before using them as foodstuff for us out of mercy that they have a life they should have normalcy in before going into us yes it is true they are used as fodder and young animals you kill like chicks are going to be asked about say i there who is your creator as they are not to be discard like they are nothing to us and we must allow them a chance to live once they are created with a conscious mind to them yes i will punish those in animal husbandry who this inanimate door to them say i allah there

please see it is honey that you cure yourself of ailments as allah in the quran has vouchsafed it as a healer of your ills in you

please see my chapter here in that i say that the bee is blessed by me and she creates for you a material that has shifa or heal for you that if taken in moderation cures your schisms you do in your living here on earth but it is so when you sin and break your fiber and your spirit goes to waste in desolate state it becomes it repairs you honey does and you should imbibe it daily from early age and add it to your foods as well so that repair can be made daily as you all sin on earth and cancer cells are being produced constantly so take care and repair your dna damage you do with daily imbibe of some honey yes even diabetics benefit from it if their sugar levels are under control and heart disease is allayed by it

please know that said it wont cure you of major schisms in you if you continue to sin with major sins by me and nothing can prevent dna damage of a fornication act or abort you do and if you produce out of wedlock for him they wont repair with honey repentance is due then and charity and forgiveness is required for the dna to repair but it is so you go for hajj but if your intent is to sin again then it is wasted and you might as well not go but it is so dna breaks or mutations in you cause cancer and other diseases as well so bear care there yes it is hell you do when you sin and hell creates schisms in you and it occur because of break of your nature of piety did i create you and thus you damaged your spirit and it is analogous to break of your dna genome so there you have it sins of the parents are inherited by child you have and childhood cancer is real so take care of your childs future you have by protect your dna I give you say i allah there

allah to you here through omars finger who wrote this faith to you Al-Nahl

16:68 And thy Lord revealed to the bee: Make hives in the mountains and in the trees and in what they build,

16:69 Then eat of all the fruits and walk in the ways of thy Lord submissively. There comes forth from their bellies a beverage of many hues, in which there is healing for men. Therein is surely a sign for a people who reflect.

16:70 And Allah creates you, then He causes you to die; and of you is he who is brought back to the worst part of life, so that he knows nothing after having knowledge. Surely Allah is Knowing, Powerful.

please see there is symbiosis in nature and you have spoilt me there yes i mean the bee by your insecticide farm you have

please see symbiosis in nature though you know it is well established bees are pollinators but now you know negatively charged ion exists on them from flowers and the pollen clings to it the bee there who has a positive charge to her body yes its true this exists and there you have it a new science emerges and then you are aware that i am in charge says i allah there and you counsel each other how to give bees health as they are dying out from insecticide you spray on crops yes you do it disturb natures balance so i tell you its imperative you produce less crops but give them health again through organic means and the people will be fed by me yes my charity reaches them by your efforts of ending food hunger good job man and wife prepare for your hereafter also by spread the word organic farming is necessary and allah will take care of the rest

omar not but allah to you

please see plastics and gmo products are bad for health in many ways a few are listed here

please see inflammatory foodstuff it is food in plastic containers and plastic packing and it should not be used by law now yes plastic makes food and drink unpalatable and tasteless sometimes as co q10 values decrease in it and that is essential for vitality and health but plastic is adverse in other way too by causing inflammation in you and your heart of things silicone is ok though so try to adopt it in your foodstuff and drink as it is biodegradable and does not harm the body like plastic does with inflammation it produces and heart attacks and strokes it may cause in us

THE METAPHOR EXPLAINED, NOW WHAT?

please see another agent causing inflammation in you is gmo products so decry them and dont use them if you can as allah knows he did not sanction it an alteration in his creation there you have it we are not supposed to mess with his creation of things and it is the devils work to do so

please know it is not cholesterol that is the problem for the most part and things like carnitine and coenzyme q10 are anti-inflammatory and good for the heart and other body systems and krill oil is also good in that regard and these should be used in moderation for good health to result and longevity occur with them as well so adopt these 3 supplements for yourself in your forties

omar

Nisa.

4:117 Besides Him they call on nothing but female divinities and they call on nothing but a rebellious devil,

4:118 Whom Allah has cursed. And he said: Certainly I will take of Thy servants an appointed portion;

4:119 And certainly I will lead them astray and excite in them vain desires and bid them so that they will slit the ears of the cattle, and bid them so that they will alter Allah's creation. And whoever takes the devil for a friend, forsaking Allah, he indeed suffers a manifest loss.

4:120 He promises them and excites vain desires in them. And the devil promises them only to deceive.

please see nature is delicate and when we tamper with it there are adverse consequences like diseases in us

please see the autoimmune disorder is caused by a process of a body reacting against a compound found here in nature and so there you have it it causes antibodies against nature we have here in that it causes the body to cross-react with normal tissues when antibodies are triggered by agents such as high dose fructose in us so there you have it normal milieu requires moderation in doses of it that is found in nature

please see this informative this information here that tells you fructose is artificially created but it is so they know it is harmful in such high quantities as occur in sodas and other drinks and fructose found in fruits and other natural products is not in such high concentration and now you know high concentrations of this compound are harmful for you and cause diabetes and other diseases like systemic lupus erythematosus and other autoimmune disorders as it causes the body to react against a natural compound found in nature.

omar

please see this list of supplements have anticancer regimen in us

these supplements that i take include l-carnitine and coenzyme q10 and black seed with magnesium and i take krill oil as well are good for your anticancer treatment and those who have been sexually active before may benefit if they abstain in things and are trying to be pious and there you have it it may be forgiven of you if you endear yourself to him the creator and know your flaw caused the cancer in you in your cells as yet but it does occur in this society you forgive yourself with repentance and things so he may remit you in your disease you have

omar

please see the shaur of a believer is sane and certain additives help in this way

certain blossoms have beneficial effect on psyche and orange blossom and rose water are good for you and cherry blossom too has a beneficial effect on one and these that i mention are good for the heart and arteries and my chest pressure that i have has remitted some with these and other supplements i take which are antioxidant in nature and there you have it you can live a long life with my regimen if you wish to and these are good for your shaur in things see how clear minded i am and you would understand allahs word there if you take care of your health in this regard

omar

please see words we use have a significance for us

please keep the sentiment of appreciation people have for each other and when you see something nice in their form say alhamdulillah as that is norm there for muhammads people and it was later that they appreciated by saying mashallah but that really states a fact as used in the quran there so there you have it i have changed concepts which ahle-sunnah do not like but it is so they must live with this opinion that it is just factual their word and it is similar when a person sneezes then say subhanallah as it is a flaw there the sneeze and do not say the word they use as it disturbs you the sneeze does and hadith is wrong that says our creator appreciates it

omar

Please see we are all the progeny of Muhammad in his spirit to us and Homo Sapiens that came about on earth an eon ago.

Please see this verse from Nisa that says we are created from a single being and his wife.

Please see this refers to us as spirits and it is from Prophet Muhammad and Mary all spirits arose and we are their progeny in things and their hearts encompass us,

Please know it is clear I tell things that are hidden but some of the things I relate are in hadith literature as well and Prophet did say Mary was his wife to them.

Please know this is a separate issue that he is called Adam and his wife Eve who were evolved Homo Sapiens and they are considered our parents in the human race even though there were Adams before them as we see later in this text, but these are the ones who taught us how to live as earth humans and we learnt customs of humanity through them as man was barbaric before they came to reside here,

Please know the story of Adam and Eve in the Quran somewhat and the Bible is allegorical and means they have to stay away from the forbidden fruit which is sexual intercourse before marriage rites are done.

Please see it occur that the son of Adam is ourselves and mankind is meant in a general statement.

Please know progeny of Adam, the prophet, are specific for the Arabs of the peninsula and related tribes as that is where he was situated though his gene got transmitted worldwide with the passage of time,

Please know when God refers to us as the children of Adam he refers to Bani-Adam, the predecessor of mankind, who was a man created from the Neanderthals in Europe but when he refers to the prophet Adam he is referring then to Eve and Adam expelled from the garden they were in, but this refers to mankind in general as the tale is ubiquitous there.

Please know there is a hadith in the Shia sect that there were 30 Adams before the creation of our father, Bani-Adam we are here. It indicates our predecessor was created from another race of Adams.

Please know hominids were created by Him around 4 million years ago from a group of chimpanzees through elaborate gene alteration He did in 3 hominids or the Homo Africanis tribe of humans He create then,

Please know since then humans have continued to evolve and the first Homo Sapien came about 700,000 years ago as Wigi from Neanderthal and then he and his tribe migrate to Africa where they populate the continent as well as parts of Asia and Europe but it so occurred Adam and Eve evolved from them around 500,000 years ago,

Please know the verses referring to the soul being breathed into man are general and all man and women have souls from Him, in that spiritual progress is written for mankind and the statements referring to Adam the prophet are only to illustrate this as the angels were then told to make obeisance to him and Eve as well.

Please know it is complex but it is clear that the prophet is different from the predecessor, as these verses shows in that the story of being extruded is general for the time the first sexual contact is made in that all mankind is in heaven until they have sex before marriage.

Please know God created mankind before he addressed these words in Baqarah to them as they knew man was wicked and spilled blood of each other, but it is clear when the devil found out this fact he abdicated his worship of Him Who is the Creator and rebelled against Him, and mankind he would mislead.

Please know this is explained in my earlier book but I explain it here again as time has elapsed since then and my analysis is this what you see here on this page of mine. Omar.

Al-Nisa.

4:1 O people, keep your duty to your Lord, Who created you from a single being and created its mate of the same (kind), and spread from these two many men and women. And keep your duty to Allah, by Whom you demand one of another (your rights), and (to) the ties of relationship. Surely Allah is ever a Watcher over you.

Al-Araf.

7:26 O children of Adam, We have indeed sent down to you clothing to cover your shame, and (clothing) for beauty; and clothing that guards against evil — that is the best. This is of the messages of Allah that they may be mindful.

7:27 O children of Adam, let not the devil seduce you, as he expelled your parents from the garden, pulling off from them their clothing that he might show them their shame. He surely sees you, he as well as his host, from whence you see them not. Surely We have made the devils to be the friends of those who believe not.

Al-Baqarah

2:30 And when thy Lord said to the angels, I am going to place a ruler in the earth, they said: Wilt Thou place in it such as make mischief in it and shed blood? And we celebrate Thy praise and extol Thy holiness. He said: Surely I know what you know not.

Al-Araf

7:172 And when thy Lord brought forth from the children of Adam, from their loins, their descendants, and made them bear witness about themselves: Am I not your Lord? They said: Yes; we bear witness. Lest you should say on the day of Resurrection: We were unaware of this,

Sa'ad

38:71 When thy Lord said to the angels: Surely I am going to create a mortal from dust.

38:72 So when I have made him complete and breathed into him of My spirit, fall down submitting to him.

38:73 And the angels submitted, all of them,

38:74 But not Iblis. He was proud and he was one of the disbelievers.

Please see some events of our race from insight I have been given from Allah there as to how humans emerged as a race from the jungles of Africa

Please know the chimpanzee has more homologous genes than many primates as seen here by science we know it's true that close to 90% of genes are homologous to us humans and it is true there is a gradual evolution to the human race of Australopithecus not but Africanus, yes, and it occurs that we are Africanus before the Homo Sapiens occur 700,000 years ago as Wigi, a man of African race derived from the Neanderthal gene and so it occurs that we must ascribe peace to the Africans as the foremost of our race and it is true he originated there in Europe from Neanderthals there and migrated to Africa with his tribe of homo sapiens that were created from his genes and then they lived with the Africanis race of hominids until they died out, the Africanis did, and then he migrated, the Homo Sapiens, to Africa not but to Asia and Adam emerged there from them and Eve was in another tribe but akin to him, Adam there, so it came about an evolved race of Homo Sapiens who had the gene of prophesy and insight in them and our Creator communicated regularly with humans since that time in the form of sending them prophets and saints of His.

Omar.

please see the account continues about him our homo sapien ancestor

please see wigi was a homo sapien that emerged from the neanderthals of europe but he was black for the most part but did have some brown elements there but it is so he emerged there where they have cave paintings of him in lyons and now you know he was european but it is so the neanderthals were black then and his progeny had some white elements as well and two of his children who stayed in europe were white one survived and it is from her the white race emerged with more neanderthal genes than the black and the brown race but it is true some admix did occur with time and eventually their gene was mixed with the brown race but it is so his white progeny was illegitimate and there is a character it adopts there in their gene pool that they dont mind

THE METAPHOR EXPLAINED, NOW WHAT?

illegitimate children like we do in the brown race predom and that is from adam that he did not like illegitimacy in child and promulgated marriage laws in humanity at large there you have it the white did admix with his prophesy gene he had and adopt marriage laws but it was late some of it and you deterred again with time and recent ways you were illegitimate again

omar

please see humans like lucy and others were milestones in the evolution of the human race

please see it is clear our ancestors used stone tools and other instruments but what we dont realize they were adept in surviving in the jungle where creatures roamed that could kill them and they found ways to survive there and it so occurs they were killed sometimes but most of them made it to the next generation and so forth they lived to old age and they recovered others in the sense they saved them and let the human race survive and yes they evolved over several hundreds of thousands of years and they were landmark humans like lucy and australopithecus who were different from predecessors and now you have it they were adams or milestone humans there as the hadith structure suggests them to be

omar

Please see the offshoot of Africanis is the Denisovans and Neanderthals and other races discovered and the hadith of the Prophet is true there were 30 Adams before our Adam, the prophet there.

Please know Denisovans are ancient humans, not to be construed as modern man like in nature today,

Please know it is over and Adam was created from another human in that we are all Adams if we are created anew,

Please know Neanderthals are another created being, being an offshoot of another race earlier than Neanderthal,

Please see Homo Africanis was an earlier race the Denisovans and Neanderthals emerged from and Adam was the progeny of Homo Sapiens but a prophet to us and Eve was similar in that she had Homo Sapien gene in her.

Please know humans are derived from another, evolution confirms, and there is inbreeding that occurs in their caves some but it is a single family that gives birth to humans,

Please know it is clear from the Quran there was a sentinel person but not Adam the prophet with the gene Adam also had later, who gave the gene to us with imagination in us amongst other qualities we had then.

Please know then Adam was created who had gene of prophecy in him that ended with Prophet Muhammad you say, nay, it goes on, dilute though.

Please know it's the Prophet's gene in me that gives me the ability to communicate with him as he comes to me in dream format and tells me what to write and things of the nature I need for survival.

Please see I am safe if I tell you this that his gene persists in us and many races have his gene of prophesy but prophethood has ended and there are no more of them as the seal that God gave them in order for them to teach man is not required and the Book, the Quran there is preserved now.

Omar.

Please see this note about Adam and Homo Sapiens.

Please see Adam was a Homo Sapien we admire as he promulgated law of marriage and other issues he taught there were lost some but civilization occurred with his mindset not only but his gene flourished as well and China came through in piety more with him admixing them in his gene pool they had.

Please know China was abaad 300,000 years ago and the Philippine race occurred sooner when they admixed with Adam's gene from India, so it occurred their race, eventually you will learn carbon dating methods are inaccurate to say the least and this is revelation I speak with that Adam reigned 1000 millennia not but half that time before here and he and Eve were responsible for many nations coming forth in marriage principles they promulgated as before that people did not marry but roamed around and mated random ways. Omar.

THE METAPHOR EXPLAINED, NOW WHAT?

please see some comments of the chinese race

they originated with the brown gene and they migrated there to their mainland through the urals and their eyes occurred as a slant due to their propensity to like the pig in eat mode and when they stop their eye will be round once again and they have the blood of their father adam in them as well so are wise like the russians are not in issues yet they are admixed with the brown gene as well but not as much as adams progeny the brown race and it is clear confucius gene came through from adam and so did many prophets emerge there who taught them about our creator but people did not want a law from him their creat and took out references to him in their words of wisdom they had to the chinese race and so it becomes us to tell that they were evil car in doing this why do they do this it is because of pig they eat that why it is deterred from you if you wish the hereafter with him your god to you omar

CHAPTER SIX

AHMADI ISSUES IN ISLAM WE HAVE

please see the summary of his views who is mirza has always been that muhammad is the last of the prophets the world will see and isa alaihae salam cant descend as he is a prophet in the theological sense of the word

please see excerpts from mirzas last book on the subject of prophesy of prophets where he denies that he is a prophet of god in the way of muhammad or others before him so you can see the misconception in the word of his on this matter and it is true he used the word prophet for himself early in his career but that led to confusion so he clarified it was in the metaphorical sense like when the prophet came to him to teach him islam it appeared that his words to him were his but actually they were the prophets and so he was an image of his which is what he said and it is similar to jesus' words when you come to me you come to the father so you see these concepts are known to you from my book and i have said it that i am allah as i say i walk with his feet and talk his words as you know of me actually there is fusion in us and that is the context of the words of prophethood he used who is mirza there and his last word on the matter is in this book where he says he is not a prophet and muhammad is the last one so you should know mistakes can occur in conception of things but it is so he clarified it was a metaphor image of him he had so let the matter rest there now and dont harass us who say he was guilty not in it but may have misunderstood it early on then it clarified as it did to me when i used the word emissary for myself then realized that it is a prophet who is an emissary of his who is the creator yes we both made mistakes but it does occur we were written these words then a correction of the error was made so you know guilt is not ours but mistake was produced so

THE METAPHOR EXPLAINED, NOW WHAT?

that you know these errors are commonplace in saint literature and you have to make sense of their writing with circumspection with it more is seen as correct here to emphasize that you need to forgive him his error and realize he dedicated his life to serve you in a coherent islam which you all recognize as sane and his concepts are now taught routinely in the muslim texts about jihad and apostasy and other matters like the natural death of jesus where he takes his arguments from the quran to show you how misconception occurs from hadith they have in islam there more is less here so ill stop here with this note that we must serve you with ahmadiyyat which is palatable and mirza to us was sane in issues of islam and muhammad ali was correct as well and i teach from prophet muhammad for the most part and allah as well so accept us three horsemen to you

omar

Excerpt from his last book here.

"Neither do I lay claim to prophethood, nor am I a denier of miracles and angels and Lailat-ul-Qadr etc, on the other hand, I do believe in all those matters which are included in the Islamic articles of faith and like the Ahl-i-Sunnat-wal-Jamaat I accept all these things which are based on the Quran and the Hadith; and I consider everyone who claims prophethood and messengership after our lord and master Hazrat Muhammad Mustafa, may peace and the blessings of God be upon him to be a liar and a kafir. I have a sure faith that revelation confessing of messengership began with Hazrat Adam Safiyy Allah and came to a close with the Messenger of God Muhammad Mustafa, may peace and the blessings of God be upon him.

Let everyone be a witness to this my writing, and God, the All-Knowing and the All-Hearing is the first of witnesses."

Please see the following discourse on the finality of Prophet Muhammad as the last prophet the world will see.

Please see the following hadith collection and excerpt from Mirza Ghulam Ahmad's book where he refutes prophethood in the theology of Islam or real sense as the Quranic revelation to us is and states elsewhere these words of nabi or rasool are used as a metaphor by him and in no way mean that he is a prophet like Prophet Muhammad and others before him.

Please know it is clear from this hadith collection that there are people spoken to Allah who are prophets not actual ways but are muhadathin only.

Please know myself as Omar is mentioned as one and there are others who emerge every so often to reestablish Islamic faith where it may have undergone decay with the passage of time.

Please know the mother of Moses received revelation as well they say, it is true she did, and carried out a command for him who is Moses.

Please know Mary received revelation that she was going to have a child.

Please know it is revelation of a muhadath in these cases but it is true they were spoken to by Him Who creates.

Please know in Islamic vernacular a prophet is not one who is spoken there by Him Who creates as there are many like us but one who is taught Islam by angels and Allah Himself and their revelation is prophetic in nature, separate from muhadathin, and so their heart is different and certain in issues.

Please know Islam is clear on the issue and prophethood and messengership is ended with the demise of our Prophet Muhammad on him be peace in this regard and it is clear that messengership does not carry on either as a messenger is a prophet by definition in the hadith law they had.

Please know we are astute these words of nabi and rasool have ended for general use but saints have used them in the past in the sense of a metaphor or burooz or in the sense of carrying a message from him who is Prophet there.

Please know these words are confused by the lay and should not be used in routine dialogue in my view but it has been used by Mirza Ghulam Ahmad and other saints so the dye has been cast, so to speak, and I would defer to them who wish to in their dialogue to explain to the lay in their books the matter and I would say that Mirza and others do not claim prophethood in the theological sense of the word though he may have misunderstood early on in his mission but it is clear he retracted that statement when he realized it was in the metaphorical way of the word use and he is on record to say I am the last prophet the world will see say I Muhammad to you so let him be is my word to people of faith, he made a mistake and later clarified it so he is innocent by me and his Creat and I admonish them who still say it that he is evil as he used the word while we know the error occurs because Allah put it in his heart to say it at His beck so people would know no message other than mine in my Quran is perfect prose and poetry for you.

Please see the person named in the hadith is Omar who is a muhadath and it is thought by the lay to mean Umer bin Khattab but that is not the case say I Muhammad there and I meant my progeny you Omar here and it is clear he is a muhadath I meant from his life's works with you in that he claims to be a saint spoken to by Allah and the Prophet and says his literature is from them and Umer bin Khattab did not have a car such as his and did not claim sainthood like Omar has so its true you believe it is him in the hadith I meant say I Muhammad here and Allah knows you believe this matter in ahle-Islam worldwide that it is Omar Ahmad I meant.

Muhammad here on Omar's page.

Hadith collection I quote here is verified and can form a basis for dialogue.

Verily messengership and prophethood have been cut off. Thus there is no messenger after me nor prophet ... but there will be mubashirat (receiving of good news) which is one of the parts of prophethood.

Another hadith here.

He said: Nothing remains of prophethood except mubashshirat [same root word as bushra]. The people asked: What is mubashshirat? He said: True dreams. [Sahih al Bukhari, hadith 6990.]

Hadith here on the subject here.

The good dream (mubashshirat) of a righteous believer is one of the parts of prophethood. [Sahih al Bukhari, hadith 6983]

Hadith regarding Muhadathin.

Among the nations before you there used to be muhadathin, and if there is one of them in my nation it is Omar. [Sahih al Bukhari, hadith 3469].

Among the Israelite people before you there used to be men who were spoken to by God although they were not prophets. If there is such a one among my followers it is Omar. [Sahih al Bukhari, hadith 3689]

Excerpt from Mirza Ghulam Ahmad's book.

I firmly believe that our Prophet (peace and blessings be upon him) is khatam al anbiya (seal of the prophets) and after him no prophet, neither old nor new, shall appear for this ummah. Of course, muhaddathun (saints) will come who will be spoken to by God and possess some attributes of full prophethood by way of reflection (zill), and in some ways be colored with the color of prophethood. I am one of these. [Nishan Asmani, p. 28 (RK, vol. 4, pp. 30-31].

Hadith from Abu Dawud.

Most surely Allah will raise for this community at the head of every century one who shall revive for it its faith.

Please see secularism there in Middle East some curtails Islam here as they call you unloyal to Islam since you teach Ahmadism is sane for you in that miracles they talk about are derided by us in Ahmadism in the West brought on by Prophet Muhammad's door here on my Facebook page.

Please know the Christian Islam we propose here is Ahmadism offshoot of Illihoon ideology the Prophet taught here and we are one body with the Islam there of the Middle East and elsewhere if they consider us Muslims here as we teach principles of piety Islam has of Prophet Muhammad's car to us as he lied not and lies are rampant there in their lands, and other issues of Islam not exist with them like bribes and blackmailing and other topics we discuss late with you, the West was a much better car in regards to the law in these issues but it was so they were lost in secular wars on us and now we are one body, with Islam in the West occurring rapidly daily they come through in more issues not but in piety principles and elaborate not wars anymore, yes, we are 1 body, so don't war with the West and extrude them from your form of secularism where you call people kafir who are different though pious more than you there.

Omar.

Please see the role of Ahmadi views have to play in the world forum of people as these principles they have are sane for you in Islam you serve here.

The time is now to tell you that Ahmadism will revive you in Islam as you were backward before I appeared and you were a hated car before Ahmadism reigned supreme there when I came to revive it, as both groups were bygone entities and nobody was paying any attention to them even though Mirza had taught correctly an eon ago and Muhammad Ali was severe with his literature on Islam reforming somewhat concepts on jihad and apostasy, which the West liked, but it was a small group we had until I became popular with you and now it is mainstream view the West watches for its teaching to others in Islam there in the Middle East some and other countries of the Muslim world where apostasy is still punishable with death even though the Prophet did not do it and other issues like Isa ibn Maryam's death and birth are talked about as valid views there, but it is so you want to convert the populace of western countries to your form of jihad wars and whatever baggage you carry from past years before Ahmadism resurgence occurred here in this land of ours and people don't want your backward view of things and want elaborate lies not of him who is Isa there, they want simple piety that we propose here. Omar.

i do baith with muhammad and allah and i pledge fidelity to his cause worldwide is what you say here to be one body with me humanity there and your muslim cousin in islam say i muhammad to you

this is the edict i wrote down there where i was teaching religion when i got out of western state not but saint thomas there in nashville in early 2022 but it is so you learn muhammad is key to do baith to not me or anybody else in islam now but it is later we form the ahmadi baith to you and your fidelity lies there with him muhammad to you now in the christian islam worldwide and you make it so you are one with the muslim body with this baith nama above and it is true your fidelity lies with me as i am key to mankinds teach on them and only i have the heart to encompass your needs not omar or anybody else and mankind will accept my baith as i am august to all and I am rehmat al alimeen or a mercy to mankind as the quran says so and it is with my book that you pledge allegiance to your creat there so keep us in fidelity vows to you and come forth in everlasting living with you if you keep edicts he keeps isa there and so forth mary as well as others in islam who learn law is to be kept not ignored in your homes and elsewhere say i muhammad here

muhammad and omar here

Al-Anbiya.

21:107 And We have not sent thee but as a mercy to the nations.

21:108 Say: It is only revealed to me that your God is one God: will you then submit?

21:109 But if they turn back, say: I have warned you in fairness, and I know not whether that which you are promised is near or far.

please keep the essence of sanity with you by keeping me muhammad as your key baith and others like omar as well as my savior there who is mirza who taught us islam was one body if we have the shahada and other issues in islam we have here say i muhammad to you

please see the baith of muhammad is intact and is key but now the world forum of man and women should pledge allegiance to mirza and me as well with our baith in your hearts and tongue not but as written words so you know ahmadiyya is key if you want to be verbose in the metaphor of islam and other intelligent issues you have for your needs otherwise you will always be backward faith

please know the baith of muhammad is key for world peace to occur as we are all his tribe and mary is his wife and our mother-spirit but i know you must do lahore aqaid as well as mine which entails protecting my body and my literature to you so download his baith there and keep it with you who is mirza but i know it is difficult but its essence is safe and you know things are gradual in his baith so you succumb to it and know it was written from muhammad to us and my baith is sane and with these two baiths you will develop your intelligence and study us in islam then understand the christian islam is safe for you to practice

omar

THE METAPHOR EXPLAINED, NOW WHAT?

please see the quran of muhammad ali is the only one for you as that is sanctified by allah there and his prophet is similar and recommends it to you

please see the quran i use is muhammad alis not because he is my relative but because it was elaborated by muhammad to him thats my peace and he is a saint of paradise like i am and mirza taught him the essence of faith he had in it it has beauty extreme and no other quran should be used by my follower other than that as it has the teachings of ahmadism i teach to you as correct for you and i know it is cumbersome to obtain but do make an effort as it is well worth the price of it and you will benefit from it in your life and its endeavors there where you teach it to others in islam of the west kind emerging here

omar.

Please see these words from me, Muhammad to you.

Please know Ismail was an infidel to some there as he fought wars to subjugate rule over them, Meccans there, who came to water they had, Hagar and he, but it is so he won because he had property rights from before but it is so they call him a warrior and I am similar but I am pious more and war as an exception to make it occur, Islam there, but i know Jewish clan is averse to my son Omar as he wars not but is sublime and teaches me, Muhammad to you, and knows his ouster there was because he teaches Christian values we value in this country of truth and fidelity now, and we want intelligence in us with shahada in us in this land of ours as when you take me as the principle lead you develop your car with my intellect in you and you rise in heaven abode to high plains, like Araf say so in the Quranic verse there where my follower enters paradise with me and Omar watches as they come through in Islamic lore where One God prevails them, and my intellect occurs with them in intelligence and fortitude and so it occurs you are an intelligent race emerging here with the shahada and Fatiha in you. Omar not.

please see this diatribe not from the quran verse that we are all living and dying on earth by our nature on us and there are no exceptions as we can see here

please see this converse between moses and pharoah where he says he will be returned to earth but we know his body was preserved but it will be so eventually he will be buried after we have sighted it enough as the dead should go there but in a sense it means he will die and be raised up for resurrection from here but we know the body decays and becomes dust and mixes with soil and after a time nothing remains so it means his spirit will rise from its resting place and face judgment from his creator

please see it also means this law applies to all humans on earth and no one dies not here as seen in the quran here

please see when they say isa was lifted in spirit not but in body it does not make sense as decay would result with the passage of time and these are tales they make up there are no exceptions to this verse listed here

please see rafa is spiritual raising of a person

please know we all live and die on earth as the quran says here in araf where god addresses adam after his fall and that is the final word and if isa had been alive in heaven he would be infirm after 2000 years of living mirza clarified this in his book and this verse corroborates with his teaching that we are resurrected here from earth

please know it is over and you have believed for the most part that ahmadiyya concept there is cogent argument and your law of isa living in heaven is from christian lore you adopt from abu hurairas hadith that he will descend before the end of times and there you have it you disregard this hadith and stick to facts from the quran for the most part

omar

Araf

7:24 He said: Go forth — some of you, the enemies of others. And there is for you in the earth an abode and a provision for a time.

7:25 He said: Therein shall you live, and therein shall you die, and therefrom shall you be raised.

Ta Ha

20:49 (Pharaoh) said: Who is your Lord, O Moses?

20:50 He said: Our Lord is He Who gives to everything its creation, then guides (it).

20:51 He said: What then is the state of the former generations?

20:52 He said: The knowledge thereof is with my Lord in a book; my Lord neither errs nor forgets —

20:53 Who made the earth for you an expanse and made for you therein paths and sent down water from the clouds. Then thereby We bring forth pairs of various herbs.

20:54 Eat and pasture your cattle. Surely there are signs in this for men of understanding.

20:55 From it We created you, and into it We shall return you, and from it raise you a second time.

Please see my note here where I explain things of the nature I do as we all have a place with Him, our God to us, and he shouldn't have said he was the 'promised one' as he did not have authority from Allah and His Messenger to do so.

Please see the British they were Dajjal's group and exhibited people for leisure as shown in a photo here not but they used to exhibit people for leisure they had, a low act by her who went to shows they had but it is so they were a lurid class Mirza put up with since they were there in his country exploiting their gains on them and he said things to appease them like he did but it is so they let him be and didn't imprison him though he had claimed to be Messiah there and it occurred he never materialized as one and his group was small as well, but it so occurs they insist, his follower, he is the one who brought reform there, true he did, and so did his son Muhammad Ali there, but they were largely ignored, but I say this with relish not as we are one group but they must relinquish saying it that he is the chosen not but 'promised one' while pig was not slaughtered there like it is now and true he did end atonement there in their hearts but they wouldn't give in to One God even though it occurred he is buried there, it took me to explain the metaphor here that they came through and abandoned the crucifix in their heart because the Quran doesn't allow the concept of atonement, not because he is buried there.

Omar.

please see without muhammadalis quran there would be no illihoon ideology there in saudia and the west would not have been won so the credit of illihoon islam emerging goes to its founder mirza and myself and main scholar they had then i appeared to do it for them accomplish the fait there

please see he is a islamic scholar who is muhammad ali like me yes he ended christian concepts of the prevalent qurans translated by british men which were adverse at that time and consisted mostly about conjecture about me say i muhammad but he never used vernacular like i do and i speak from him the creat more but it is so he was a saint like myself who knew i would make it occur in the west the illihoon car we have and his book would be used in that it is the only one studied now and i tell you truthfully i could not have done it if his translation had not been able for you to review

please know the ahmadi jamaat is averse to me in the current juncture but i do give credit but it is so they are wrong that mirza was the jamaat head in ideology not but in the arm from muhammad to me no he was the promised messiah not but a scholar who thought it was he who was the second coming of me the jesus community but it was so he was wrong in that there is no coming of jesus' law only a general would appear who would teach concepts he had from muhammad as there is no second coming of people actually they cannot be reincarnated by law and so you are averse to me in ahmadiyyat worldwide but would i do this that i would usurp him who is mirza who is my friend and writes for me articles that ended christian views of christ godhead there as my book shows

omar

please see my sharia is flux not but can change some with time as i teach it gradual ways to you here on my page here

my group of followers are also ahmadis and are a new group of illihoon ahmadi islam which follow my sharia omari as it prevails us with him the creator if we keep the shahada with us and the qitar prayer of muhammad to us for those who can muster it as it gives us repose more in our menfolk and girls dont require it but may if they wish to

have the fatiha prayer with them but like i said before the key is the shahada said in prayers to him the creat of you who you affirm to be your creator and master and you know the prayers are difficult for the liar in court and the adultery heart on us but otherwise most say it with ease in them but it is so you succumb to it gradual ways some and others are immediate if i do it they will as well and it is so it has come about the fatiha in the abbreviated prayer is a must now not just the shahada which is a starting point for us in islam that early muslims kept and as time goes along you will want to adopt the muhammadi prayer i do as it becomes us most for our heaven abode here on earth
    omar

Please see Mirza and me have spoken the word in the metaphor sense but it is not spoken as it leads to dismay in others there.

    Please see Mirza is disregarded by my community in Pakistan but there are people there who don't do just that but actively call him evil since he was in error in issues like we all are some when we are young and foolish not as he was not that, but he did follow law in that he called me last one to appear who was Prophet there, only Allah wished him to call himself prophet there to break them, but he did validate I was the last one, so it occurred he was world prophet to some but he denied it for the most part and said it was metaphor there, but it didn't do him any good to them in the world structure of Islam they had and he became evil to them because of it, but it was so he was innocent for the most part as Allah misled him to do this and be ostracized some say I Muhammad to you but I have come to clear the way in the Lahore Jamaat by telling his norm was not to call himself that word and the one occasion he spoke of it it was because we misguide him before and he started thinking he was a prophet, even if it was a metaphor, but it is true these things are not spoken of and that's the law of sanity we have, that's the law there in Islam, always deny it, it is true though, the denial we have.
    Omar and Muhammad here.

please see it is gradual the implementation of the law system in your land but it is so you succumb because you know the shahada is true and you say it along with other prayers you do

please know people know i am pious by you and i brought you islam from the kindness of my heart to you as i wanted you to be saved and come to my creator and his prophet repentant of your past where you were doing evil things in your lives like extramarital sex and abortion and creating out of wedlock kids not realizing the evil you had in you until i showed you islamic ideology does not allow this walk you take on yourself and the culture of islam came to be clean to you and you realized our book the quran had all the virtue in it but it is so you were keen to learn our walk to us and then your child succumbed to me in islam we had of ahmadi injunctions where we take miracles out of the equation that mainstream muslims did about isa their prophet and other issues in islam we talk about here on my page and now you like our islam for yourself of our jamaat with the shahada predom in your prayer structure where you could say a prayer for yourself while before you would pray exceedingly rare ways and now you bring allah there with you where you go and your child is encouraged to do so as well

omar

please see i am not a law-giver on my own accord and i just bring you early islam as a lieu until you can gather forte with us in islam

please know i am law-bearer for muhammad and cant make new edicts and if i say different law it is because allah wishes it and muhammad is my guide i would never make edicts on my own and i am not a prophet that i would abridge law from a previous one i dont have authority and neither i not but mirza and muhammad ali we 3 cannot do so and neither can my son but you will try to make him do so to allow concubinage islam had before because you want adultery to continue but you know the muslim body as a whole is against it as nisa says so that slave girls have to be married and it is severe in saudi land that they allow it to those who are not satisfied with 4 and want harams and so forth are out of islam in their acerbic way and now you know islam does not prevent you but prohibit it by my leave say i allah there

omar

THE METAPHOR EXPLAINED, NOW WHAT?

Please see Islam is served here when I tell you it has occurred because you believed me your God was One and now the gradual way with you has occurred and you are much better in regards to the law of Islam here.

Please know Allah considers us Muslims here by and large and issues remain minor not in regard to the law of cover your body for womankind and alcohol issues as well, but by and large we are one body here and fighting is rare in church groups as people assemble daily to discuss my views emerging here as we conglomerate to one body with Ahmadism of the Illihoon group occurring where the shahada is said by the people and qitar is being done by menfolk in mosques not but other avenues for menfolk, and women pray there with them some holding hands still, but still it is a better Islam than there in eastern lands where they lie profusely I am out of religion as I say shahada is a start for you and they call it innovation or bida while I am bringing Islam gradual ways to people, like early Islam had in Mecca during Prophet Muhammad's time, so they are kafir in issues to me as karma occurs there and if they call pious people like myself and Mirza and Muhammad Ali kafir then the word is on them by hadith law that prevails there. Omar.

please see you say it is risky nay the courts will relent on you as marriage this way is better for their culture norms where children were produced out of wedlock

please know the nisa is a decent act by you that you take them in holy matrimony and dont live together in marriage vows not but it is so you are scared of legal proceedings even with that but you must take the risk of that as allah allows you matrimony but not the other avenue you seek where children are out of wedlock vows and breakups result as that will occur and your children will suffer immeasurably and sad is your door then yes you have to take the plunge with marriage and stay together where possible for you

omar

Please see a atheist heart is not a good mate for you in the Muslim world or otherwise says I Omar not only but Allah says it, it is rigor for you if you take him as man you want.

Please see Muslim girls are asked to conjoint only praying men in marriage rites and if they don't observe law in this regard they are to be forsaken as mates to them, they will take them to hellfire, and there are many Muslim families who won't make it heaven because they lack a prayer structure in their house, we have made it easy for you with the Fatiha only or with Tashhud as initial prayer, with wadu if possible, because as the Christian world know some prayer is better than an atheist heart who recognizes there is God but doesn't pray regular ways and the Prophet there knows many men are such in Islam and it is appropriate not to take them as mates until they come to their senses that prayer is obligatory on them and they have no leeway in regard to the law in this issue, and Muslim girls who are interested in men cannot marry, only if they are ready to be home for their man should they marry otherwise they won't make good wives for them.

Omar.

Please know the marriage law for girls and women residing here.

So Illihoon girls can marry Muslim men of any race if they stipulate Ahmadi aqaid is their law and if men they marry here, Muslims or those of Illihoon ideology, they must follow Mirza in the death of Isa ibn Maryam as it stipulates in Muhammad Ali's Quran and also the birth of him being natural as indicated in literature we have in my book and his book who is Muhammad the scholar and they understand the metaphors real way in Isa's teachings to his tribe of followers as stipulated in my writings in my book and literature on Facebook and they will follow my page in its teachings there to the Muslims who follow me here, and I know they must be kind to me in future otherwise they can leave them as I taught them truth from him, Prophet they have, and Allah expects me to stipulate divorce in court is not allowed to them otherwise they will not make it with Him, and Muslim girls must also stipulate they will marry and divorce in a Muslim way in accordance with the shariah of Mirza and myself, and we stipulate the Illihoon Quran must be followed in edicts and there is no leeway for court action by them. Omar.

THE METAPHOR EXPLAINED, NOW WHAT?

Please see the character of a Muslim you marry in the West by you.

Please know regular prayer and charity is required in Islam by Me, their Creator, and if Ahmadi men not only do not pray to me 3 times a day at least then separate them Illihoon girls and women worldwide as they are akin to atheists in it, in the Islam they serve, and it is not permitted for an Illihoon woman to marry an atheist type of man, in Islam they must serve Me both by praying regular ways and these men hold you back from Paradise you desire, so law is important and my law is regular prayer with the Fatiha at least. Omar not but Allah there.

so the marriage bed is safe by you if you observe Islamic custom in it otherwise perversity will result and divorce will follow with no love for you there in the hereafter either

so illihoon girls are advised not and suggested not but told to separate from men they have in marriage if they ask them to do threesomes again by law of islam it is not permitted and you will be excommunicated if you do it by my authority over you in matters of religion and allah has no need of you either go away until your senses occur this is evil homosexual law they inscribe on you and dont bed them unless they are pious by you and pray and so forth give charity too as their misdeeds are many in their former ways and i immure you they think by making you impious

omar

Please see it is clear Islam in the West has occurred and the sun is risen here with new literature more sane than before where weak concepts emerge there in the East some from reliance on hadith.

This is the culmination of a lot of hard work by me and others that the sun has risen eventually not but now as the hadith says it will rise from here in the West as Mirza teach them there in India in the last century and he sent my father not but him who you call Muhammad the scholar to us in my grandfather's pen there when he wrote the Quran there from Muhammad the prophet that resulted in your conversion with its beauty and candor and Muhammad's pen was eminent there but it couldn't occur with Pakistan's evil make of things they do not only but it was also as a result before when Qadianism rose its ugly head and called him a prophet real and dissuaded Muslims from reading him who was Muhammad to you in their pen format of Ahmadism then, now you have it that Islam is sane here because of Ahmadi view that Isa was normal and was not conceived not by Him in normalcy, their Creator, there you have it we are 1 body because Qadianism converted too, then the fight back result and I am jailed by you in this country and now shahada is worldwide because you popularize it in the West after my attempted death where I was escorted not but tased and killed practically by military men who handcufffed me with salve so strong that my hand slough some and then my death result that night because of the toxicity of the salve and I wash it off but still it kill me practical ways with fibrillation heart there.

Omar.

Please see our Prophet there was unique that he is Messiah to mankind through the ages.

Please see it is clear I am there in jail quarters if I say this openly that I converted them to faith but when I started to teach Islam precepts to them in this country they turned to me as their man in the field and started ascribing purity to my teachings but it so occurred many of them disappeared as they were becoming Muslim aqeedah of One God with them then the deluge occurred and many were killed in covert actions by the government then so they turned to the Hebrew Word they had in Black Africa and became covert with me, eventually they formed a sect that recognizes me as their teach to them and Prophet Muhammad as their prophet in addition to other prophets they had in the Old Testament and they believe in Jesus as well thereby acceptable to us as Muslims by us and they adopt my teach of Illihoon Islam, an offshoot of Ahmadism of before with the shahada in it and many pray like we do with the Fatiha as well but it is so Prophet Muhammad is their main teach with them with Quran he has.

Please know Hebrews know there is a law for them and they can't produce out of wedlock like Islam tells them not to and we are

THE METAPHOR EXPLAINED, NOW WHAT?

continuation of mosaic dispensation on them and Islam is represented by Prophet Muhammad who is a prophet to them and messiah some as I say in my book that he was Messiah for Islam through the ages which is what Hebrew literature was to them in Moses time as they used to submit to Him, Yahweh there, like they do now in Hebrew Israelite clan currently prevailing in the black community of this land, and so it occurs there is a continuation of prophets they have but they should go by the Quran which is a testament there that law is complete with it and there is no prophet after him who is Muhammad, as the Quran tells them, and Jesus had elements of truth preserved there in Bible literature of the past and he was Messiah there to his people of the Jewish faith residing in Israel during his time and they should recognize him as a representative prophet they have, and Jews around the world need to understand these issues as cogent for them that the Quran is the continuation of the mosaic law they have and is the last Word in the law structure from Him, the Creator to them.

Omar.

Please know Hebrew Israelites as a group are sane with us as yet and eschew Israel's policy of hate to that man, Muhammad, they say.

Please know the Hebrew Israelites are closer to the Islamic faith than many of the Jews of Israel residing in their land as they recognize our Prophet as a prophet there in Arab lands who taught monotheism, like they did in Israel to them, and it is clear they are our brother faith as Moses predicted him who is Muhammad in his text to them and there you have it they should not be extruded from us in Islam of the West emerging where 1 God is inherent in our belief and they too should recognize the Quran as true, like the people of the West do, and they are sane if they understand a new world order emerged with the Quran coming forth and they should adopt its teachings in their lives as it is very similar to their law structure from the same Entity of worship we have in our faith of Abrahamic traditions to us.

Omar.

Please know these are the Hebrew Israelites who recognize me and Muhammad to us.

The Jesuits to you are Catholics, are they, they follow the law of Bani-Israel closely and belief in Jesus' spirit in things but it is so it is a Hebrew branch that developed close ties to Catholicism late but it occurred they were law abiding more and made their follower follow law, and the Jesuits of Ethiopia follow the law precepts of Jesus and Moses as well and recognize me as their rahber who brought them Prophet Muhammad's Book, the Quran, and my teachings to them, and are with me in Heaven one day when they adopt formally our Book, the Quran I teach from, as they are hesitant about purity as yet.

Omar.

please see drew and malcolm x were clean by us and had misgivings of their own but were true to the spirit of islam with them

please know drew ali was a white faith in the sense of being a pure man but it was so he couldnt muster islam in his follower as he was profligate in his youth and somewhat later as well when he became independent of us in islam of the west as he was ahmadi from mirza to us yet he taught differently from him who was mirza and muhammad ali and they sent farad muhammad to reform him but he couldnt muster either there were too many inconstancies in his teaching to be accepted by us in islam so he had to be relinquished and the nation of islam appeared which farad took over but they didnt trust him he was pakistani fitrat of long prayer structure so they relinquished him the blacks did and elected his protege elijah to lead so it occurred black Islam movement here with ahmadi literature and you became evasive to black men emerging here and jailed some including drew and marcus and then killed him who was drew

omar

please see some history of the nation of islam

the nation of islam is a relatively small movement now but was a force in its time of ascendency in the 1930's but it is there misconceptions arose and they called an ahmadiyya imam god in the incarnate sense *and elijah muhammad a prophet of his but they do believe in allah the creator and prophet muhammad as a messenger of his but should be derided in concepts they have that take them out of mainstream islam the ahmadis propose for themselves in the future as a force now that they have become in the west from mirza myself and muhammad alis teach there but it is so they should not be extruded actually as they are an offshoot of the islam of fard muhammad who was a lahore ahmadi who was teaching correctly from the books of muhammad ali the scholar there of the lahore jamaat and it was elijah who changed his teachings around and called him god and all that they say*

it was practically dissolved in 1975 by warith deen muhammed but unfortunately farrakhan gained ground and certain heretical elements resurfaced there but it is so they are getting better with my coming and are following mainstream islam of the ahmadiyya faith more in their teachings and so there you have it they teach from muhammad alis quran and their outlook is similar now

omar

please see black america is my car as they come through and adopt the shahada and fatiha some

please see black america has come through for us in islam we serve you of 1 body if you serve the shahada to you and the nation of Islam now also pray there the shahada some and other prayers as well and they are our brethren faith but do take prophethood to be ongoing which is wrong so ahmadi principles are better for now where we believe prophethood has ended with muhammad as there is no need for them with the completion of faith we have as the quran tells us in its final verse there in maida entailed below

omar

Maida.

5:3 *Forbidden to you is that which dies of itself, and blood, and flesh of swine, and that on which any other name than that of Allah has been invoked, and the strangled (animal), and that beaten to death, and that killed by a fall, and that killed by goring with the horn, and that which wild beasts have eaten — except what you slaughter; and that which* is sacrificed on stones set up (for idols), and that you seek to divide by arrows; that is a transgression. This day have those who disbelieve despaired of your religion, so fear them not, and fear Me. This day have I perfected for you your religion and completed My favor to you and chosen for you Islam as a religion. But whoever is compelled by hunger, not inclining willfully to sin, then surely Allah is Forgiving, Merciful.

Please see the Jesuits are well intentioned but Israel won't budge as yet and hate him who is Muhammad to them.

Please see I'm a Jesuit not but a Muslim mu like my Prophet was and the Jesuits are keen Israel follows their lead in recognizing Prophet Muhammad as their rahber there when he was teaching them in Madinah precepts, but they didn't relent to him and were extruded to Khaibar where they stayed until they converted to Islam of monotheism, where they follow the Quran precepts instead of following their own whims like they do now where Torah is a watchword not but only an avenue of abuse on others and piety there is ignored, like taking care of your neighbor's yard is not followed and rights are usurped there of others under their care, there you have it they don't follow the spirit of the Book and are like the Bani-Israel of before who would relent not on Mary and called her a fornicatress and walked out, and Jesus was disregarded as a prophet of theirs and killed in their hearts intents.

Omar.

Please know the Salafi movement had a credit with some there but it was interim in ideology until I could come forward with my pen to Muhammadi men like Omar and Mirza and Muhammad Ali as well.

This is Salafism of the 18th and 19th century, a backward movement to those in the West but still forward during those times when western influence was increasing and people were becoming apostates, and so they gained independence issues of Islam as well in the sense they did my teach but other issues they did create which I was not a party to and as they were subjected to rule from the West then they initiated jihad as well which Mirza abrogated on my behalf as they were too strong and I went on to teach with pen to my pious one, Mirza there, who they *ostracized for removing a tenet of Islam, but it is so I removed it as it would have annihilated men which we did not want and we wanted Islam resurgence in these quarters here in the West rather than their backward style of relying on hadith as there were too many errors there, so I abrogated it, their Salafi move with the advent of Mirza's teach there and saw it was outmode with jihad movement which I did not teach them, they thought it appropriate to war an occupying army and they had the tenet in Islam of defense warfare, which I did too, say I Muhammad here, and Wahabism also stemmed from Ibn Taymiyya teach but these Salafi movements relied on hadith and we abrogate hadith to you in the West for the most part but i know Wahabis are good Salafi and are willing to adjust to Ahmadi tenets as they make sense to them, a character of my son Wahab there who listened to me in my spirit do I come there, and now there you have it I am a lieu there until they come through with me and Mirza and Omar say I, the august one.*

Omar not but Muhammad to you here.

Please see the mosque structure here is averse to my literature but they need not be here if they adopt and adapt not to truth of Ahmadism we teach of the West to them.

Please see Memphis mosques are upset I teach Ahmadi aqaid or principles on certain topics and make it law if they want to marry local girls that they insist on virtue topics on them as we insist on in Islam of Ahmadism, in men they marry, those of them that are on my Facebook page being an avenue of peace there as it is incumbent they must educate themselves on Islam emerging in the West if they want to stay here with them and it is incumbent on them to learn Islam again as much has been lost with hadith they create abrogating certain verses of the Quran which they did not like, henceforth the whole Quran is considered as sacred and congruous while hadith are abrogated by me say I Allah to them and if they don't adapt piety we teach of Ahmadi aqaid then their car is parked in their lands not here. Omar not only here.

the imam in the mosque is not well with us in islam as he thinks his property in the sense of his religious belief is over and they are derided in islam there in their middle eastern values they have of making money unjust means and what else they teach them there

the imam at the mosque is angry with me over issues that i change religion they have from prophet muhammad to me but it is so i am quiet now as issues have occurred that will extrude me here if i continue to teach differently but it is so people trust me as i have no bone to fight with them as i used to pray with them before i was asked to separate and not pray behind imam structure who are averse to my teachings but it is so the imam of the islamic center here is sane and gives in to people and their requests for peace with us who are people of illihoon jamaat of ahmadism that emerges slowly now they say nay it has emerged and is rapidly becoming the law here as people comprehend it as sane and they in the imam people are not well in issues and people are nice now and help each other and child is brought up with nice etiquettes and it is all because of girl structure with us especially the one in 7th heaven with us eventual ways yes the girl who was in western state with us and taught that you had to be subversive in order to get your way with the government but it is true she held me there and taught i was kind to her and did not want things like sex from them girls in this land here in this country by us

omar

please see i am harassed because of my success with you if i had been a little-known scholar they wouldnt have bothered me the way they are doing in public places where i eat and meet them who like my car

please see public places do this intimidation on a scholar of islam here that they harass him to teach him a lesson not to come to their restaurant and eat there and i could file discriminatory notices in court proceedings but i want to wait just yet and let them take a hint that people will leave their abode as i am their star who taught a nice faith there different from mainstream islam they have in middle eastern countries which they dont care for in this land of ours as they as a group there dont understand me or prophet they have as i write from him while you do in christian islam emerging in western lands of ahmadi aqaid or principles of brotherhood with them in the christian door they have and god knows they have come forth in fellowship to us in ahmadi lands here in the western hemisphere where jesus is taken as god not anymore and nature is his door in that he had a natural life and birth and death as well as a prophet of his grace to him

omar

please see the ahmadi car is extant by you in this land and the west as well.

please know there are some in the muslim world who are me negatively and say i innovate things and things of that sort and deride ahmadi edicts about isa and other issues we have so dont associate with them they are not worthy for your culture and are similar to your church groups who deride me they are liars to you so stay away from such people and the pious one by you knows i am good for you and brought you tranquility and a quiet heart to you and are those who understand issues and learn as we go along and now you have it those who deride me are evil car as i do his bid the creator there who sends me prophet muhammad to teach things to you and me as well.

Omar.

Please see they were a backward class and the ruling elite has to educate them there in piety principles Islam has for them.

Please see the Taliban infrastructure removed with time from my home town not but country of Pakistan some as there is no need for them now that Ahmadi aqaid are being followed and army is sane to start praying camps instructing populace to pray the shahada at least while they work, and to pray the other prayers with the Fatiha in them when they can, as it is incumbent in the land of having a structure of piety with regular prayer in it and the qom or country was wayward with Allah and the Prophet in that they were evil class who didn't pray and made their money unjust means and now they must amend to Him if they want to have credit with Him and the world community as well,

they were not going to make it to Heaven because of these issues we speak of here.
Omar.

Please see traditional Islam likes to take the credit of converting people there in India to Islam but Ahmadism taught these principles of brotherhood with them in the 19th and early 20th century.

They are a erudite group, the IREA are, but wrong in issues there that their scholars of traditional Islam brought it out as Ahmadism brought out these facts that their scripture in the Hindu lore was from God as well, well over a century ago by an Ahmadi scholar named Vidyarthi who taught us in Islam that they were Muslim in India at the outset and they followed One God teachings as they were taught this by prophets and saints of their culture, it was a later innovation they had of idolatry that they ascribe godhead to them, purportedly to bring them closer to Him Who creates and now their culture in India is averse not to Ahmadism emerging as it is much better than the Islam there where they took advantage of them and killed many in the wars they had with them, and people like Modi and others like my candor and Mirza too before my time and Muhammad Ali is a scholar by them, immense in degree, and so it occurs they are ready to teach their people about One God principles we have here in the West and they don't want to be left behind in this culture of alacrity the West inculcates as good there for them.
Omar.

CHAPTER SEVEN

PROPHET MUHAMMAD IN SCRIPTURES AND WRITINGS WE HAVE

please see this passage that exonerates him muhammad to you and confirms him as my mercy to you or rehmat al alimeen say i allah there to some who listen on to my diatribe not here

please see the soul intact and the spirit unchanged

please see muhammad on him be peace in that regard that he never had a major sin to his credit not and it is true he was pious and never had a lie to his name or any other sin apart from some mistakes we talk about in the quran some

please know he had a spirit intact and that is why he is my choice to teach you as the most pious by me is the most clear-minded of my creation as his brain has never been perturbed by sin and he knows clarity not to do it sin in him so both play a role

please see his spirit was intact so his soul grew and never diminished like we all have it occur say i omar here but it is true he grew wise quickly and not through experience of the adverse kind we all learn from in life and it is so because you are a witness as to his life from the quran and the hadith lore you realize omar too is confirming this on his page to you and he is not a liar or exaggerator to you and speaks plainly of prophets of yore and you know i write for him and you trust my word there in arabia and middle east some not but here in christian islam you have where you recognize this form of communication exists for some as indicated by hadith and your literature and you know the prophet did say nothing would be left of prophesy except clear visions and thoughts from him and these people would be called muhadith so you know there is a basis for saint here and revelation by means of angels who read book passages to him has end with muhammad and these are clear thoughts and visions he has omar here and mirza and other saints before have been recorded as saying they see and write from him creator they have but back to the point i make that prophet has intact spirit and thus was perfect in aplomb and clarity and knew no doubt that it would occur islam there but did not know i would make it worldwide through his pen there

please know he had a perfect thought process which is what mind is and the mind is the spirit in things as you can see the word has come that when your mind is muddied it is because of some sin in you and you have to reform in piety with repentance and prayer helps in that regard and the prophet was always clear in his mind more or less as we all travail some when we live on earth but it was so he had a perfect balance and knew not to sin so there it is he is my chosen one for all eternity as he proved it in his life what a perfect slave of mine he is and because his spirit is intact he will always have the most clarity of my servants that i create and he is also my wise one who is my companion always

omar some but mainly allah here

Al-Anbiya

21:106 Surely in this is a message for a people who serve (Us).

21:107 And We have not sent thee but as a mercy to the nations.

21:108 Say: It is only revealed to me that your God is one God: will you then submit?

please see the quran was revealed to a man who fulfilled it in his life there

please know it is a book that is perfect for you and the fulfiller of it is likewise

please know it was the prophets custom not to lie and even his enemy declared that to the sovereign of the eastern roman empire when he met him and was questioned about him and he told him that he had never known him to lie

please see he fulfilled every letter of the quran in his entire life thats why we were indebted to him for bringing us the law book to us

please know the quran could not have been given to another man

THE METAPHOR EXPLAINED, NOW WHAT?

please see his heart is the repository of it and it is the only heart that could assimilate the words of it

please see heraclius converted and did not fight him as he knew he was noble and that he was true in his claim to be a prophet of them the arabs and so he withdrew his army from the war field at tabuk in the last year of the prophets life

please see we are indebted to this man muhammad they know as he alone completed faith for humanity for his creator and it is his book we read there in our daily prayers so be grateful to him and allah as well for creating him a witness of us and an example we follow to get to paradise for us who fulfill the words of the quran to us yes no one can enter it unless they are like him who is muhammad to us and now you adopt it as no other book can take you to high station of firdous to us

please see aisha the wife of the prophet bore witness to this fact that his morals were that of the quran and isa and myself bear witness with her and he isa says he did say to the people that he will send the spirit of truth to them to complete faith in things that they did not have heart to bear at that time and so there you have it he is a witness with us aisha and myself here and you know other prophets also predict his coming there in arabia so you know it is clear from history that he was to come as a teacher to us

omar

Al-Ahzab

33:21 *Certainly you have in the Messenger of Allah an excellent exemplar for him who hopes in Allah and the Latter day, and remembers Allah much.*

Al-Ahzab

33:45 *O Prophet, surely We have sent thee as a witness, and a bearer of good news and a warner,*

33:46 *And as an inviter to Allah by His permission, and as a light-giving sun.*

Hadith

Qatadah reported: I said to Aisha, "O mother of the believers, tell me about the character of the Messenger of Allah, peace and blessings be upon him." Aisha said, "Have you not read the Quran?" I said, "Of

course." Aisha said, "Verily, the character of the Prophet of Allah was the Quran."
-Source: Ṣaḥīḥ Muslim 746

Please see that without fidelity to him who is Prophet there you won't make it to Heaven Abode with you and that holds for all mankind as he is extant and you must be kind to him in words you use, like the Muslims do.

Loving the Prophet and auliya and prophets of Islam is incumbent on one and you have to respect them in that they serve Him Who creates them to bring piety to you and if you disregard them that's different but if you deride them or their works to you then a punishment awaits you and you won't enter paradise with them, it is clear we have to show respect to those who do Allah's work for Him, but the person who is key is Muhammad on him be peace on this issue and if you deride him hate will follow you in your life and those People of the Book who call him evil are evil by you as you can't find flaw on My near perfect one in all his life's endeavors, other people you may but he was upstanding with you, and you won't receive peace from Me, your Creator to you if you deride him or auliya we have.

Please see hatred will always be your life and you will fight with others around you if you disregard him who is Muhammad as he is to be treated with respect by Me but if you are ill about the issue and call him bad I will create sadness in your life as bad affects you and you become sad in it say I Allah the August One by you, so don't do it, call him bad to you, and live in piety like Muslims do in this issue and dare Me not in this matter.

Please see you know he is true and good to you and your soul will reject you if you call him bad there and love will not occur in your life and you will start hating Me as well.

Omar.

Nisa.

4:107 And contend not on behalf of those who act unfaithfully to their souls. Surely Allah loves not him who is treacherous, sinful:

THE METAPHOR EXPLAINED, NOW WHAT?

Please see One God occurred with you and you realized Omar was telling it true that Muhammad was the best person to lead us, then Illihoon descend here and peace occur in your hearts about the life Hereafter.

Please know they are taken by Him, the Qadianis are, by their Creator as they were creating law that he was nabi actually, who is Omar and Mirza, as they call him that but it is not so they don't in their heart but it is mischief they do, some of them.

Please know Ahmadi Muslims are my identity as they want qitar but it is not required in Illihoon as we are 1 body now and the shahada is sufficient for us but the qitar is beneficial in the fight in us but it is so simple prayer is sufficient and as we said when Islam occurred there in China and Middle East it was wrapped up, the world was.

Please know in your heart you know, I, Muhammad is the head of humanity as Omar's book lists him as the best person to lead and Isa and Mirza as well say so in their writings and in your shaur as well you know he was Allah's companion before others and he still is and is in his shaur the best to lead in world affairs, in his spirit he does now, so it occurs you trust Omar in this and so forth and the world is wrapped up as you trust Omar and Mirza some in this matter as they both praised him effusively you say, yes, it was effusive say I Muhammad.

Please know it was when Omar took you as a witness that I was the best person the world will see you succumbed to him and Allah was One with you so you succumb and say he is true who is Omar to us and Allah decided to end the world in its previous structure and descend heaven to us and now there you have it we are one structure in the world community and battles fought are in statutes and sanctions for the most part and it is true the world is wrapped up in its structure of impiety it had.

Omar not here but Muhammad there in spirit to you do I write this.

please see sin-free means only that they have achieved it perfection with him the creat and do not sin anymore not that they have never sinned that is inconceivable there

please see it is clear we sin when we are on earth as the hadith says so that when we wade through water we will get wet but i know you know minor sins occur to all of us and some not but all mankind fall with major ones as well and our prophet was an exception not as it says here in these two sections but rest assured he was the most pious of us and knew no sin in an overt way but he did have the thought of shirk as did abraham as the quran explained he searched for god and realized him in thoughts and speech but it is so it is a dhanb or sin to do so but it is forgiven if you clear in your thoughts as he was well-intentioned in it and our prophet was similar but it is so all mankind has a major sin or dhanb and the prophets all go through soul searching and things like that and some sin overtly but it is clear muhammad never explained what his was in hadith lore we have but it is so he was sinless after that except for minor issues we all have as we travel forth on earth and there you have it i am told his sin was a thought about him being god but it was a thought only placed there by allah on him as he searched for purity in things and it is clear he never touched a woman outside marriage and other sins were unknown to him but it is so he did not have a fall with women while all other prophets had and it is just words they say that they are sinless and it is so we learn from our mistakes and are forgiven and learn when we repent and major sins aside minor ones are forgiven when we pray and ask forgiveness in things but i know you say he touched women but it is so he did say to companions that he never touched outside wedlock and there you have it he was sinless in major ones and mistakes or khata are different and are forgiven when you repent it your flaw there but there you have it it is because we all have a major sin or more in our life we must be humble in it and bring others to sinless state he has there when he submits to god his flaw and he forgives him and allows intervention for us when we too ask him the creator for forgiveness and so forth you realize the hadith is there that the prophets will be approached on the day we are judged and they will say ourself not but 'myself' because of some sin they had and they wont intervene for them the people who ask them to and they will eventually approach muhammad and he will submit himself for judgment and then mans forgiveness will commence and people will start going to heaven

THE METAPHOR EXPLAINED, NOW WHAT?

when muhammad enters there so we know he has a sin according to muslim teach but according to our law he was least in sin so there you have polemic from christian door who say he sinned and jesus didnt but it is not so according to our law there from hadith and we all sin and that is what makes us human and god is sin-free actually and has created evil to test us and so forth he saw the best there was in thought his sole major sin with him and others have sinned in kind and deed according to hadith structure we have and it is so my son isa and musa there did predict him so he is august to you and isa did say of him that he will complete faith for them so obviously he had a more complete faith than my son who did sin some in his youth there while my hubby muhammad never did and omar knows he is not him in sin free existence of no lies to his credit thats why he is the chosen one there in our before-life to bring islam to world structure and people know its blasphemy people of faiths different do when they say their man never knew women or sin but we know they all do says maryam here and it is just words of aggrandizement they say as we know all are human and only allah is sin-free and now you know if muhammad had a sin they all did as his intercession there is a document with us and you in islam believe he is the best man because of it this intercession he had for mankind and the quran calls him a mercy to mankind and so forth his message is for all man and women and their child so do honor him as the best of us all humans we are no gods in us as we are all men you like actual ways and bless in your prayers as those who gave you law from him the great creator of us with the culmination of faith with the quran there from muhammad to us

omar and maryam here

Al-Mumin

51 We certainly help Our messengers, and those who believe, in this world's life and on the day when the witnesses arise—

52 The day on which their excuse will not benefit the unjust, and for them is a curse and for them is the evil abode.

53 And We indeed gave Moses the guidance, and We made the Children of Israel inherit the Book —

54 A guidance and a reminder for men of understanding.

55 So be patient; surely the promise of Allah is true; and ask forgiveness for thy sin and celebrate the praise of thy Lord in the evening and the morning.

Muhammad

47:19 So know that there is no god but Allah and ask forgiveness for thy sin and for the believing men and the believing women. And Allah knows your moving about and your staying (in a place).

Al-Furqan

25:68 And they who call not upon another god with Allah and slay not the soul which Allah has forbidden, except in the cause of justice, nor commit fornication; and he who does this shall meet a requital of sin —

25:69 The chastisement will be doubled to him on the day of Resurrection, and he will abide therein in abasement —

25:70 Except him who repents and believes and does good deeds; for such Allah changes their evil deeds to good ones. And Allah is ever Forgiving, Merciful.

Please see the Prophet succumbs to you if you are sane in things and make it gradual, your love for him, but we know he deserves it more than Jesus as he gave you comfort where you had none and were sad in things you do here.

Please see this verse of the Quran hasn't come true but it is there in the archives and Allah will make it appear soon so you can see it for yourself, they say it is the Comforter or Paraclete who is referred here but that is a word used that is separate and not to be confused with this name here, but rest assured he is the one who praises his Creat there as you can see from the Quran words and his hadith structure where he is full of love and virtue to Him, his Creator, and we should learn from his example and be effusive in the worship and praise of the One Who gave us a living conscious brain and mind that is able to appreciate things and a body that enjoys pleasures and all that we do in virtue with it, more here is required, I too am Ahmad but I am not the one spoken of in this verse and rest assured it is our Prophet who came to comfort you there was a God and that we have a Hereafter where we will be given things if we are pious in this life, so you succumb to pious life now as you have seen death and despair with hardship to you and you love piety in you where you are loving me, your friend, from his office, the Prophet there.

Omar.

Al-Saff.

61:6 And when Jesus, son of Mary, said: O Children of Israel, surely I am the messenger of Allah to you, verifying that which is before me of the Torah and giving the good news of a Messenger who will come after me, his name being Ahmad. But when he came to them with clear arguments, they said: This is clear enchantment.

Please see the seal is Muhammad as can be seen from this Biblical lore here.

Please see this verse from Isaiah that speaks of the seal being given to an unlearned man, this refers to Muhammad, on him be peace as it is clear he could not read at that juncture and he said those words as recorded in biblical text not but in hadith lore we have, but it is so he was the seal mentioned here.

Please know Omar's arm wants it explained but i know the words have been altered some but the context is that after the sleep the prophetic seal would be offered to him who is Isaiah there.

Please know he would not open it as he knew other prophets would appear.

Please see it would then receive grace with him who is myself, Omar not, but me Muhammad and I would say those words and the seal would occur.

Omar.

Isaiah 29.

10 For the Lord hath poured out upon you the spirit of deep sleep, and hath closed your eyes: the prophets and your rulers, the seers hath he covered.

11 And the vision of all is become unto you as the words of a book that is sealed, which men deliver to one that is learned, saying, "Read this, I pray thee": and he saith, "I cannot; for it is sealed:"

12 And the book is delivered to him that is not learned, saying, "Read this, I pray thee:" and he saith, "I am not learned."

13 Wherefore the Lord said, "Forasmuch as this people draw near me with their mouth, and with their lips do honor me, but have removed their heart far from me, and their fear toward me is taught by the precept of men."

please see the reason we were created here from earth material and why we were sent from our heaven of before when we were spirits who roamed the earth here it was a plan though with us in islam that i would test you eventual ways since you demurred my wisdom before say i allah there

please know jokes and games are fun to do but industry is severe for you but it is required adam was sent out of eden for industry to occur in him i could have created heaven for you in the first go but you werent coming through you were all jealous of my chosen one muhammad there and you thought i was partial to him in unjust way most of you thought that so i gave you the world to prove your worth and all of you testify now you are not perfect like he was to you this is the reason for my creation of you from earth material say i omar not but allah there that you will bow down to my wisdom in future as you will not want earth again after i give you heaven afresh there in the hereafter for you omar not

please see it is clear communion or isra is commonplace amongst my saints but know it is not the communion i had there with my beloved son muhammad and his dream not but motion was real to us

when you have a communion with me your mind is my mind in you and your thoughts come from me as repose i have in you but it is so you are one body with me in your meet of me in your thoughts to you and muhammad had seen this communion too when i spoke to him in isra prayer he had and you know it is a mutually appreciative act prayer is to me your creat there as you give me peace and i through my soul there in you give you peace too and we love too in it when this peace result in us yes my soul grows and so does yours in this prayer you have and

i am pleased with you and you are too pleased with your creator and love flourishes between us and then you start loving others with this repository of love i give you from myself there you have it only one god issues prevail you and now you know others who learn from you love you in similar ways as you give them peace and love occurs in them too with the prayer they do to me their creator this is the nature of heaven i create here say i allah there
    omar not here

    please see the salafi movement does not represent me say i muhammad to man and i dress in modern clothes that are modest in nature here in my follower with you
    please know the way of the prophet is truth and integrity first and later the clothes and the beard as that law is late now with the orthodox salafi not move we teach and they say to them salafis first clean your house before you preach in the west true say i muhammad here and you must be truth bear and law abiding before you teach or else you will be taken away as hypocrites now as many imams are in this land of illihoon people who dont bear it in their testimony to man and there are some imams who berate me for bringing islam gradual ways with hadith not in it and early quran law of virtue and piety there that early islam adherents had there but it is so people of the west love my simple piety and law-bearing and they like nice men who dont berate them on minor issues of islam while at the same time encourage them on major issues they have but it is so the salafi move away from me even though i bear truth and integrity with them here in the western culture of piety emerging by you with you in your midst in the world forum as you teach me in prophet muhammads garb for his simplicity to emerge with you
    omar

    please see terrorism is on the wane here in the west and east both areas are safe more or less
    please see it is politically incorrect to do this that you say terrorism is the creed of muslims there in this day and age when i am teaching islam from prophet muhammads group in paradise as these concepts are

not there in islam he had and what i teach is different concepts from them in middle east where they take verses of war in an out of context manner and apply it to civilians further the number of thousands of attacks since september 11 is arbitrary and made up there is very little terrorism now as i have been teaching prophet muhammads islam to them and they agree to lay down arms too and in the recent years there have been few radical attacks on targets here and the west so dont bother with these propaganda pundits they do this jewish elements who hate islam coming to you and your nation of one faith we have now of mono god here which you export to them in the western hemisphere and east as well

omar

Please see the Prophet's acclaim that though he had the instinct to bed women before marriage he abstained from the touch even as he knew in his heart it was wrong to do.

We all desire sex in our youth, the Prophet did too in the touch to him but he abstained and didn't talk about it, he thought it bad in him and suppressed him in it and stayed away from girls as he wanted to preserve himself for marriage, he had virtue in his intellect to him and he thought as you did that good men don't bed women before getting married to them, and he lived in a culture where he could stay apart if he wished, but he knew it was over, he was impious as he wanted women out of wedlock say I Allah there, I put it in your heart all mankind to desire every member of man and women in your psyche if they were attractive to you and some follow through on this impulse on their living here in earth but it is not possible to bed everyone you like, you have to marry and settle with one and maybe later with another or so if you're male by law of nature I gave you as you roam more by nature in an attempt to procreate as many as you can, a law of survival we have for man and women as well, but they are satisfied in creating for one male by her nature of procreation in marriage rites I give her for her safety to occur, and so you know that Hell is full of people who try to procreate out of wedlock and if they inhibit it, the child to them, it is still a sin as it leads to an ill man or woman who do this procreation act and inhibit childhood from occurring in them by abort or contraception. Omar not here.

EPILOGUE HERE

Please see I end here this note to you in that we are kind in Islam to give you a reckoning with Him, your Creat, as you thought you were going to make it to Heaven without accountability and you were leading impious lives full of sadness door and didn't know it, you thought it was norm to be suicidal in thoughts but is it, nay, it is not and you must have aplomb there is a Heaven eventual ways with you as my book here says but you must come through in piety before it materializes for you and you must observe law He gave you for your betterment and happiness to occur and you realize you can live without extramarital sex, yes, you are happier that way and soon you will come to know the loving embrace with your partner is worth more with you but you live for the day that your Creator embraces you with love from Him as you are ready for that to happen when you sin not in significance with us in Islam and yes Heaven evokes you and you wish to be Muslimkind of people who submit to the will of their God just like your savior did, Jesus to you, and you realize many saints do that and Prophet Muhammad also had that door on him so you want to be with him and Isa and others in Islam who serve you with piety in their hearts and our Creator is there with them in Heaven above us and Mary and other women who have made it with Him are there as well, one happy family at the feet of their Creator wishing for Paradise with you who are pious enough to make it with them.

Omar.

www.ingramcontent.com/pod-product-compliance
Lightning Source LLC
LaVergne TN
LVHW041909070526
838199LV00051BA/2551